D1175584

The Church is Charismatic

Edited by
Arnold Bittlinger

Renewal and Congregational Life
World Council of Churches, Geneva

ISBN No. 2-8254-0673-2

© Copyright 1981, World Council of Churches,
150 route de Ferney, P.O.B. 66, 1211 Geneva 20,
Switzerland

CONTENTS

Introduction

I.   Towards a Dialogue

II. Letter of the General Secretary of the WCC
     to the Member Churches and Reactions of
     the Churches

III. The Bossey Consultation

INTRODUCTION

The World Council of Churches' report on "The Church
for Others" (1967) envisaged an accelerating secularization of society. And in a sense the world is indeed
becoming more secularized, particularly in many countries of the Western world. Parallel to this trend of
secularization, however, a new religious wave is sweep-
ing through societies. We live in a time when one can
win elections on the ticket of being "born again", when
a non-Christian producer can make a fortune with a
musical about "Jesus Christ Superstar", when a British
actor can fill a theatre night after night just by
reciting the gospel of Mark.

This religious wave is not restricted to the West, as is
demonstrated by the fast-growing independent churches in
Africa, by the religious revivals in Poland, the Soviet
Union, and other Communist countries, by newly emerging
religious movements in Japan and Korea, and by the fierce
religious commitment of politicians and military leaders
in the Middle East.

These religious revivals are a mixed blessing. Some of
them strengthen the prejudices and the power of an unjust status quo; others, however, open up new and creative opportunities. Whatever we think of these religious outbreaks, religion, in both its destructive and
creative forms, is going to stay with us for a long time.
Sociologists, economists, development specialists,
medical researchers, and politicians are slowly coming
round to the idea that they have to reckon with these
religious forces. Is it not time that theologians take
note of them too, without hastily stating that Christianity has nothing to do with religion? Perhaps the
gospel has a twofold function within and over against
these religious phenomena: namely to discern in them
that which is good, human, and possibly in the service
of the kingdom of God and to indicate that which is
evil, inhuman, and possibly in the service of the "old
liar", the enemy of humankind.

In this context the Charismatic Renewal can be seen as
a Christian variation of a worldwide religious revival.

It is therefore important for the World Council of Churches (WCC) to help its member churches come to terms with a phenomenon both inside and outside the churches. That is how we would interpret the unprecedented response which the study programme on the Charismatic Renewal received worldwide from the member churches. It was announced by a simple letter signed by the General Secretary of the WCC. The letters from individuals and churches and the study reports from various committees, convinces the staff of the WCC that the Charismatic Renewal was something which preoccupied the minds of its member churches and that their questions and comments had to be fed into a worldwide consultative process.

The process started with a decision of the working group of Renewal and Congregational life at a meeting in Stony Point, USA, followed by the meeting of a small task force at Schloss Schwanberg, FRG (1978), where an attempt was made to produce a descriptive and evaluative consensus paper. As contributors to this task force came from very different geographical and ecclesiastical backgrounds, it was difficult to find a common language. What emerged in the end was a compromise: the different contributions were edited in such a way as to produce one paper. Due to the nature of this paper some of the most important experiences of the task force were lost. There was, for instance, a member of the task force who did not take part in the discussion. She simply prayed and fasted. She also had a number of visions, which translated the research process into a language which is probably easier for readers from different backgrounds to understand than the propositional language of the Mediterranean culture.

The Schwanberg experience called for a drastic rethinking of the study process, especially since the WCC by now was determined to make the Charismatic Renewal the topic of one of its major study projects. At the Bossey Consultation (1980) the participants came from an even wider variety of backgrounds than the members of the Schwanberg task force. There were well-known theologians from Roman Catholic and Protestant Charismatic Renewal groups. There were also the members of the working group of the WCC's sub-unit on Renewal and Congregational life, people whom one usually describes as

ecumenical church bureaucrats. In addition, a nuclear
physicist, who happened to be the chairman of the cabinet
of the chef spiritual of the Kimbanguist church, and
the General Secretary of the Israel Nineveh Church (two
independent African churches, both members of the WCC)
were present. A black choir from the Church of God in
Christ in England came with their pastor, a driving
instructor by profession. One of the worship services
was led by the Senior Apostle of the Cherubim and Seraphim Society from England (an African Independent Church
widely known throughout West Africa) according to the
liturgy of his church, which is word for word identical
with the old Anglo-Catholic liturgy - except that he
celebrated it without reference to a printed liturgy
and with all the dramatic panache and deeply felt reverence of an African who actually knew and experienced
that he was praying in the presence of angels and archangels, the cherubim and seraphim and all the company
of heaven. Prophecies and speaking in tongues fitted
easily into this age-old liturgy. At the final eucharist the Anglican Archbishop of Cape Town confessed that
the Scripture reading of that day had spoken personally
to him. He had a grudge in his heart, he said, against
those people who thought he was not outspoken enough in
South Africa's race struggle, while in his own country
he was continually up against members of his own church
who thought he should restrict himself to religious and
politically neutral language. The Archbishop prayed
this grudge be taken out of his heart. The General
Secretary of the WCC, the West Indian Dr Philip Potter,
who took an active part at the whole consultation, went
forward and embraced this representative of one of the
leading white churches of South Africa. Discussions
were introduced and interrupted by spirituals from the
black choir by testimonies from participants. Praise,
prayer, and Bible studies accompanied the theological
debate.

Such was the climate of the Bossey consultation. For
those who had to prepare papers for this conference
it was vital to insert their contribution into the spirit and the letter of this agenda. Dr Philip Potter
solved the problem of introducing the study process by
describing his own thoughts, joys, comments, and critique when reading through the thick file of responses
to his initial letter. By personalizing his theological

analysis, he made it possible for everybody to follow his critical analysis. Peter Felber communicated his feelings, his worries, and joys (and not just his thinking) about the reactions to the Schwanberg paper, and he thus was able to transform these contributions into a plea for sharing.

These lived encounters made it possible for the reports on the worldwide Charismatic Renewal, on the churches' reaction to it, and on possible models for interpreting such diversity from the New Testament to be taken seriously, because by now the participants had themselves become part of that which was to be analyzed and evaluated.

We hope that the following pages will encourage similar encounters in the congregations and churches and that they will help church leaders and leaders of Charismatic Renewal groups to experience in and through their different theologies and spiritualities a creative challenge for a church united and renewed in the Spirit.

Walter Hollenweger
University of Birmingham, UK

I.
Towards a Dialogue

1. Stony Point, 1978

From 29 August to 5 September 1978, the working group of the WCC sub-unit on Renewal and Congregational life met at Stony Point, New York, USA.

One of the topics of this meeting was a discussion on "Spirituality and the Charismatic Renewal". This discussion opened with a paper by Arnold Bittlinger on the theme "Charismatic Renewal -- An Opportunity for the Church". It ended with a resolution to hold a consultation in March 1980 on the significance of the Charismatic Renewal for the churches. At Stony Point the sub-unit also adopted a statement on "Renewal", which is included in the opening paragraphs of the Bossey Report, printed in Section III, below.

A. CHARISMATIC RENEWAL - AN OPPORTUNITY FOR THE CHURCH ?

Arnold Bittlinger

A movement of spiritual renewal unprecedented in the history of the Christian church has been spreading through the churches of the world since the beginning of the sixties. Unlike earlier such movements, this contemporary renewal movement, sometimes called "the Charismatic Renewal", is spreading all over the world, within all confessions, and among all social classes.

I. A first charismatic upsurge in our century started in Topeka, Kansas, USA on New Year's Day 1901, within the "Holiness Movement", an offshoot from Methodism, and in a few Baptist churches. This spiritual uprising was not accepted by the mother churches and therefore became an independent movement, the so-called "Pentecostal Movement", which began to form its own churches. It subsequently spread throughout the world and is at present the fastest growing branch of Christendom, especially in Latin America and Africa. It is estimated today to embrace anything from 30 to 40 million adherents. The most interesting branch is the independent African churches with about 8 million members.

A second charismatic upsurge with many precursors began
in the USA in 1960. Beginning among Episcopalians and
then in other Reformation churches, especially Lutheran
and Reformed, it spread to the Catholic Church in 1967
and thereafter throughout the whole world.

Many hundreds of thousands of Christians (the million
mark has probably long been left behind) in the various
churches identify themselves with this movement today.
Exact statistics are not available but the growth rate
may be inferred from the attendance figures for the
annual conferences of the Catholic Charismatic Renewal
movement in the USA from 1967 to 1974 held in Notre
Dame, Indiana. In 1967 there were 70 representatives

1968	150
1969	500
1970	1,500
1971	5,000
1972	12,000
1973	23,000
1974	37,000.

Since 1974 these meetings have been decentralized and
comparable statistics are no longer available.

In this movement there are thousands of pastors and
priests, as well as a number of bishops, archbishops
and professors of theology. The spokesman for the
Catholic Charismatic Renewal movement is Cardinal Leo
Suenens, Primate of Belgium, who regards the movement
as the main hope of renewal in the church and who has
been appointed by Pope Paul VI as official go-between
for contacts between the Vatican and the charismatic
renewal movement.

Following statements issued by a number of Catholic
Episcopal Synods on the charismatic movement, the Vatican's Unity Secretariat in 1971 inaugurated a five-year
dialogue with representatives of the pentecostal movement and the Charismatic Renewal. This took place from
1972 to 1976 (a complete description of the prehistory
and of the sessions of this dialogue is found in my book
Papst und Pfingstler, Peter Lang-Verlag, Bern and Las
Vegas).

On Whitmonday 1975 in a service in St. Peters Cathedral
in Rome Pope Paul VI adopted a favourable stance towards the Charismatic Renewal movement.

Within the evangelical churches various synods and church authorities have also adopted a generally favourable attitude towards the Charismatic Renewal movement. In May 1976, for example, the Conference of Bishops of the United Evangelical Lutheran Church in Germany issued a statement part of which read:

> "We watch attentively and hopefully the Charismatic Renewal in countless Christian communities throughout the world. Many people hunger for fellowship and a new spirit but do not yet see how they are to be achieved. In our view this clearly shows that God claims the whole man with his intellect, emotions and actions. Man can evade this claim only at the price of missing the meaning of his life. We therefore beseech God graciously to further the work of renewal in his church and its congregations also in and through the charismatic movements."

The World Council of Churches, too, has given increasing attention to the concerns of the charismatic movements; for example, at Nairobi, at various courses at the Bossey Institute, at a consultation in Rostrevor, Northern Ireland, and by the appointment of a consultant on Charismatic Renewal.

II. The rapid spread of this movement cannot be explained simply by the fact that the world has shrunk to a neighbourhood or by the improvement in means of communication. It is also and primarily due to a threefold longing on the part of Christians:

- the longing for a truly spiritual life, in reaction against an over-cerebral Christianity.

- the longing for real fellowship (one in which the gifts of the individual are taken seriously), in reaction against a Christianity which reduced church members to minor supernumeraries.

- the longing for strength, in reaction against a Christianity which denied or explained away the miracles and mighty works attested in the New Testament.

III. Although this threefold longing is in some degree
the common characteristic of the whole charismatic uprising, what is called the Charismatic Renewal today is
far from being a uniform phenomenon. To avoid confusion we need to distinguish at least three main streams:

1.   the classic Pentecostal movement

2.   so-called neo-Pentecostalism

3.   the charismatic congregational renewal.

1.   The "classic" Pentecostalists belong to the "classic"
or "free" Pentecostal movement which began in the USA
in 1901. They are organized in their own churches and
produce their own theology (mostly with an evangelical
fundamentalist basis).

2.   The neo-Pentecostalists derive from the charismatic
upsurge of the sixties. Though largely adopting the
theology of the "classic" Pentecostalists, they do not
form their own churches but remain within their traditional churches. They do, however, attend regular
(usually interconfessional) prayer meetings.

3.   The representatives of the "Charismatic congregational renewal" also stem from the charismatic upsurge
of the sixties. Unlike the "classic" Pentecostalists,
they do not form churches of their own but remain (or
become) faithful members of their own churches in which
they often occupy (or come to occupy) important posi-
tions. Unlike the neo-Pentecostalists they do not take
over their theology from the classic Pentecostalists
but interpret their spiritual awakening in the light of
and within the context of their own theological tradition. Nor do they establish prayer groups independent
of their congregations; rather, they seek to renew
their own churches charismatically.

In the following remarks, I want to concentrate on this
third stream of charismatic congregational renewal.
What precisely does this involve? Whereas Christians
with a pietistic background look for charisms chiefly
in prayer circles, socially committed Christians will
look for them in their own action group and the litur-
gists in liturgical worship. The "charismatic" with

psychological interests will seek the effective deployment of charisms in therapeutic groups or teams while the church-oriented "charismatic" will look to a similar effect within the normal life of the congregation. The politically engaged charismatic will look for charismatic contributions (gifts of prophecy, wisdom, discerning of spirits, leadership) in everyday democratic processes, while the charismatic theologian will hope for deeper insights into his theological work. The same applies to parents, teachers, doctors and other callings and professions.

IV. What then _is_ a charism? Purely as a phenomenon, nothing whatever is in itself "charismatic" or "spiritual". All phenomena are the realization of possibilities within this world. But everything, however ordinary or extraordinary, can be made use of by God for the neighbour's or the world's salvation, and thereby becomes a charism (there is no Christian who always acts charismatically, but there is also no Christian who never acts charismatically).

V. This brings me to the basic question: How can charisms become effective within the Christian community? How far is the Charismatic Renewal movement an opportunity for the Church?

1. An opportunity for the individual church member. The individual church member is set free by the Holy Spirit to be himself. Prayer becomes in consequence the outpouring of the heart so that the person praying can express and spread out before God what really moves him in the depths of his heart (even his aggressive feelings).

Where the Holy Spirit is at work, he will also make Christians more receptive to what God is saying to them in the Bible and more conscious of his command to the individual, to the Christian community and to society.

2. An opportunity for worship. Where the Holy Spirit is at work, there can be a fresh experience of worship as a conversation with God, in which God speaks with his people and his people with him.

When those participating in worship are set free to be themselves, it becomes possible to introduce creative elements (such as improvised singing, painting, dancing, etc.).

3. <u>An opportunity for the church's diakonia</u>. Where the Holy Spirit is at work, Christians develop their imagination and sensitivity for difficult situations, for when people become receptive to the reality of the Holy Spirit they can no longer ignore the distress of their fellow human beings.

4. <u>An opportunity for the leadership of the church</u>. Where the Holy Spirit is at work, human beings become more important than things, the common good more important than individual advantage. In meetings and decisions, therefore, the important thing will be that all should be able to contribute in the way best suited to each, and not that the individual should impose his view on others. Even the fumbling hesitant word must be taken seriously (perhaps with the question: Have I got you right?) and the shy person helped and encouraged to voice an opinion.

5. <u>An opportunity for pastors</u>. A pastor who is filled with the Holy Spirit realizes that in the last analysis it is not he but Jesus Christ himself who is responsible for his community. This will give him a joyful confidence, even in difficult situations.

But he also knows that Jesus always works through people. This will enhance the pastor's sense of responsibility, above all his resolve to remain dependent on the Spirit of Jesus so that <u>he</u> may be able to act and speak rightly through him.

The "spirit-filled" pastor knows also that Jesus works through all the members of his body and not just through one. This will deliver him from any desire to monopolize the action and enable him to delight in the gifts of others.

6. <u>An opportunity for the ecumenical movement</u>. Where the Holy Spirit is at work, he first of all points clearly to what is important and valuable in a person's

own confession. But the spirit-filled Christian will also be eager to discover what is lovely and of good report in other confessions. When something seems strange to him, he will try to understand this too.

With caution, he will even be able to adopt certain things which are better in the other confession or which are perhaps neglected in his own. Many "charismatics" from free churches, for example, have in their contacts with members of the Catholic Charismatic Renewal movement rediscovered the importance of the Eucharist, while Catholic "charismatics" have very readily adopted the practice of bible reading and spontaneous prayer.

When Christians from different confessions come together to pray and to celebrate, to work at theology and to render practical service, a common tradition has come into existence which could prove stronger than that which has hitherto divided Christians from one another.

(Translated from the German.)

B.   SPIRITUALITY AND THE CHARISMATIC RENEWAL

(excerpt from the Stony Point minutes)

Churches and congreations all around the world are presently aware of movements of spiritual renewal, which in some instances are revitalizing, in some instances divisive. Many churches have begun to study those movements, especially the charismatic movement, and numerous documents have been published. There is an obvious need to engage in direct dialogue with the Charismatic Renewal in a broad ecumenical context.

Therefore a consultation should be held in conjunction with the next meeting of this working group, in March 1980:

- to clarify understanding of the Charismatic
  Renewal and its meaning for the churches;

- to study the responses of the churches to
  the Charismatic Renewal.

The 40-50 participants should include, in addition to
members of the working group:

- leaders in member churches;

- leaders in the Charismatic Renewal;

- participants who are laity, theologians, women
  and youth - with and without personal experience of the Charismatic Renewal.

Detailed plans for the consultation will be worked out
at a meeting of a consultative group in December 1978.
Member churches will be invited to help identify the
issues. Suggestions and plans will be presented to the
Executive Group of the sub-unit, meeting in 1979. It
is anticipated that, as a result of the consultation,
the working group will be submitting a substantial report on this issue to the August 1980 meeting of the
Central Committee.

2. Schwanberg, 1978

*A "consultative group" met in December 1978 at Schloss Schwanberg,
Bavaria, Federal Republic of Germany.*

*Reports and testimonies were presented on different aspects of
the Charismatic Renewal, and an introduction was given to Rex
Davis's book Locusts and Wild Honey. Christoph Ziemer, of the
German Democratic Republic, read a paper on "Charismatic Renewal
in the Work of the Churches of the GDR: Aspects of the Problem."*

*The results of the Schwanberg discussions were summarized in a
paper entitled "Towards a Church Renewed and United in the Spirit."*

The consultative group met a second time in December 1979 in Nidelbad, near Rüschlikon, Switzerland, in order to work on programme details for the Bossey Consultation.

A. CHARISMATIC RENEWAL IN THE WORK OF THE CHURCHES OF THE GDR: ASPECTS OF THE PROBLEM

Christoph Ziemer

(Translated from the German by the WCC Language Service.)

When we speak of Charismatic Renewal, what precisely do we mean? Is it a dimension of the renewal of the church or is it a particular practical religious form? What is its goal? A charismatically renewed church or the charismatic movement?

In our church life and work we are dealing here in the first place with a particular practical religious form, the charismatic movement. This does not mean we should lose sight of the utopia of a charismatically renewed church but certainly that we should distinguish between the two.

1. The charismatic movement can be understood as a reaction to the present situation in the church and in the world. It draws attention to shortcomings and, by offering a practical alternative, challenges the church to examine its life and work critically. For example:

- renewal by the Spirit in contrast to the pre-
  dominance of rational technical nostrums in
  the modern outlook (including church strategies for renewal).

- direct religious experiences in contrast to
  tendencies to intellectualize and institu-
  tionalize the faith.

- a committed religious life in contrast to
  the lack of commitment and the optional
  character of folk-church life.

- close-knit fellowship and focus on central
  religious issues in contrast to lack of
  focus, uncertainty about mission, and identity problems (e.g., in full-time church
  workers).

The issue here is knowledge of the "signs of the times",
a knowledge based on the gospel. Is this a correct
diagnosis? Does the charismatic movement remedy the
disabilities it diagnoses?

2. In the life and work of the church, Charismatic
Renewal appears to be ambiguous. There is a tension
between attractive features and repellent ones, between
points of agreement and points of criticism. While
charismatic piety enjoys a high degree of plausibility
within the movement, there is a corresponding shortfall
in communication with other groups in the church. In
actual practice, Charismatic Renewal finds it difficult to communicate with other efforts to live by the
gospel. For example:

- although, in the use of the Bible, the "nasty
  ditch" between text and situation is bridged,
  other gaps open up, e.g., between charismatic
  biblical exegesis and other views of Scripture.

- vitalization of doctrinal contents easily ends
  in absolute identifications: God, sin and new
  life become clearly identifiable quantities.

- the religious certainty of Christians with
  charismatic experiences smacks of self-assur-
  ance to Christians with a different background
  and encourages a potentially divisive distinction between the religiously rich and the religiously poor in the congregation.

- for religious practice the discovery of fellowship remains an ecclesiastical one, and is
  usually even limited to the group of those
  thus renewed instead of leading to a genuinely
  social religious experience.

16

- the real pivot of renewal - i.e., the submission of everything to the operation of
the Spirit and the interpretation of renewal as strictly God's doing - contrasts
with the systematic direction, religious
control, and even production of salvation
almost as a manufactured ware, in the life
and practice of charismatic groups.

In the charismatic movement are we not confronted with a
piety which puts into practice precisely what the church
has always been saying? But how is what the church has
always been saying related to what the church is called
upon to be and do today?

3. In the Charismatic Renewal movement, the church is
confronted with "dangerous memories" (Metz), though
usually these are hardly noticed because they are pre-
vented from becoming dangerous to the church or to the
charismatic movement by a premature attempt at integration. For example:

- "immediacy" conceals a potential which can call
in question all institutional forms of the encounter with God.

- in the charismatic experience, God is mater-
ialized, so to speak. Does this not entail
a radical secularization of the religious
experience?

- the gift of prophecy hauls the prophetic
mission back into the congregation. But
how are we to ensure a prophetic praxis
which surmounts the restriction of prophecy
to the domestic guidance of a congregation?

- in the charismatic movement it is only in
marginal groups that social commitment appears as a central concern. The focus of
expectation there, however, is on encountering God in the disadvantaged and oppressed.
What does this imply for religious practice
and for our understanding of the Spirit
(Spirit even outside the church, pneumatol-
ogia crucis)?

There is in all these aspects a dimension of "enthusiasm". In other words, they require clarification in
the light of the Word of God. At the same time, however, they are spurs and stimuli which should not pre-
maturely be suppressed. They can highlight the fact
that truth is never a possession but always the object
of a common continuing search.

4. What characterizes the relationship between the
charismatic movement and the church is the fact that
while the charismatic movement on the one hand stands
in and wishes to stand in the church, on the other hand,
as a movement it stands over against the church. This
raises the question of plurality within the church but
also the question of the unity of the church. How are
we to surmount the tensions which surface here? What
suggestions can we make here?

   - we need dialogue between experiences and not
     just between convictions. How do distinct
     experiences - charismatic and others - be-
     come mutually communicable? What can be
     learned here by comparing the different con-
     texts?

   - there is need for a distinguishing of the
     spirits, one which is recognized as a task
     of the whole community. "Experience of the
     Spirit", therefore, "not only precedes doc-
     trine but also leads on to the separating
     of the spirits whereby doctrine emerges and
     the community is maintained in the act of
     witnessing to its unique Lord and trusting
     the voice of his Word" (C. Hinz). The re-
     cognition of discernment of the spirits as
     a charisma could also add that the exer-
     cise of this gift involves a prophetic act
     in which the gospel and the "signs of the
     times" are brought together.

   - models are needed for the cohabitation of
     different styles of groups within the church
     (tolerance, integration, dialogical plur-
     ality).

B. THREE VISIONS BY A PARTICIPANT

One of the participants at the Schwanberg conference was a woman who prayed and fasted throughout the conference. While doing so she had several visions:

First vision: I am cycling through B on a bicycle. Just near the school I see a big house being built, higher than all the others. I dismount and think to myself, "This is it!" The sun is shining on its steep gables and the tower next to it. The workmen are hard at work. It won't be long until the roof is put on. There is something wrong with the gear transmission on my bicycle. It's not a big job to replace the broken screw.

One of the participants interpreted this vision:

Perhaps the world-wide charismatic movement is the big, ecumenical house that is being built and we can say, "This is it!" Beneath its roof Christians who in the past have avoided one another, whether out of ignorance or fear, can perhaps learn to work together in mutual respect and fellowship. At any rate, that's what the reports from all over the world seem to suggest. The trouble is, that in me and many other observers there is obviously something wrong with the transmission. We are lagging behind with our "transmitting" and "understanding". There's a screw which needs replacing.

Second vision: I am in a high, church-like barn, with a beautifully shaped roof. High in the roof gable stands an earthenware pot holding a rose bush in full bloom. The pot is standing on a long staff fixed to the wall at the side by four wires. A psychologist says, "I like that. The pot is safe."

I realize that the roses are artificial. The psychologist's wife shakes the rose bush and says, "Some of the blossoms are real."

Then real petals of crimson roses come
falling down. You can distinguish the
real roses from the artificial ones:
all the real ones have several roses
growing from one stem -- the imitation
ones each have only one.

One participant interpreted this second vision:

The discussions are much too "elevated".
Some of what is said is artificial and
unnatural, but some people seem to like
this artificial "elevation".
Yet there are some real blossoms there
too. Some real things also fall to the
"bottom" so that even simple people can
understand.
It is important to distinguish what is
real from what is artificial.

Third vision: I am in a sheltered garden protected by
high, old walls on two sides. On the other
two sides there is a view over a wide
stretch of beautiful countryside. The
garden is full of luxuriant fresh green
plants. I ask the old woman working there
whether the plants are sown or planted.
She explains that some of the bushes are
many years old, some sown, some planted.
A lot could also be transplanted.
Now I see MALLOW in bloom. The new mallow
shoots are growing from an ancient thick
root, and young shoots are also growing all
around the trunk. The old woman says the
root comes from SINAI.

There was no interpretation of this third vision.

C. TOWARDS A CHURCH RENEWED AND UNITED IN THE SPIRIT

WCC consultative group paper

Revised and abridged by W.J. Hollenweger

1. Hopes and Expectations

1.1. A number of leaders of charismatic movements from the reformation, non-conformist and Roman Catholic traditions, who came together for prayer and study at Schwanberg Castle (Federal Republic of Germany) in December 1978, formulated their expectations for this study process as follows:

As the ecumenical movement is itself a renewal movement, it is astonishing that it took the World Council of Churches longer than the Vatican to recognize the necessity for a study of the charismatic movement. This omission is now remedied as it is recognized that the Charismatic Renewal contains great promises and poses a number of problems. Both are to be explored and tested.

In the process of this testing and exploring we expect the experiences of contemporary spiritual initiatives to challenge the churches and the ecumenical movement. Equally we expect the experiences of the churches and of the ecumenical movement to challenge contemporary movements of renewal.

1.2. The Charismatic Renewal has the potential to extend the contemporary ecumenical movement to communities within Christendom which have so far kept aloof from the development of ecumenism. This is particularly true for the majority of the churches in Africa and Latin America, which are not separated from the World Council of Churches by a conscious theological decision but by an appalling lack of communication. There are few bridgebuilders (pontifexes?), few intercultural theologians who bridge the abyss between the statements of an international bureaucracy and the stories of Third World congregations, struggling successfully for spiritual and physical survival. Whether or not the liturgies of the Charismatic Renewal contain such intercultural bridge-building elements, has yet to be tested.

1.3. In dealing with the Charismatic Renewal, the
ecumenical movement and the churches will be confronted
with "dangerous memories" of their own past (J.B. Metz),
i.e. with a spirituality which does that about which
the churches always talked. This raises at least the
question whether the church today is called to do what
it has always said it should do.

1.4. The temptation is great to brush aside and suppress these dangerous memories. One way of preventing
a fruitful appraisal is to greet charismatic renewals
too readily with unqualified admiration, to applaud it
and thus to freeze it as it stands now. Another way
is to reject it totally on the basis of the false conviction that the church has already dealt with "these
enthusiasts" once and for always.

1.5. We venture to express two hopes for the emerging
dialogue: Firstly: We hope and pray that the Charismatic Renewal will not be too hastily classified, label-
led and thus isolated. We note and endorse the desire
of many exponents of the so-called "Charismatic Renewal" to avoid the term "charismatic" as possibly misleading and giving the false impression that there are
"uncharismatic" Christians. Their preference is for
speaking simply of "congregational renewal" or "renewal in church and society". These terms emphasize that
the charismatic impetus should not result in a distinctive movement or an isolated spirituality, but that it
should seek rather to open up the fountain of faith
which is common to all Christians, namely, the Holy
Spirit promised to all Christians. In the final analysis it is God himself who is renewing his church.
This prevents the work of the Spirit from being exclusively identified with any particular renewal movement.

Secondly: At the same time we hope that new initiatives
will be able to take on a special profile of their own
before they begin to become fruitful for all Christians
and all churches, for in this way they will be an identifiable force. In other words, the possibility of a
renewal will be all the greater for the churches if
there is an identifiable Charismatic Renewal. The
churches will only be able to receive something whose
authenticity demands reception. In this process of reception, the encounter with the reality of the Charisma-

tic Renewal will precede theological interpretations.
That different theological interpretations of one and
the same reality are possible, is suggested by the
three following paragraphs on the Spirit in an eccles-
iological, cosmological and sacramental context.

2. The Spirit - an Ecclesiological Approach

2.1. Since the baptism of Jesus, the Holy Spirit has
taken the form of the church. People were able to see
and hear something of him in the spiritual gifts of
Jesus (Matt. 3:16, Acts 2:33). In the power of the
Spirit, Jesus began to evangelize, came forward as a
new prophet, as the unique and final witness of God,
as the healer (Matt. 4:23), having power over all the
evil forces of separation and division (Luke 4:18ff;
Acts 10:38). Through the Spirit, Jesus offered himself
as a sacrifice to the Father (Hebr. 9:14) and so established the unity of all humankind in his own body on
the cross (Eph. 2:14). In the hour of death, Jesus
transmitted his Holy Spirit and the rich variety of his
spiritual gifts into the history of sinful humankind
(John 19:30). Since his resurrection his spiritual
gifts are continued in the church. Baptized with the
Holy Spirit, we experience (Acts 1:8) his resurrection
in the spiritual gifts by which we serve one another
as stewards of the manifold grace of God (I Pet. 4:10).

2.2. We thank the Lord for having granted us a new experience of the church. This new experience can properly be described as a social experience of God, not in
isolation from or at the expense of others. The Holy
Spirit is God "in between", or "the Go-Between God".
His purpose is to establish relationships between us
and to produce a common experience among us; this includes human experience, yet at the same time trans-
cends and purifies it and connects it ever more firmly
to the cross of Jesus Christ.

2.3. We belive that this Holy Spirit is present as one
and the same Spirit in the still divided churches, and
that he distributes his gifts in every church as and
when it pleases him. Divisions are not his doing but
due to human sin. This being the case, we confess that
no church is able to express the fullness of the Holy
Spirit in its life. Everything accomplised by him,
therefore, in the divided churches contributes to their
mutual upbuilding (I Cor. 12:7) and towards their unity.

2.4. "The reason why many people feel that God is dead, is the absence of communities in which they can experience his presence" (H.M. Schulz, Damit die Kirche lebt, Mainz, 1975). Few will question the truth of that statement. It describes the poverty of our churches. Yet it is in "the fellowship of new life" (H. Gollwitzer) that the social and historical experience of God acquires shape and form.

2.5. Our physical life is not something we bestowed on ourselves. God is our Creator. He creates us by giving us a mother and a father. It is through these human beings that we receive bodily life. So too, it is through other human beings that we receive the life of our souls. We have not chosen our inclinations and instincts for ourselves. We are always conditioned by others - not so much by our ancestors and the biological inheritance we received from them, but much more through the people who have made up our human world, the people whom we encounter and who inspire us to trust and distrust, joy and fear, courage and cowardice.

2.6. Faith, too, is something we receive through the mediation of others. This is why Jesus attaches such importance to the calling of a new fellowship, the company of the disciples. In a world marked by sin and separation, we need a fresh start, a new form of human fellowship.

2.7. Here we have the focal point of the political and social task of Christians. Admittedly there is much conflict and dispute about this. But on one thing there can hardly be any dispute: the fellowship of the new life shows its spiritual character by being a concrete and social fellowship. Whether the experiences and insights of this fellowship apply to the world at large is debatable. But it is not debatable that the world needs to see in this fellowship an alternative to its own behaviour - not a life of undisturbed harmony, but of conflicts shared with mutual respect. The Christian community should and can become the model of a renewed society.

3. The Spirit - a Cosmological Approach

3.1. The Holy Spirit renews creation and bestows fullness of life. At the same time, this dawn of a renewed creation is "not yet" the full light of the day. It is a sowing in hope, a sign of things to come, hidden beneath human weakness and the ambiguity of everything religious.

3.2. Within the context of this renewal of creation we expect healing of social relationships, healing in our relations with our own human self, healing of bodily sickness. We expect God to disclose new possibilities (written into God's work of creation) of human inter-communion and patterns of life, of prayer and intercession. Therefore speaking in tongues, prophecy, dance and vision are not infused, supernaturally imposed extras of the divine being. They are, on the contrary, disclosures of patterns of human life "in the presence of God", disclosures brought about by God's own Spirit.

3.3. These disclosures bring us in contact with the heritage of primal and other religions. We have to look for bridges between the wisdom bestowed by God on all peoples and the historical experience of Israel and the community of Jesus. We reject any dualistic interpretation of the world, and, in the confession of God as Creator and Father of all humankind, we seek to discern in the diversity of human religious life the unity of his creation. This openness sets us free from anxiety and self-centredness, from an ethno-centric misinterpretation of the Christian faith. We get a new sense of the way in which the stories of the biblical witnesses - those shepherds, hunters, farmers, and city dwellers - speak home to people living in different cultures. Such an openness does not relieve us of the task of critically sifting and examining both the archaic heritage and modern technological civilization.

4. The Spirit - a Sacramental Approach

1.4. The Holy Spirit and his gifts are bestowed on a person in baptism, which presupposes and includes conversion. Conversion is a once-for-all event, impossible to repeat with the same personal intensity, a once-for-all authentic decision for God (Hebr. 6:4). Constant "readiness" for conversion, present only as intention, can be a hindrance to genuine conversion. Conversion is a once-for-all event which needs constant and repeated renewal and reinforcement by the power of the Holy Spirit.

4.2. Baptism, too, is a once-for-all initial experience. At whatever age it may be administered, baptism does not operate automatically, but by personal acceptance. In keeping with the process of individual development to maturity, this permanent offer of the faithful God must be accepted afresh again and again. The repeatable, explicit renewal of baptism is a great help in this respect.

4.3. By confirmation, power is given to the baptized Christian to place the spiritual gifts which he or she has received consciously and deliberately at the service of church and society, and to maintain continuity with the Holy Spirit's operation at the beginning of the church's existence (Acts 8:14-17; 11:15ff). The explicit prayer for the renewal of the grace of confirmation - also in the presence of the congregation - allows the Holy Spirit to introduce the individual still more deeply to the mystery of his activity in history, history which is always a history of sinful human beings. Every charismatic fresh start carries within itself the seed of potential division. In the renewal of confirmation, the Holy Spirit himself overcomes this danger. The renewal of confirmation also saves leaders from the danger of abusing their spiritural gifts or of attaching people to their own person.

4.4. For ordained leaders, the renewal of ordination is often a radical process in which they allow God to rekindle in them the gift of grace they earlier received (II. Tim. 1:6-10) and are roused from resignation, routine, error and their own arbitrary tactics, to become once again pastors led willingly by the hand of God (Rom. 8:14; John 21:18).

5. Gifts of the Spirit and Discernment - Some Practical Considerations

5.1. The Holy Spirit refuses to be identified with the patterns of a particular historical and cultural situation. The continuity of his work does not consist in his always doing the same thing but in his always establishing the authority of the same person, i.e. Jesus Christ, in the life of the individual and of the community. Hence the community has the freedom to become receptive again to the suppressed and forgotten gifts of New Testament times, as well as to rediscover the activity of the Holy Spirit in new and different charisms. Spiritual gifts are specific forms of grace, which by their variety will reflect the fullness of the Spirit and the universality of grace.

5.2. In practical dealings with spiritual gifts we need to remember:

- that the gift is never a possession but remains dependent on the giver; that it is never a question of having (something new), but always a question of being (somebody new);

- that the individual does not make his or her gift the measure for others but the others become the measure for the exercise of his or her gift;

- that delight with the visible appearance of the Spirit in specific experiences should not result in the trivialization of the Spirit but rather in the acknowledgement of his mystery; the freedom of the Spirit's action is thereby safeguarded and we are able to experience God even in ways which run contrary to our expectations and desires;

- that all experience of God's immediacy remains a mediated immediacy; that the Spirit does not wish to work without or outside the given processes of nature and history; and that the recognition of these mediations (cultural, historical, social psychological, etc.) cannot possibly imply any diminution but only the enrichment of our knowledge of God.

5.3. The community which is receptive to the gifts of the Spirit and which leaves room for the diversity of his operations will necessarily recognize its task of clarifying these experiences in the light of the gospel. For the discernment of the spirits, the Christian community will be guided by the following criteria:

- are the gifts and experiences of the Spirit
  controlled by the life and practice of Jesus?

- do the gifts help towards the upbuilding of
  the Christian community for its service in
  church and world? Do they help the church
  to develop and take visible shape as the
  "Church for Others"?

- does the exercise of the spiritual gifts
  reveal the presence of faith, hope and
  love as the fundamental acts of Christian
  life?

5.4. Since the whole Christian community is responsible
for discerning the spirits, special importance attaches
to the question as to how it can do this. If the discernment of the spirits is understood as a charism,
there is a danger of it being assigned only to particular
individuals who themselves are not subject to control.
We have here a problem which can carry the seeds of
division within it.

But if the Christian community itself as such under-
takes this task, the reaching of decisions is then
understood as a communication process, since it is a
question of discerning "the signs of the times", a
question of recognizing and affirming the activity of
the Spirit today. A Christian community which accepts
this task will view itself as a "pathfinder", a "search
party" which, while not shrinking from the venture of
reinterpreting the gospel, recognizes at the same time
the provisional nature of its knowledge. In some
churches the episcopal office has an essential function
here.

D. PLEA FOR SHARING IN THE SEARCH FOR A "CHURCH RENEWED AND UNITED IN THE SPIRIT"

Peter Felber

1. Presentation

I hope my paper will help us to find a sincere unity in all our diverse experiences - a unity which takes into account all the things which separate us.

In 1978 the WCC Advisory Group held a conference in Schwanberg and drew up a paper. This "Schwanberg paper" was then sent to various people asking for their reactions, and I was asked by Arnold Bittlinger to evaluate them. My paper begins with a short evaluation of the main topics discussed.

When I read all the reactions my impression was that the diversity expressed was not so much rooted in the different theologies themselves but rather in the different experiences which lay behind the mask of these theologies. I therefore wrote my paper based on that understanding.

However, because my way of thought, my theology and my "preaching" are rooted in my experience, I do not want to force them upon you but rather to share them with you. In order to do this I am obliged to tell you my story, which is not only the story of my Christian life but also the story of why I am attending a consultation on Charismatic Renewal organized by the World Council of Churches.

I am Swiss, I belong to the Reformed Church, and I was born and brought up in the dry structures of the established church in Switzerland. I had my basic Christian education in that church. When I made the decision to study theology and when I was actually studying, I felt increasingly the gap between what full Christian faith could be and what it was in the cage of my confessional church context.

Then I found a notice in my seminary advertising the job of steward an an ecumenical conference. I applied and was accepted. This was the first time I was in-

volved in the ecumenical movement, but not the last.
(Stewards are young people invited by the WCC to help
out at conferences and thus to learn more about the
World Council.)

This experience of ecumenical fellowship at WCC gatherings was for me the big experience in my Christian faith.
I cannot say "I was born again", but after that experience my faith was renewed. I cannot say I was
"baptized in the Spirit", but after that experience I
had an insight for the first time in my life into what
the Spirit is doing. Most of the richness of my present Christian faith stems from the experience of the
ecumenical richness of our faiths, and from that time
onwards I was able to fill my confessional cage with the
richness of the gifts which I found in other confessions, churches and Christian lives.

So when, in 1979, Arnold Bittlinger told me about the
Charismatic Renewal, I found that I had experienced
many of the things he told me about in the ecumenical
renewal. Everything in my paper comes out of this
ecumenical experience, in which I found the richness
of Christian faith.

Now a few remarks about the different issues in my
paper:

The Schwanberg paper is a well-formulated consensus
document - the only paper we have here of that kind.
Because that paper is the only one written in the form
of an ecumenical document, there is the danger, now that
we have experienced our unsettled diversity, that we
will seek help in the formulations of that paper. I
have felt this danger already at other ecumenical conferences, so I feel that we should try to formulate and
express in our final documents what we have really experienced here together. So let us go back to people's
experience and ask each one the following questions:

1. what is your significant experience?

2. what is your situation?

3. what helped you - for instance, a charismatic
   experience - to solve a problem in your situation?

4. how do you analyze your situation and the
   solutions you found helpful for the future?

5. what answers do other people in your situation have to the same problem?

I found these questions helpful every time - in ecumenical dialogue, in the dialogue between different situations and ways of thinking, and dogmas - because they
lead to the most common level of human life: the experience and shaping of the world, which is our life
task as Christians and as human beings.

Let us profit by our diversity and the quarrels arising
out of that diversity, because we belive that "He's
got the whole world - including our diversity - in
his uniting hand." God is strong enough also to tolerate our human quarrels. Knowing that, I am free to
quarrel not in the Spirit of hate and separation, but
as an engaged human being for what I think is God's
will in my experiences, and I shall see what God thinks
about me, about my formulated experience and about the
interpretations I have given to this experience.

2. Plea for Sharing in the Search for a "Church Renewed and United in the Spirit"

The task of this paper is to consider reactions to the
"Schwanberg paper". The main issues in these reactions are the following:

- the Schwanberg paper makes a strong connection between God as the creator of the uni-
  verse and the Spirit as a gift for the whole
  of created mankind. Many persons were not
  pleased with that and requested a more strin-
  gent connection between the experience of the
  Holy Spirit and Christ's deed of salvation
  which he has done once for all. In theological terms: it is the question whether
  pneumatology is a function of christology
  or vice-versa.

- for some persons the connection between
  ecumenical renewal of the church in the
  ecumenical movement, especially in the

World Council of Churches, and renewal
through the Spirit through the Charismatic
Renewal which we are experiencing today
all over the world was not clear.

- another point which appears several times
in the reactions is the "sacramental approach" to the Spirit in the paper. In the
paragraph about sacraments the "one for all"
character is mentioned on the one hand,
while on the other it is stressed that some
sacraments need renewal. It was felt that
the connection between these two aspects
must be clearly worked out.

- it was further remarked that we should pay
attention to the work on sacraments done by
the Faith and Order Commission of the WCC.
This would give us an opportunity to test
the work of the WCC on sacraments and see
if it is helpful for the experience of the
Spirit made in the Charismatic Renewal,
and also to clear that experience in the
ecumenical context of our Christian faith,
as worked out by the WCC.

How should we deal with this paper and these reactions?

The danger of ecumenical conferences: It seems to me
that one of the greatest dangers of conferences is to
underestimate what is really happening in the conference itself. So many conferences, anxious about the
result, do not wait for something to happen but begin
with the "safety-belt" of an input paper, which they
rebuild into an output paper. But is it not true that
by having prepared a clandestine "result paper" from
the outset, one runs the risk of passing by a spiritual
happening? Let us avoid this danger in our consultation. The different live spiritual experiences that
each of us undergo during the consultation are more
important than documents. The Schwanberg paper (and
others) which we are considering should therefore only
be a guide for our work.

The adventure of an ecumenical conference: Every new
gathering can be an adventure if we let it. One does
not know in advance what will happen during a conference. This openness can be beneficial or dangerous.

32

One of the dangers is that participants from different cultural and ecclesiastical backgrounds lose a lot of time through misunderstandings. The organizers of the Bossey consultation have sent the paper "Towards a Church Renewed and United in the Spirit" to churches, congregations and individuals all over the world in order to avoid misunderstanding right from the beginning. So the reactions to that paper are rather a model for the conference and a pointer to where differences could arise during the consultation. By studying the responses we can also see where differences arise due to misunderstandings and where there are real differences among the participants. These reactions should therefore rather help us to be more open for the arrival of the Spirit and make the consultation itself more efficient. The evaluation of reactions has shown the following difficulties with which we might be confronted in Bossey.

The three levels of human experience and communication:
I had the impression from the reactions that we human beings live on three different levels when it comes to experience and communication:

1. The first level is that of basic experience. Each of the persons who reacted to the paper has undergone an experience of God and the Spirit. This immediate and unformulated experience was so strong for each of them that it provided their motivation for engagement in the renewal of the church through the Spirit. But these immediate experiences seem to have been made in different contexts. One person said: "Authentic human community" as an aspect of the experience of the "fellowship of the new life" and of God "is (more readily) found in a basketball team (than in the church)." Other people have had an immediate experience of that reality in some congregations of the Charismatic Renewal, with its specific forms of worship and life. This means that we have to take note of the fact that each participant comes with his own basic experience. And individual experiences will no doubt vary, at least insofar as the context in which the experience of the Spirit took place. So we should not judge the experiences with which we are confronted as legitimate or false, but we should rather ask our fellow Christians: "What are your experiences? What help is it to you to experience the presence of the triune God? Do you feel a gap in your life has been filled through the experience of the Spirit?"

2. The second level of our human experience is <u>formed</u>
<u>experience</u>. We live in different cultural and eccles-
iastical contexts. This <u>context</u> gives us the <u>background</u>
<u>and the forms</u> of our experience. On that second level
the experience becomes "language": not "language" in
the sense of spoken and written words, but "language"
as a cultural form of immediate experience. Man
enters through this process of experience, becoming
language in the world of communication. Let me give an
example: a South American Pentecostal's experience of
the Spirit is in the form of a spiritual dance; an
English-speaking European gives it the form of a prayer
in biblical language and an African sings. Now we live
in a world dominated by Western word-culture. Therefore,
in the worldwide Christian church the form "word" for
our spiritual experiences (including the form "verbal
confession") has an advantage. We appreciate more the
spiritual experiences which can be given in Western verbal form. I have the feeling that we Americans and Europeans should beware of this behaviour. It is a sign
that we are in danger of excluding our Christian sisters
and brothers who have experienced the Spirit in forms
which are outside our community. Why are all the reactions only from Europeans and North Americans? The only
one from Africa was an oral one: "A wonderful paper,
but how can I bring it to my people? They wouldn't
understand this Western theological language!" (There
were other reactions along the same lines, even from
participants in the Schwanberg conference who were not
able to communicate their thoughts because of the difficult theological language used by the experts.)

I feel we should be careful and listen to all the different forms in which the Spirit speaks, and not only
to the written and spoken "word" approved of by Western
theologians. It is easier for Europeans and Americans
to ignore them but in doing so we perhaps exclude some
other aspects of the Spirit and his (or her - many
people stressed the feminine character of the Spirit!)
impact on the world today. And perhaps we pass by the
renewal effect of the Spirit and some of his/her forms
for the Western churches and congregations.

3. The third level I would like to mention is that of
the <u>interpretation</u> we give to our experiences. Human
beings, after having experienced something in a cultural

form, and after the immediate experience has become expression, try to incorporate this experience into their
system of thinking and believing. We try to interpret
its meaning within our already formulated faith. The
interpretations are very different and sometimes quite
dogmatic. I think it would be preferable for us to
remain open-minded regarding these dogmatic questions
and not confuse our human thinking and interpretation
with the reality of God and the Spirit. Let us be
more open during the consultation and tolerate the
interpretation of the experiences of each of us as
rooted in our own lives, and listen to the reasons
why each individual is convinced that his/her own particular interpretation is helpful to him/her personally
and to his/her church in the situation in which it
confesses its faith.

II.

Letter of the General Secretary of the WCC to the Member Churches and Reactions of the Churches

To: Member Churches   3 August 1979
    National Councils
    Regional Conferences
cc: Members of the Central Committee

Re: A CHURCH RENEWED AND UNITED IN THE SPIRIT:
    A Consultation on the Significance of the
    Charismatic Renewal for the Churches

Dear Friends,

In March next year, the World Council of Churches' sub-unit on Renewal and Congregational Life will gather some fifty people to work on the above topic.

Their task will be to clarify understanding of the Charismatic Renewal and its meaning for the churches, and to study responses of the churches to the Charismatic Renewal. Through and beyond the quest for understanding, participants will be seeking a clearer picture of that renewal in faith and obedience to which Christ is calling his church.

This is a request for your help in identifying the issues to which the consultation should address itself. We have tried of course to track down official statements on this subject made by member churches, but we may not have found them all. In any case, past statements may not be adequate formulations of the issues as you perceive them today, and indeed many churches have not expressed themselves officially about the Charismatic Renewal at all.

I should be grateful, therefore, if you, or someone else in a position to advise us on behalf of your church, could take the time to outline what in the light of your experience and of your situation are the main questions that call for attention at the March consultation. A response by 1 November would enable us to draw upon your questions and insights in giving final shape to the agenda.

Thank you, in anticipation, for your help.

                              Philip A. Potter
                              General Secretary

1. Responses of the Churches

(compiled by Arnold Bittlinger and Peter Felber)

An anthology of the reactions to the letter of the General Secretary of the World Council of Churches concerning the Charismatic Renewal in the churches.

(See page 59 for list of all churches and organizations who have responded. The numbers given after quotes in the text refer to this list).

I. HOW THE CHURCHES ARE AFFECTED BY THE CHARISMATIC RENEWAL

The experience of the ambiguity of the Charismatic Renewal

"The Spirit of God is moving within our nations today. He is moving where he wills in the lives of men, women, boys and girls...

"Worship is changing many congregations. Lay people are seeking and taking a new role...

"But hand in hand with this revival is confusion. In some congregations and circuits all is not well...

"In other congregations the people are divided, both groups claiming to follow the truth...

"Where this movement of the Spirit is part of God's plan of salvation for his church, the united church must face the challenge. There is the danger that we may be opposing God's plan for salvation.

"It often helps to break down denominational barriers. There is the new found freedom that allows Christians to worship and witness with other church groups...

"There is an involvement in social witness. The gospel is seen once again to have the power to bring about social change.

"The Sixth Assembly calls on every minister and pastor to be open to the movement of God's Holy Spirit in every congregation and locality.

"We want all the Christians and especially our leaders in each place to know that where the Holy Spirit of God moves, there at the same time the Devil is active. (22)

"I was extremely interested in your letter, the more so as I myself am at the head of a church which is at present experiencing a charismatic revival, brought about by the spiritual awakening which took place in the Congo in January 1947 and which is still going on. This movement, I admit, did an immense amount of good to the church but it also caused quite a few difficulties and sharp misgivings." (5)

The reactions of the churches: consulations, reports, "task forces"

"I am glad to report that we had a very interesting and useful time at our consultation at Ely on 9-10 October, and I shall hope to be sending you a copy of the preliminary report of it shortly. We are hoping to produce a popular pamphlet for the Church of England on the subject subsequently, and to stage a debate in the General Synod, with a report by our own Board, in February 1981.

"Meanwhile, we are now very interested to see how your own worldwide consultation in March will develop. (39)

"Our General Staff Council authorized a task force...

"The objective of the task force is to prepare and present a report to the denomination which would propose "guidelines or criteria for the proper understanding, acceptance and place of the Charismatic Renewal and of charismatics within our denomination." The work of the task force continues...

"The Charismatic Renewal movement has been evident within our fellowship, but not in a uniform or dominant way. Its early appearance several years ago was marked by some divisiveness, tension and fracturing of congregational life over issues of elitism, extreme emotionalism, glossolalia, the authority of the pastor and "elders", and denominational relationships.

"The movement was also marked by an upsurge of commitment, renewal of faith, and joy in worship and witness." (6)

41

Some member churches are a product of earlier charismatic movements

"The Kimbanguist church, in whose midst there are permanent charismatic manifestations, although not yet having made an official declaration on this subject, wishes to participate and provide a living witness of its experience in this matter. (4)

"The history of the Salvation Army, and particularly its very rapid expansion from a small London mission to a world movement in 20 years, is only intelligible as a work of the Holy Spirit. For this reason, the Salvation Army could itself be called a charismatic movement and its early meetings resembled - in freedom from traditional forms and in the expression of joy and mass emotion - charismatic meetings of today." (63)

An Orthodox point of view

"For us in the Orthodox tradition, the term "renewal" usually applies to the life of the believers in community, and not to the church as a whole, which we regard as an organism with Christ, the Blessed Virgin, the apostles, martyrs and saints and all the departed faithful in it, and we do not presume to renew that church. It is always new by the presence and power of the Spirit. We do not equate the common life of the Christians now living on earth with the life of the church; the latter has so many dimensions.

"For us, renewal of the spiritual life of our believers is a work of the Holy Spirit through the teaching of the word of God and participation in the mysteries of the church - especially the sacraments of repentance and communion, or confession and eucharist. It is only by returning to God from our sinful ways and seeking to be united with him through the Body and Blood of Christ our Lord that our spiritual lives can be renewed...

"Nor do we believe that the charismatic movement as such, which exists also in our church, brings about the renewal of the church...

"We have sought to help our charismatics take more leadership in the church, but they do manifest some

Montanist tendencies and keep themselves aloof from
other members of the church, seeking guidance mainly
from their own charismatic leaders... (20)

"If the sub-unit can do some preliminary work on ecclesiology and pneumatology in relation to renewal, the
consultation can be useful."

II.   EXPERIENCE AND THEOLOGY

New society - new experience

"Experience of God is primarily a social experience of
God; to know and practise this is vital for the growth
of the congregation and the charismatic congregational
renewal movement helps to develop this knowledge and
practice.

"The transition from a static naturalistic experience
of life and the world to a socially dynamic one, a
transition which can rightly be described as "epoch-
making", summons the modern human being to a socially
mediated, personally binding religious decision.
This approximates closely to the authentically New Testament witness to a spiritual experience which is related primarily to the Holy Spirit in our midst rather
than to the Creator God above. The future of the
people's church largely depends on that church's becoming increasingly a fellowship of personally committed Christians mediating their faith to one another
and to the world in a social form. The theological
basis for the emphasis on the existence of the church
in this form is found at the point where the doctrine
of the Trinity, christology, pneumatology, and ecclesiology intersect. In short, "spiritual experience is
basically experience of the dual divine We and, at the
same time, experience of its in-dwelling in the plural
We of the disciples of Jesus..."

"More important than liturgical movements and innova-
tions in worhsip is the transition from a structure of
worship dominated by the single voice of the pastor to
one which is charismatic and congregational. Although
this transition is not simply a matter of organization,
appropriate developments in the congregation can help
to bring it about. (45)

"It is due to the change which was realized in the last
decades in the society in which our church lives and
to which it is to a certain measure bound in its work
and style of living that our church has to rethink the
problems of its own charismatic renewal. (32)

"Is it perhaps easier for modern man to experience and
to conceptualize God's presence in terms of the presence
of the Holy Spirit?" (48)

Cultural background and religious experience

"Is the charismatic experience itself of God or of man?
Granting there are counterfeits, but what of the experience itself? (8)

An Australian voice:

"The cultural relativism of the phenomenon. My own view
is that the Charismatic Renewal is a massively culturally conditioned religious activity and part of a clear
cultural spectrum of the seventies. Both its cultural
dimension and its dimension of religious response need
major study...

"The Papua New Guinea experience. I note because it
may not get noted elsewhere that the experience of renewal in the highlands of New Guinea, while it may be
expressed in charismatic language, in fact is deeply
dependent on traditional responses in animistic religion and is a superb illustration of the cultural relativism of spirit type responses." (30)

The Pacific Islands:

"The use of laying on of hands with prayer in many
meetings run by charismatics inside and outside Pacific
Island churches has been more beneficial than otherwise,
since it is usually done under spiritual direction that
controls mere emotionalism. The same may be said of
the casting out of evil spirits, which are a source
of great worry and misery to many people in most Pacific Island cultures. Is this a regular ministry seriously neglected within the orderly and often more
beautiful liturgical framework offered by the main
churches? Should new and satisfying forms of regular
public worship with this in mind be devised by the churches themselves?" (21)

An African voice:

"Until recent years, there was no freedom in the older churches to express Christian joy by rhythmic clapping, dancing, or singing in Ghanaian style. Only 45 years ago one teacher, proud of his African heritage, was dismissed from his post in a key teacher training institution because of his insistence on wearing traditional dress to go to church and to preach...

"We need to stress that he (God) is active in healing and miracles. We know healing demands prayerful preparation by the pastor and the whole membership of the congregation, and that if we take it seriously we must be prepared for Satan's counter-attacks. Africa is well aware of the reality of evil spirits (and as the West loses the prevailing influence of the gospel the awareness is coming back there too). We who have the answer, in Christ's supernatural power, must pray and act in accordance with our underlying conviction." (3)

A European insight:

"...occult ties play an important role." (34)

An answer from the Indian sub-continent:

"In response to your request, I submit for your reflection some questions and insights which I have been feeling in my heart for many years in my meditations and yoga, i.e. silence, devotional recitation in my mother tongue (Tamil), and mystic liturgical chants...

"Can the monastic ashram community life be conducive to Charismatic Renewal?" (23)

"Charismatic forms" and cultural estrangement

"Are imported forms of group praise hailing from lower and middle class culture in America or Europe, and widely used by charismatics, alienating Pacific Island peoples from their own cultures?

"Is it not important to build a bridge to forms of group ecstasy already there in local cultures rather than culturally alienating people by the use of stereotyped imported material?" (21)

Experience of God must become theology

"How can "charismatics" be encouraged to give a theological explanation of their experience with the living
Lord, in such a way as to avoid the charge of "charismatic existentialism"?" (56)

What is the purpose of theology?

"It seems to me to be rotten theology to suppose that
any religious movement has in it any automatic and in-
fallible defence against error and degeneration. The
fact that there really does seem to be justification
for the claim that the charismatic movement "of the
Spirit" does not mean that we are all suddenly going
to become incapable of sin. I'm hoping, therefore,
that the URC is going to keep its eyes wide open to
the dangers at the same time as it learns to open its
mind and heart to the Spirit." (61)

Why not pneumatology?

"Why was and is pneumatology (doctrine of the Holy
Spirit) taught separately and not integrally in European theology?" (46)

Theology and the congregational experience - the present gap.

"The oft-lamented gulf between academic theology and
congregational piety is bridged neither by the popu-
larization of academic theological works nor by a retreat into pragmatism or the practical sciences, but
only by mutual receptivity to contemporary operations
of the Holy Spirit and their theological implications.

"It is not far short of tragic that some of the severest
criticisms of the charismatic movement come from certain pietistically inclined groups, particularly within
the fellowship movement." (45)

III. ABOUT ECCLESIOLOGY - WHAT IS "CHURCH"?

Church and renewal

"A working definition

The term Charismatic Renewal is used rather than Charismatic Movement, for the latter could imply an organization working inside and/or outside the churches
which one can join, which does certain recognizable
things, whereas Charismatic Renewal we understand to
be a term which describes the individual and corporate
experience of Christians who claim a fresh realization
of the Holy Spirit as the one who empowers the Church
in all the concrete and specific ways described in the
New Testament." (61)

See also page 42 on "Charismatic Renewal also in the
Orthodox Church". (20)

Established churches and Charismatic Renewal

"The charismatic movement as a critical question to
the church (its possible contribution to the spiritual
renewal of the church).

"The appeal for a conscious decision for Christ, for
committed discipleship, is a clear challenge to the
established church. (34)

"Is the church the community of the baptized of the
faithful or only of the renewed? Or should the church
cover all three? (58)

"It must be critically questioned whether you can separate the decision for Christ and the receiving (experiencing) of the Holy Spirit. Can there be a decision
for Christ without the help of the Holy Spirit (see
Luther's statement on the Third Article and the relation
between baptism and the Holy Spirit)?" (34)

The question of baptism

"Matters relating to "Christian initiation", i.e. how
does a person become a Christian and what place does the
"baptism of the Holy Spirit" have in this process?
Questions relating to baptism/confirmation/conversion/
sacraments, etc. (3)

"It is a theological question of some note as to when
members of the Body of Christ received the Holy Spirit,
in particular how to relate sacramental inclusion,
conversion of the so-called "baptism in the Holy Spirit"
of those who have been both baptized as infants and
have been strong believers for a number of years. (8)

"Which kinds of understandings about baptism are found
in the charismatic movements and which baptismal practices lead to misunderstandings (re-baptism!)?

"To what extent are traditional baptismal doctrines a
hindrance to a charismatic renewal of the congregation? (4

"It is surprising that in charismatic circles baptism
is rediscovered as the objective date basis in the life
of a Christian and that the Lord's Supper is held in
such high esteem. (34)

"It is significant that oral confession is anew being
taken seriously as a liberation possibility which sets
free powers for the whole church as well as for the individual." (34)

Present church structures and the sources of the church

"Are the main-line churches finding a threat to their
tradition-hallowed structure in Charismatic Renewal?
If yes, why? If stealing of sheep is one of the com-
plaints how does the shepherd lose the flock? Was it
not because the Christian community lost track of
Christian spirituality? Is not Christian spirituality
the way a community organizes itself in order to open
itself to the transforming power of the Holy Spirit,
which power is the power of the gospel? (23)

"First it is the problem of the function of the whole
organism of the congregation. The question of the charismatic concept of the Christian congregation had to
come necessarily if the thinking was really sincere and
thorough. Our theology had to rethink the complicated
problems of the institutionalized church facing the law
of the development of the institutional form of any
organization and taking more and more into account the
developed institutional form of our church. On the
other hand, we know that any institution has to return
to the sources from which it was fed at its birth and

strengthened in its early life-time if it does not want
to reach the stadium of morbid stiffness and hypertrophy." (3

Some suggestions for study by the World Council consultation

"An examination of Charismatic Renewal must include a
comparison of what was "normal" in the New Testament
church, and what is "normal" in today's church. The
great appeal of the charismatic movement has been: "You
can live New Testament Christianity today!"

The Reformed Church, and by the same token the World
Council of Churches, would do well to address itself to
the reasons why so much of church life today is "subnormal" compared to the New Testament church. The report quoted states "Every Christian is eligible for
every work and gifts of the Spirit." This is a fine
theological statement, but it begs the more important
practical question: "Why then is so little of the work
and gifts of the Spirit in evidence?" (10)

The ordained ministry

"Should we not recognize that the celebration of the
eucharist before it became the preserve of the ordained
ministry was the legitimate and natural function of the
layman and that structured hierarchical ordination
bottled up the Holy Spirit with the laying-on-of-hands
of ministers (order) with all the succeeding wrangles
of "apostolic succession" and the loss of charisma? (23)

"What sort of "authority" can a local Methodist minister
claim, by virtue of his office, in the affairs of a
charismatic group? (53)

"Wherever the concept of the charismatically renewed
congregation is thought of the concept of the one-man-
leadership in the congregation is as well problematized.
The same is discussed also in other contexts. This concept of the one-man-leadership in the congregation was
help practically even in our church work. Its main
characteristic is that a single man, the pastor, was
the preacher and the teacher at the same time - the only
one for both functions in the given congregation. This
concept of the congregation's work is not problematized
there where there were several other persons around
this pastor helping him in his many-sided daily work.

It is problematized there where the charismatic congregation prays for the fullness of the gifts of the Holy Spirit as well as for the preaching service and also for the teaching one. In this new concept the pastor becomes only one of the many gifted members of the given congregation." (32)

The ministry of unity leads to division:

"One function of a bishop is to be a centre for unity in his diocese, though quite often he is a centre for division, since if he exercises any real leadership, he is likely to displease some of the people all the time and all of the people some of the time." (2)

Church renewal through tensions and division: positive and negative aspects

"The basic problem with regard to the "charismatic movement" is its strong spiritual closeness with the Pentecostal movement, with its permanent divisive effect. Question: Is the charismatic movement a renewal within the church and a spiritual congregational renewal? Will a new dimension of Christian spirituality come to light through it? Does this mean: renewal or breaking away?" (49)

Positive aspects:

"From our research this year it is obvious there are areas of exciting movement within the church, and there are also areas of tension. We are convinced that such tensions, while indeed they may be unpleasant for a time, are signs that the church is alive and growing. They become opportunities for everyone engaged in the life of the parish to explore at depth the meaning of Christian life. (28)

"The continuing charge of divisiveness needs to be looked at. To me it's a non-question. Jesus said that he came to divide; he split Judaism irrevocably, and will return to divide the just from the unjust. All growth is achieved by division (i.e. cell and parturition, etc.). Every renewal movement in the history of the church has caused some dislocation and division; to my mind the present one is remarkable for how little it has divided. But the evidence needs to be tabulated for people to look at. (1)

"When facing the problems brought on by the movement, one should keep in mind that during the history of the church there has never been a revival that was without problems for the churches and the congregations experiencing the awakening. (40)

"Paul asks that worship be done decently and in order. Are the somewhat ephemeral choruses and ditties used in charismatic groups comparable with, for example, the great hymns of Charles Wesley on the Holy Spirit or the majestic local forms of singing, and Bible-drama of, for example, Tonga, the Lau Group in Fiji, or the "prophet songs" of many Melanesian churches?" (21)

Negative aspects:

"But there are also dangers: One much-loved priest said to me: "Some of these groups have widened their vision to accept new limitations"! (2)

"Sometimes, too, the Charismatic Renewal is eclectic. One of my correspondents writes: "Instead of being the leaven in his parish church one man I know travels 30 miles each Sunday (each way) to be with a charismatic group (passing dozens of parish churches on the way!)." These groups are too often inward looking and much talk of renewal of Christians tends to imply the inadequacy of those outside. They are divisive in the sense that the unity they proclaim "across denominational barriers" is a unity of the like-minded, of those who share the same experience. They are not open to others.

"Question: Does the Charismatic Renewal renew congregations and build up the Body of Christ? How far has it succumbed to the dangers of a "holier-than-thou" attitude? Does it forward ecumenism, or hinder it by putting a new exclusivism in place of traditional denominational barriers? (60)

"Are there other church factors which obstruct renewal action or on the contrary promote them? (for example, a too-narrow conception of the institutional ministry?)

"Are there forms and action from groups within the range of "Charismatic Renewal" which in themselves show the impossibility of integration?

"Are there wrong turnings or wrong teachings which should
be rejected?" (34)

Church outside the churches?

"While the classical Pentecostals are separatists, the
neo-Pentecostals are active on the fringe or beside the
churches." (49)

"The majority of those who have been helped by this experience in the Pacific seems to be composed of people
who were previously rather shy and not easily able to
speak out in public. For them, the experience has been
important and valuable, but does it follow that it is
necessary for others, or for all? (21)

"Admission to the ministry of the older churches has
always been limited to those of better education, and
the way into the ministry passed through many a committee and examination. Thus many of the newer churches
which have burst out of this situation are headed by men
of little education who have gifts of leadership which
they could not exercise within the older churches. (3)

"In some situations the charismatic fellowship has been
found to be the most significant means of attracting
and converting the "outsider". Those newly converted
do not fit easily, however, into the more traditional
patterns of worship and institutional church life. (53)

"Material concerning what is actually happening in the
churches should be collected so that the consultation
does not end in just theoretical speculation. We think
that a mapping of the attitudes of the churches towards
the charismatic revival - and vice versa - should be
undertaken. We also think that it would be worth-while
to find out whether the charismatic movement has created
other types of contact than the churches." (57)

The conditions behind renewal

"The relationship of the Charismatic Renewal to the
historical development of the church, i.e. why has it
happened in this way at this time? What is its relationship to the past history of the church?" (31)

African insight:

"The so-called Pentecostal experience of the baptism of the Spirit and the related spiritual gifts, especially speaking in tongues, has come into Ghana.

"...through a spontaneous reaction of African Christians to the cold and undemonstrative forms of Western liturgy which have been introduced into the country by the missionary churches. This reaction is not only against the Western forms of liturgy but also against the older churches' bureaucratic organization and conservatism...

"The historic Pentecostal churches came into Ghana in the 1920s and 1930s whereas the older Protestant denominations, Presbyterian, Methodist, and Anglican, have been in the country for over a century. Nearly all churches are growing faster than the rate of population growth, which is about 27% over a decade: however, whereas the older churches are growing at between 30 and 45%, the Pentecostal churches seem to be growing by nearly 70% over the same period. (3)

"As the manifestations of the Spirit can be experienced only periodically - in Switzerland the last time was several years ago - the question arises of what happens when the effects of the Spirit decline again or fail to appear altogether?" (58)

IV. THE ECUMENICAL SIGNIFICANCE OF THE CHARISMATIC RENEWAL

The community of the "charismatics" - the ecumenical dimension

"Within the charismatic movement there has been a real attempt at the local level to develop a sense of the church as "community" and at the broader level to find practical expression for the church as the Body of Christ (i.e. the remarkable ecumenical aspect of Charismatic Renewal). (30)

"As may be expected, this entails a split. Some people have special gifts, while others seem not to have them. Those who do not possess apparent gifts, often feel inferior, even though no declaration of inferiority has been expressed on the part of the charismatics. If a doctrine of baptism in Spirit is presented in addition to baptism with the use of water, Christian life is often in an imprudent way directed towards an experience of baptism in Spirit. (40)

"For many people, the label "charismatic movement" conjures up in the first place only such "exceptional" charisms as glossolalia, etc. But the primary concern of this movement is actually to take seriously the endowment of all Christians with charisms...

"The Charismatic Renewal movement in the congregations is expressly opposed to any overemphasis on certain charisms. The charisms of social criticism (in conscious contrast to a spirituality which is indifferent to secular responsibility) and financial administration are just as much gifts of grace as diaconia and prophecy, when practised in a personal and social relationship of faith in Christ. (45)

"How far should the diversity of the churches be considered as a gift of the Holy Spirit? (58)

"The Holy Spirit grants many gifts of graces through which different Christians are commissioned and enabled to participate in the salvation work of Christ in their congregations and in their own way.

"In the divided Christianity the gifts of grace are so distributed that each confession conserved the gifts which correspond to them, but which they have also multiplied and exaggerated.

"Each confession is inclined to be satisfied with the scope of gifts present among them as if no other gifts existed. This leads to impoverishment and paralysis.

"Confessions need one another because no one possesses the fullness of all the gifts, but on the other hand no one lacks any gifts.

"The Holy Spirit who is working for the gift of graces urges all confessions to aim for the fullness of the gifts which are only present in the whole church.

"In ecumenical encounters each confession realizes, in encountering the gifts of other confessions, the limitations and one-sidedness of its own gifts. (55)

"The Charismatic Renewal of the congregation is the beginning of a common ecumenical tradition and constitutes
a great hope for Christian unity.

"Whereas in the past, charismatic Pentecostalist revivals
usually tended to divide congregations, the Charismatic
Renewal of the congregation must be seen as a strongly
unifying movement. Spiritual experience in the most
widely divergent traditions is nothing less than the
start of a common ecumenical tradition and gives every
ground for high hopes. Far from being accompanied by a
blurring of confessional differences, it usually leads
in fact to a revival of one's own tradition as well as
to its relativization as a "charism" required for
strengthening the unity of the whole. A "convergence"
takes place between the different traditions in the
course of a lengthy process. At the level of the congregations, an ecumenism which is often sterile or in-
tellectualistic undergoes a spiritual revival and acquires a witnessing role inasmuch as it "magnifies"
Christ for us and we find our faith being strengthened
by Christians of other traditions... In this respect,
the evangelistic thrust in the Roman Catholic Church
with its more markedly hierarchical structure is something new which opens up far-reaching prospects for
national evangelism and ecumenical endeavour. (45)

"How can the dimension of reconciliation and unity be
further explored, especially between the Roman Catholic
and the Reformed disciplines? (56)

"Therefore many leaders think that we have to recon-
sider God's plan with a charismatic or spiritual renewal;
where and how did we fail, and what has in fact been the
fruit of the renewal? It seems as if the prayer groups
were meant to be schools for future church life, giving
the believers an experimental understanding and reception of the gospel, leading us to a new way of life.
Therefore we have ahead of us a new phase of the renewal
where the body of Christ will find its healing towards
real unity. This has as a necessary pre-requisite
unity and love among leaders - also among leaders of
different denominations, and willingness openly to accept the work of the Holy Spirit in groups, congregations, institutions, etc., which have not yet been known
as charismatic nor have named themselves so. (43)

"The president supports this attempt by the WCC to clarify
understanding of the charismatic movement. There already
are signs in this church of a new movement of the Holy
Spirit, for which we praise God. As you are aware, this
renewal can cause division and confusion, but in no way
does the Samoan Methodist Church believe this should in
any way deter or hinder God's plan for the spiritual
awakening of the world. We firmly believe that the churches of the world are approaching an exciting era of
happenings and miracles similar to those described in
the book of Acts. Also we find, to anyone who has been
spiritually baptized, there is an awareness of the ecumenical power of the Spirit of God."

The charismatic renewal as grassroots ecumenism

"The release of the Spirit has brought a great number of
Christians nearer to Christ and thus nearer to each other.
They have found a common vision and a common worship. A
number of prayer groups are interdenominational. At
the Dutch national convention, Protestants participate
in the Catholic eucharist and Catholics in Holy Communion. No doubt we can speak about a grassroots ecumenism -
an ecumenism of the heart. As the Holy Spirit is given
to the church as a "bond of peace", the Charismatische
Werkgemeenschap Nederland wants to be an instrument of
the Spirit in working towards "a church united"...

"The CWN is a part of a worldwide movement of the Holy
Spirit and has a number of international contacts.
Also it refuses to be an association, focusing only the
personal and vertical aspects of Christianity. (42)

"With respect specifically to the ecumenical movement,
I agree with Dr Kevin Ranaghan, a Roman Catholic layman,
who said at the 1977 Kansas City Conference on Charismatic Renewal: "I believe that this is the largest
grassroots ecumenical movement in 800 years." The charismatic movement, with its emphasis on the experiential
aspects of the life in Christ, has proven to be a
vehicle by which the Holy Spirit can mould Christians
together more deeply and quickly than by any other means."

"The significance of the Charismatic Renewal for the World Council of Churches

The World Council of Churches has brought together
Catholic and Protestant traditions, but it has not been

a grassroots movement, nor does it have the potential of becoming one as long as it is based mainly on discussion. The charismatic movement, in the few years of its existence, has begun to bring together, in significant numbers, the Catholic stream, the main-line Protestant stream, the evangelical Protestant stream, and the Pentecostal stream. This is exactly what bishop Lesslie Newbigin had visualized in 1953 as a basic requirement for a renewed, missionary church. The future of the ecumenical movement depends on a grassroots renewal by the Holy Spirit!...

"For that reason, I am excited that the World Council of Churches has decided to explore the significance of the Charismatic Renewal for the churches...

"The conference must address itself to the ecumenical implications of on-going Charismatic Renewal, both in World Council churches, and in non- or anti- World Council churches. Will institutional ecumenism benefit from charismatic ecumenism? If so, how? It seems a matter of observation that without ongoing spiritual renewal further progress towards Christian unity will be minimal.

"Therefore, the question must be raised: What can the ecumenical movement learn from the charismatic movement? Characteristics of the latter must be examined: spontaneous; lay-oriented; dynamic; worship and mission-oriented; trans-denominational. Examine the promise of further reconciliation between the main Christian traditions, implicit in Charismatic Renewal.

"The role of the "third world" churches in the World Council. These are the churches that at present are most open to "Pentecostalism". Some of these churches are in the Council.

"Since the Holy Spirit is a Spirit of unity, emphasis on the Holy Spirit will lead to a renewed search for Christian unity, based not so much on doctrine or church order, but on shared life in the Holy Spirit. The charismatic movement is an ecumenical movement! What kind of future does the World Council envision for itself? " (10)

Ecumenia, alliance or a third way

"In a recent publication Kalevi Toiviainen, Bishop of
Middeli, has the following to say of Finnish attitudes
to ecumenical affairs: "Many Christians in Finland regard ecumenia as at best an acceptable pursuit, half
superfluous but on the other hand a matter of such in-
difference as to be not worth opposing. It is seen as
a kind of luxury which may interest the sort of person
who imagines he already has everything he needs. There
are on the other hand still those Christians in this
country who consider it a desertion and a disloyalty to
the Lord.

"It may at least be said that many Finnish Christians
subscribe to a mode of thought deriving from the conservative theology of neo-pietist and evangelical movements, for which ecumenical aspirations are to be feared
as leading to some kind of generalized religiosity or
into the lap of the Roman Catholic Church. Frequently
these same circles are heard to criticize the World
Council of Churches for laying too much emphasis in its
activity on socio-political endeavours.

"Even among those members of local congregations who in
principle endorse the ecumenical movement there are some
who regard the ecumenical work of the World Council as
excessively leader-centred; results of their work are
difficult to apply in practical parish activity. This
criticism is something to be reckoned with in as much
as the leaders of the church cannot hope to get very far
in their own discussions unless ecumenical thinking
finds sufficiently broad acceptance among members of
the congregations...

"Failing this, the contact of the leadership with the
field will be severed. At least the Finnish charismatic
movement has succeeded in drawing into its sphere many
of those associations and individual Christians who look
askance at ecumenica.

"How can the interest in interdenominational cooperation
aroused at congregational level by the charismatic movement and the results achieved in meetings arranged by
church leaders and especially the World Council of Churches and in bilateral church conferences be better coor-
dinated, and seen as an expression of one and the same
aspiration to church unity?

"Within the sphere of the charismatic movement there have also been from the outset centres and congregations un-affiliated to any denomination. In Finland likewise the advent of the charismatic movement brought with it the foundation of the first Bible school common to the mem-bers of all churches and religious groupings, together with its charismatically oriented publication." (48)

"How the WCC can be used by our Lord in giving assis-tance to educate and prepare the world church is a prime issue that must be given in depth thought and prayer. You can create magnificent structures and models of what you see as the ultimate ecumenical church but it surely will fail if people are not made aware that the Holy Spirit himself is the real power who makes this happen. (19)

"Do not the workers and writers of ecumenical agreements need to look at the possibility that people in the Char-ismatic Renewal may have found a dimension of unity that they have not found? (8)

"Finally, are all members and staff of the WCC itself aware of the significance of being born again, John 3:3 and Galatians 2:20? This is the real issue this confer-ence must face. Have all members and staff asked for and received the baptism by the Holy Spirit - is every-one experiencing the power of the Holy Spirit in his or her life? Get this in order first then surely the Spirit of God will lead you into areas of church unity that now seem so far away." (19)

V. CHURCHES AND ORGANIZATIONS WHO REACTED TO THE GENERAL SECRETARY'S LETTER

AFRICA
1. Anglican Church of the Province of Central Africa/Malawi
2. Anglican Church of Mashonaland, Zimbabwe
3. Bible Reading Association, Ghana
4. Church of Kimbangu, Zaïre
5. Evangelical Church of the Congo

AMERICAN CONTINENT
6. American Baptist Church
7. Church of Brethren (Ill./USA)
8. Episcopal Church (NY/USA)
9. Evangelical Lutheran Church of Canada

	10.	Hope Reformed Church, Canada
	11.	Lutheran Church in America
	12.	Presbyterian Church, Canada
	13.	Reformed Church in America
	14.	United Church of Canada
	15.	United Church of Christ (NY/USA)
	16.	United Presbyterian Church/USA
ASIA	17.	Anglican Church of the Province of the Indian Ocean
	18.	Batak Church, Indonesia
	19.	Methodist Church in Samoa
	20.	Orthodox Syrian Church, India
	21.	Pacific Conference of Churches
	22.	United Church in Papua New Guinea and the Solomon Islands
	23.	United Church of North India
	24.	Youth with a mission, Tonga
AUSTRALIA AND NEW ZEALAND	25.	Anglican Church in New Zealand
	26.	Baptist Union of New Zealand
	27.	Methodist Church of New Zealand
	28.	Presbyterian Church of New Zealand
	29.	Uniting Church in Australia
	30.	United Theological College
	31.	Vision Ministries - Temple Trust
EUROPE Eastern-Socialist	32.	Church of the Czech Brethren, CSSR
	33.	Evangelical Church of Rumania
	34.	Evangelical Lutheran Church of Saxonia, GDR
	35.	Theologische Studienabteilung of the Churches in the GDR
	35A.	Arbeitsgemeinschaft Missionarische Dienste in the GDR
Western	36.	Baptist Union in Great Britain and Ireland
	37.	British Council of Churches
	38.	Conference of European Churches
	39.	Church of England
	40.	Church of Norway
	41.	Church of Scotland
	42.	Council of the Churches in the Netherlands
	43.	Ecumenical Council of Denmark
	44.	Evangelical Churches in the FRG

45. Evangelical Churches of Westfalen - FRG
46. Evangelical Church of Berlin-Branden-
    burg - West-Berlin
47. Evangelical Church of the Rhineland,
    FRG
48. Evangelical Lutheran Church of Finland
49. Evangelical Lutheran Church of Wurt-
    temberg, FRG
50. Evangelical Reformed Church of France
51. Fountain Trust, GB
52. Lutheran Church of Sweden
53. Methodist Church in Great Britain
54. Netherlands Reformed Church
55. Nordelbische Evangelical Lutheran
    Church, FRG
56. Presbyterian Church in Ireland
57. Swedish Ecumenical Council
58. Swiss Church Federation
59. United Evangelical Lutheran Church
    in the FRG
60. United Society for the Propagation
    of the Gospel, GB
61. United Reformed Church in Great Britain

ORGANIZATIONS 62. Lutheran World Federation - Institute
              of Ecumenical Research in Strasbourg,
              France
          63. The Salvation Army, Headquarters
              London, GB

ANNEX TO "RESPONSES OF THE CHURCHES"

A. Response of the Ghana Baptist Convention

Observations:

1. Most charismatic Christians feel proud as superior
   believers and look down upon non-charismatic believers.

2. The charismatics go to the extreme of making speaking in tongues the only hallmark of being a Christian.

3. Many charismatic churches go to the extreme of over-emphasizing praying, speaking in tongues and healing the sick, and as a result neglect the preaching and teaching of the word of God.

4. Most charismatic pastors depend solely on the power of the Holy Spirit in ministering to their people and as a result do not believe in seminary education or training. This is also an extreme view, though none can minister effectively without the power of the Holy Spirit.

5. The non-charismatics are also guilty of going to the extreme of having nothing to do with charismatism.

6. The non-charismatics are again guilty of doing well in preaching and teaching the scriptures but doing less in the area of praying and spiritual healing.

7. Many non-charismatic churches are guilty of singing foreign hymns in which the majority of the worshippers do not participate because they are illiterate. Thus they make most of their services formal and lifeless to many.

8. It seems to me that while the charismatics pay more attention to the physical needs of the people, the non-charismatics are more concerned with the spiritual needs of the people, such as salvation and Christian growth.

Suggestions:

1. To make a careful and spirit-led study of the scriptures about the Holy Spirit and appropriation of his gifts.

2. To give equal importance to all the gifts of the Holy Spirit such as teaching, preaching, prophesying, healing and administration (I Cor. 12-14, Rom. 12:3-8).

3. To realize that speaking in tongues is not the hallmark of being indwelt by the Spirit, but rather love,

joy, peace, patience, kindness, goodness, faithful-
ness and self-control (Ga. 5:22-23).

4. To realize that to be proud religiously is sinful
    (Luke 18:9-14). Therefore both charismatic and non-
    charismatic should respect one another's faith.

5. To seek the middle ground in worship, healing, pray-
    ing, preaching and teaching of the Scriptures - this,
    for both charismatics and non-charismatics.

6. Finally, to emulate Christ our Saviour and Lord in
    all things.

May the Holy Spirit himself lead the committee responsible for this work in all their deliberations.

B. <u>Response of the E.K.i.D. (Federation of Protestant
   Churches in the FRG)</u>:

(Translated from the German by the WCC Language Service)

...Relationship to the church is clearly determined only
by the spiritural orientation. If social concern is
not at the same time an expression of spirituality, it
remains without significance for membership of the church.

...No religious problems are solved by social commitment alone. But anyone governed by religious axioms
desires to see these honoured also in social matters.

...Contours of a new life-style are beginning to emerge:
a move in the direction of simplicity (in dress, for example), concern for the originality of nature, voyage
from the visible to the invisible (meditation), growing
sense of solidarity with the whole of creation...

...What brings most young people into these groups is
not convincing argument but the fact that they feel themselves emotionally attracted to them...

...The question theologians must ask themselves is whether a one-sidedly cognitive (intellectual) approach to persons is not bound to mobilize in resistance to itself the emotional make-up (world of feelings) of those persons...

...While individuation, socialization, and communication take place in the same area as the operation of the Holy Spirit, their frame of reference is different and limited...

...The church of the Word needs a theology of the Holy Spirit. Such a theology will need to look for a contemporary understanding of the mystery of the incarnation and for possibilities of a conduct of life controlled by the Spirit...

...The Holy Spirit was not first brought into the world by the biblical message but also shared in the work of the Triune God at the creation.

...Besides its lack of pneumatology, Protestantism has a third shortcoming: in practical theology there is no systematic reflection on piety and the religious life.

...The Holy Spirit not only helps us to believe in Christ but also creates for itself a world of its own focused on Word and sacrament, a world which takes the form of ministries and services, fellowships and groups. This area, while in one respect an altogether human world, is also in another respect a world directed towards God.

...The Bible is the instrument provided by God for reflecting on and ordering our lives before God and the world. Without the Bible, Christian spirituality would be a self-contradiction.

...By meditative reflection on biblical passages, the imaginative level of our being can be reached and renewed and access thus be found to the biblical passages.

...The critical study of biblical passages which throws light on and critically analyses the contexts in which they originated is not opposed to the meditative approach to the Bible.

...The Bible offers an independent instrument of religious wisdom, one which is not dependent on the approach to reality of the natural sciences. It embraces scientific knowledge of reality without conflicting with it.

...Whereas earlier renewal movements, with their dominant interest in conversion, sanctification, fellowship and witness, were often critical of and even hostile to the official mass church and its institutions, the present-day fellowships are often active in their churches and in the decision-making bodies of these churches.

...The prayers of the individual Christian will be all the more effective as a source of spiritual renewal the more these prayers are enfolded in and supported by the prayers of the worshipping community.

...The repetitions, symbolic language, biblical texts and prayers of the liturgy can be a constantly accessible potential source of patterns of religious experience, a source immediately available in critical situations in a way not to be achieved by reliance on rational information. A free form of worship will also all the more certainly strike the right note the more it is supported by a prior discipline of this kind.

...Christians must not let themselves be robbed of their patience for the sake of human beings, however much they are stirred into action by their manifest needs.

...Spiritual experience is regarded in the New Testament as essentially a gracious gift, a charisma for personal development and for service in the congregation. The fundamental charismata are "verbal gifts of grace", i.e. ministry related to the biblical message (apostles, prophets, teachers, according to I Cor. 12:28). But prophecy, healings, speaking in tongues, the ministry of leadership, and simple forms of assistance are also biblical charisma. For assessing such spiritual ministries and experiences, one critical test is the attitude to the crucified and risen Lord.

Every normal living congregation is a setting for this experience. But even beyond the bounds of one's own church, in neighbouring churches and free churches, in religious retreat centres, in religious houses, charismatic groups, fellowships, evangelistic teams, etc. experience must be taken seriously and meditated on.

...Whereas conversion and rebirth are specially emphasized in pietism, the tradition of the church provides a
broader development. This picks up Luther's exposition
of the Third Article: calling (baptism and proclamation),
enlightenment (knowledge of sin and grace), conversion
(personal decision), repentance (self-examination), faith
(personal appropriation), justification (God's promise),
rebirth (fellowship with Christ) and sanctification
(good works).

...Spiritual individualism is a way which holds out no
promise for the future, any more than does an institutionalism concerned simply to administer laws and con-
stitutions. While faith is personal in approach, it is
not a private matter. An institution is implicit in
faith in Christ, otherwise God's incarnation in human
life would have remained incomplete. By his incarnational action, God has established the fixed points
which lie outside the subject, the individual: word and
sacrament are signals for God's incarnational action.
The ministry which accompanies word and sacrament and
the use made of these are consequently the very centre
of all ecclesial institution. Thus the whole gospel,
the forgiveness of sins, the whole of justification,
is contained in the Lord's Supper. In the faithful
celebration of this within the congregation, the "institution", i.e. that which has been "instituted" by
God, is present. Here, too, is the point of integration where the individual and the "church as institution" meet.

...All specific areas of the work of church congregations can be made fruitful, enriched and deepened by
the inclusion of this spiritual dimension. This needs
to be kept in mind every time work plans are being made
for church agencies and associations. It must also be
remembered, of course, that the spiritual dimension
cannot be achieved merely by organization and planning
but points us to the deeper levels where renewal must
begin.

III.
The Bossey Consultation

TOWARDS A CHURCH RENEWED AND UNITED IN THE HOLY SPIRIT:

a Consultation on the Significance of the Charismatic Renewal for the Churches, Bossey, Geneva, Switzerland 8 to 13 March, 1980.

Programme

SATURDAY, MARCH 8

I SHALL POUR OUT MY SPIRIT ON ALL FLESH. (Joel 2,28; Acts 2,17)

Morning and early afternoon: Arrivals

16.00   Tea

16.30   Worship in the Chapel

17.00   Plenary session in the Conference Hall

Opening remarks - Dr. Oscar McCloud, Moderator of the Consultation.

Address - Dr. Philip Potter, General Secretary of the W.C.C., who will set the consultation in the context of the overall concerns of the W.C.C., based on the responses of the member churches to his letter of August 2, 1979.

18.30   Supper

20.00   Informal introductions

SUNDAY, MARCH 9

NOT BY MIGHT OR POWER BUT BY MY SPIRIT SAYS THE LORD OF HOSTS (Zachariah 4,6)

08.15   Breakfast

09.30   Worship

10.30   Coffee

11.00   "Towards a Church Renewed and United in the Holy Spirit" - the story of a revival told by Dr. Walter J. Hollenweger

12.30   Lunch

15.30   Tea

16.00   Group discussion on the responses of the member churches and on the presentations of Philip Potter and Walter Hollenweger

17.00   Plenary discussion

18.30   Supper

20.00   What the Spirit is doing in our day - I: World
        survey led by Dr. Arnold Bittlinger

MONDAY, MARCH 10

THERE ARE VARIETIES OF GIFTS, BUT THE SAME SPIRIT.
(I Cor. 12,4)

08.15   Breakfast

09.00   Worship

09.45   Bible Study: I Corinthians 12: 1-13 (short
        introduction by Dr. Philip Potter)

11.00   Coffee

11.30   Discussion on paper "Models of Christian
        Community in the New Testament"

12.30   Lunch

15.30   Tea

16.00   Discussion on papers: "A Survey of the Worldwide
        Charismatic Renewal" and "Church Reactions to the
        Charismatic Renewal"

18.30   Supper

20.00   What the Spirit is doing in our day - II
        Afro-European Group introduced by Dr. Walter
        Hollenweger

TUESDAY, MARCH 11

AND THE SPIRIT OF GOD CAME ON THE MESSENGERS OF SAUL,
AND THEY ALSO PROPHESIED. (I Samuel 19,20)

08.15   Breakfast

09.00   Worship

09.45   Bible Study: I Samuel 19,18-24 and I Kings 22,
        15-40 (short introduction by Dr. Rodman Williams)

11.00   Coffee

11.30   Plenary session on paper "Plea for Sharing in the
        Search for a Church Renewed and United in the
        Spirit"

12.30   Lunch

Between 14.00 and 18.00 participants will meet in small
groups to produce material for the Drafting Committee

18.30	Supper
20.00	What the Spirit is doing in our day - III Informal presentations by participants and local charismatic group

WEDNESDAY, MARCH 12

THEY LAID THEIR HANDS ON THEM AND THEY RECEIVED THE HOLY SPIRIT. (Acts 8, 17)

08.15	Breakfast
09.00	Eucharist (Anglican: Archbishop Bill Burnett)
09.45	Bible Study: Acts 8: 4-17 (short introduction by Dr. Andrew Walker)
11.00	Coffee
11.30	Plenary session for report
12.30	Lunch
15.30	Tea
16.00	Plenary session for report
18.30	Supper
20.00	Open session

THURSDAY, MARCH 13

THE GRACE OF OUR LORD JESUS CHRIST AND THE LOVE OF GOD AND THE FELLOWSHIP OF THE HOLY SPIRIT BE WITH YOU ALL. (2 Cor. 13, 14)

08.15	Breakfast, followed by departures.

MESSAGE AT THE OPENING WORSHIP

Arnold Bittlinger

You have on page 2 of your programme a symbol of the
whole world - the big, round, world. If we think of
this wonderful planet earth, we think of mountains and
seas, of forests and deserts. But our picture is not
of the geographical aspect of the planet, but of people.
And we are all people.

Everyone in this chapel comes from some part of this
beautiful planet. We are people from many different
countries - from Canada and Papua New Guinea, from
Norway and South Africa, and from many countries between. We are also people from different races and
cultures. And - what is most important for this consultation - we have different experiences.

We are all characterized by our past experiences. I
hope that we will now begin a process of listening to
each other, taking seriously the experiences which
others have had. Taking an experience seriously means
taking a person seriously. There is no person without
an experience; and if the experience of a certain person seems very strange to us, it is still the experience
of that person, and we have to take it seriously whether
we like it or not.

Above the symbol of the planet earth and its people on
page 2 of the programme, there is a word of Scripture:
"I shall pour out my Spirit on all flesh". Behind this
verse are placed two biblical references, one from the
Old Testament and one from the New. You can quote this
verse either way.

There is another well-known Bible verse which you can
quote either from the Old Testament or the New Testament: "You shall love the Lord your God with all your
heart, and with all your soul, and with all your mind,
and with all your strength" and "you shall love your
neighbour as yourself". We cannot love God and we cannot love our neighbour without the Holy Spirit. Thus,
the outpouring of the Spirit is an outpouring of love.

If the Spirit does not come as love it is certainly not
the Holy Spirit. As Paul wrote in I Corinthians 13:

"If I speak in tongues of men and angels but have no
love, I will be as a sounding brass or a tinkling cym-
bal. And if I have prophetic power and understand all
mysteries and have all knowledge, and if I have all
faith so as to remove mountains but have no love, I
am nothing. If I give away all I have and if I deliver
my body to be burned but have no love, I gain nothing."

We know that all manifestations - whether it is speaking
in tongues, or prophecy, or diakonia, whether it is
called "charismatic" or not - have nothing to do with the
Holy Spirit if they are not an expression of love.
This is the one side. The other side is that love is
not a sentimental feeling. Love manifests itself, and
where there is love there will be manifestations such
as prophecy and other charismata.

Therefore, the promise of the Holy Spirit is a promise
of love, and the promise of love is a promise of power.
The promise of the Holy Spirit is thus the only real
hope for this beautiful but wounded world. It is the
only hope because love is the only hope. If we really
believe that God loves this world, we should also believe that he will fulfil his promise: "I will pour out
my Spirit on all flesh."

A. CHARISMATIC RENEWAL AND THE WORLD COUNCIL OF CHURCHES

Philip Potter

Dear Friends,

I fear you're sorry that we're not in Trinidad. I am,
obviously, for it is home for me, but I'm glad to welcome
you in my adopted professional home here in Geneva and
indeed this is the best place you could be, in Bossey,
which for the last thirty-two years has been a place
of encounter where God's Holy Spirit has been at work
with thousands and thousands of people. So it is a
great joy for me to be with you and to express this

fruit of the Spirit. This meeting, I know, has been much prayed for and we have looked forward to it. What happens during these days, let us pray, will be the action of the Holy Spirit. There's one thing I learned - intellectually, but also in actual experience - from a Jewish thinker, Martin Buber, in his very creative book I and Thou, that "I" and "Thou" is a real encounter between God and ourselves and between ourselves and each other, and the "and" represents the presence of the Holy Spirit. And this is what I pray, that we will all be as an "I and Thou" to each other, remembering that the "and" is God's Holy Spirit in the midst.

I have to thank you - and you see the words "thank" and "joy" already and the word "grace" (I haven't used it yet, but will now) are related to the gifts of the Spirit, because the Grace of God in self-giving love is "charis" and curiously enough the New Testament when it speaks of thanks says "charis" - the same word. French: grâce - action de grâces. And joy is "chara" - the same word, the way we express ourselves, our ecstasy at being finally outside of ourselves because of what God has done and our response to it.

And so what I have to say first of all is a big "thank-you" for the responses to the letter which I sent to you in August last year. I do not remember in the history of the World Council of Churches any letter coming from the General Secretary which was so generously and copiously responded to - and that is saying something. There were nearly 70 official replies and with those replies were many documents taken out of synods and General Assemblies of churches and many personal experiences expressed. It has not been easy to digest this material and Walter Hollenweger as usual - he's a Pentecostal man but he's always good at giving orders - wrote me a letter instructing me that I must read all those replies and this was a unique event in the ecumenical movement. (I obeyed him, but I think the Spirit would have meant me to do it anyhow.) There is a document which you have received which is an attempt at summarizing what was sent to us but of course it is very inadequate; it's only to give you a little taste of what was said. But you represent what was said and that is what is most important.

It is very humbling and exciting to have read these documents, humbling because of what God is doing through his
Spirit to people and communities around the world. And
exciting because of what He is doing to renew and unite
Christians and the church. I have to make a confession
to you. I didn't realise how vast the phenomenon of the
Charismatic Renewal was and the vastness of the literature. I went to the library the other day and I found
that there are four shelves of books in our library in Geneva on the Charismatic Renewal, books that have been
written in the last ten to fifteen years. This was
quite a discovery for me.

Now, I want to put the cards on the table. I realise
the difficulty of this consultation being held by the
World Council of Churches. First of all there is the
"image" of the World Council of Churches and in that
"image" there are a number of points. First of all,
it is a council of churches, and what does "churches"
mean? Well, you know what we mean by churches. It's
very official, we have to write very officially to the
churches. We have all these concepts of the churches -
unreformed, unrenewed, official and all the rest of it.
So the World Council of Churches is representing the
churches you think of being all these things that the
charismatic movement is against. That's the first point.

The second point is that the World Council of Churches,
as you know very well, is concerned about the unity of
God's people, the unity of the churches. Now, what
happens? The image of the World Council of Churches is
that it is a place where a number of very erudite theologians meet to discuss the dogmatic issues of the unity
in the church, comparing the points which divide us and
sitting down working out consensus statements as they
are now doing on baptism and the eucharist and ministry - anything but the life of the Spirit. Whereas the
Charismatic Renewal is uniting people anyhow. That is
another "image" of the World Council. And the third
"image" of the World Council of Churches is in regard to
mission and evangelism. It is not only the criticism
of the World Council that it is interested in evangelism. I don't know whether he would admit it now, but
Walter Hollenweger was Secretary for Evangelism on the
Commission on World Mission and Evangelism, at one time,
and he did his thing and he does it still. And there
are others here who have been involved. But the World

Council of Churches is identified with missionary societies and mission boards and things like that; and
when we think of such things we think of institutions;
we think of money, power, and all these other things.
(We also criticise the power but you don't know that.)
But the World Council is identified with the mission
boards and so on of the main line churches, not in terms
of evangelism as the work of the Holy Spirit reaching
out to persons and renewing them.

Then the fourth "image" of the World Council of Churches,
and it must surprise you that I haven't used it up to
now, is that it is a socio-political body, Marxist in
orientation, Third World, supporting terrorists, and
revolutionary groups of society. There is a certain
irony in this in that, for example in the replies, some
of the most significant things said came from churches
in the socialist states - churches which do not dissociate themselves from a socialist standpoint in society.
And some of the most significant replies come also from
the Third World, where people are struggling for liberation and justice. Nevertheless the World Council is
associated with socio-political things over against the
spiritual. Therefore, that's an "image" of it and of
course the Charismatic Renewal is regarded as something
which goes to the priority with individuals and so on
and the rest will take care of itself.

The fifth "image" of the World Council of Churches is
of course, by association with the churches, that it is
a bureaucracy, it is institutional, not inspirational,
lacking spirituality. When the structure of the World
Council of Churches was being renewed, for the third
time in twenty years, in 1970/1971, one of the points
that was raised was that we should give a great deal of
emphasis to spirituality because there was a crisis of
spirituality in our world and that any structure of the
World Council of Churches would need to build into its
life a deep spirituality. So, you see there could be a
certain suspicion in your minds about this meeting sponsored by the World Council. What does it want? Is
there a hidden agenda somewhere? Is it manipulating, or
something of the sort? I should imagine that that's
in the minds of some.

Well, let me put my cards on the table. I'll start with
myself, and that's very important - that's normal for

a charismatic, isn't it? I start with myself because
you can't dissociate me from the World Council of Churches. I happen to be its General Secretary, and I am a
Methodist, and in terms of what I can see of the charismatic movement, John Wesley did a lot to start the whole
problem. John Wesley started by his understanding of
sanctification. That it was possible through the work
of the Holy Spirit that one could have the blessing of
being holy and committed to God. The only trouble with
that is that John Wesley was much more nuancé than is
often put down, because for him sanctification was not
just a question of me and my God. For him, he said, we
know nothing of individual religion, what we know is
social religion. Sanctification is perfect love. I
have to declare my own interest in the matter. John
Wesley was very influenced in terms of sanctification by
two things: Roman Catholic piety, especially the mys-
tics, and the discovery of the Moravians. And the Moravians, if you do not know it, were an explosion of
something that began with the early Orthodox mission
of Cyril and Methodius in Moravia, which in the six-
teenth and seventeenth century exploded into what became the Moravian movement which had to migrate to Germany. He was very deeply influenced by the Moravian
movement with the deep sense of the Spirit and the community of faith and life. But another factor of the
Moravians was the deep sense of redeeming the whole of
creation. His brother Charles, what is not often realized, was a patristic scholar in the University of
Oxford and most of his hymns are drenched with the
works of the Fathers. And a great deal, for example
Basil's study of the Holy Spirit, is his. And the religious society of the eighteenth century was very much
charismatic. So that is my background. Of course there
is a sociological factor to it because Methodism grew
out of the period of colonial expansion and the Puritan
movement in Britain and the industrial revolution when
the whole of society was changing radically and the
whole church basis of the parish and so on did not
function any more. There was this movement which set
the world bursting out of the system of that time. It
was also related to the romantic movement in literature and art and all that, over and against the enlightenment,the Puritan enlightenment and the political
situation.

So, that is my background. And the Pentecostal movement
of the nineteenth century was a product of the Methodist
movement.

My own spiritual history in the Caribbean islands is a
background of slavery, coming out of a family with big
estates and hurricanes destroying things, the colonial
situation and the economic problems. For me, faith became a bit "in spite of". And the Holy Spirit, when as
a teenáger I was conscious of it, opened my eyes, not
just to myself but to the world around me. And that was
at the age of eleven - no surprise that I was carrying
a political banner in a political march "No taxation
without representation". And of course my background
is that of being an intellectual. I have studied in
Europe, I have worked in Europe - London University -
I have even been President of the World Student Christian Federation and I worked as a pastor in Haiti among
a people 90% of whom were illiterate.

So, my spiritual background is shaped by being an intellectual on the one side and having to work with the
marginalized. And of course through all this my conversion to the world was through the ecumenical movement.
Meeting young people after the war, 1500 of them from
all over the world and sharing with them their agonies -
that is my own background. And I tell my own story because it is the story of the ecumenical movement of the
last forty years. The story of people who in the midst
of our world have experienced the Spirit, the Spirit
making them ecstatic and getting out of themselves,
making them see God's world with all its disorder and
committing themselves to that world. So, for me, an
evangelical thing and a deep belief in the Holy Spirit
as God's way of bringing new things into this world have
always been related to radical political change. That
is my own stand and if I stand here in my office as
General Secretary of the World Council of Churches it is
with that commitment. Therefore I feel at home in the
Charismatic Renewal. It starts in my traditions - it
is nothing new to me. I regard it as very exciting,
humbling and challenging. So whatever I have to say
is not as an outsider but as an insider.

Now why is the World Council of Churches interested in
the Charismatic Renewal? Now various answers can be
given to that. First of all, the Charismatic Renewal

certainly confirms the goal of the ecumenical movement. It is a means of drawing people of different communions together. It has done that very clearly. All the reports of people who, in local situations caught in their confessional boxes and patterns, suddenly are exploded out and meet each other, pray, able to express their doubts together, even to break through the rules of worshipping together.

Moreover, when we think of John the 23rd and his call for a new Pentecost, I don't know whether the story is apocryphal or whether it is true, but it is certainly told of John XXIII that one of the old cardinals, very much a man of the counter reformation of Vatican I, came to him and expressed great concern that John XXIII was calling a second Vatican Council. It was winter, and the old man took the other old man to the window and opened the window and a terrific breeze, cold wind came and these two old men were kind of battered down, and John XXIII smiled and said, "Well, that's what Vatican II is about. Perhaps it will do that to the church". And this is what the ecumenical movement is - opening the window, wherever we are and at whatever time we are so that God's Spirit may blow into us, cleanse the atmosphere, do new things to us. Of course the instruments that God uses for this are not the official ones. The great thing about the ecumenical movement has been the accent on the participation of the laity, the people of God, the whole people of God, men and women, people of different generations, being involved and playing a role. That has been sacred in the ecumenical movement. And that is what has been happening in the Charismatic Renewal. So that is one of the reasons why we are interested in the Charismatic Renewal.

The second point I would make is that the Charismatic Renewal provides a link between the churches of the Reformation and both the Roman Catholic Church, the conservative Evangelicals, and with the Orthodox being true to their historic faith. In the life of the World Council of Churches we have had the churches of the Reformation and the Orthodox churches from the very beginning. The churches of the Reformation have tended to be very christological in their approach. The Orthodox have always given a much more Trinitarian approach to their faith, with a great deal of accent to the Holy Spirit and to the eschatological goal. Now, we have learned something from the Orthodox but the Charismatic Renewal has involved a great many Protestants and Roman Catholics. We can also think of many who have been in the church what we call main line churches and those who have been in the conservative Evangelical group. Therefore it has enabled us to have a new kind of dialogue both with Roman Catholics at the base level and conservative Evangelicals. And that is important for the ecumenical movement.

A third point about why we are interested in the Charismatic Renewal is that it does take seriously what I call the dialogue of cultures in our world today, which is described as a global vision. In the same way that young people, through their styles of music, dress and so on (you will find those styles going all over the world) and the counter culture that we have seen over against the domination of the industrialised society with a homogeneous kind of culture which makes us consumers, which makes us little atoms and lonely people, there is a relationship between the Charismatic Renewal and the whole counter culture in the kind of world in which we are living, with the pluralism and diversity and the different ways in which people express themselves. And what the Charismatic Renewal movement has done for us is to help us to express the way, the life of the Spirit as we are, and against the hard and fast – whether traditional cultures and forms of church life (or exported forms of church life which we in the Third World had adopted) and enables us to be liberated from them and to express ourselves in new ways, diverse ways, fluid ways, in the Spirit. That's an important factor.

A fourth reason why the World Council of Churches is interested in the Charismatic Renewal is this. The attitude of the member churches to the World Council of Churches is not very different from their attitude to the charismatic movement. They are very suspicious of both and, similarly, the attitude of the charismatic movement and of the World Council of Churches to our member churches is also a bit guarded. Now that might seem strange to you, but when I read the replies that you sent about the charismatic movement and the churches and read what the churches said about the charismatic manifestation, it is not very different from their attitude to the World Council. Because the World Council of Churches does not do the kinds of things that those

churches like. It doesn't behave in the manner that they
like. It does odd things from time to time. And the
churches are very annoyed. It's a question of authority.
And the churches regard the World Council as not being
sufficiently under their authority, and certainly the
World Council does not have authority over the churches,
so they are not sure how it will move. And of course
the World Council of Churches by its very nature is very
critical of the churches in their captivity to the traditions of the past and their unwillingness to be open
to the present and the future, and their unwillingness
to change. So there is a certain similarity in mood
and attitude between the Charismatic Renewal and the
World Council of Churches.

When all this is said, the fact remains that as Peter
Felber said in a paper for this meeting, the ecumenical
movement is in itself a renewal movement. This is an
important point which has not been sufficiently discussed.
The impression is given that the World Council has only
just recently become interested in the Charismatic Renewal while other churches, like the Roman Catholic
Church, has been deeply involved in it for a long time.
It is important to remind you that the whole ecumenical
movement has been in fact a Charismatic Renewal, a movement of Charismatic Renewal. Starting from Edinburgh
in 1910 with the concern for the evangelisation of the
world in this generation, it was a manifestation of God's
Spirit to send people out into the world as witness to
all the nations. Or if you take the Life and Work movement of Archbishop Söderblum, that came out of a very
deep sense of the chaos of Europe and the world after
World War I, a deep sense that Jesus was crucified and
has risen and that his Spirit was calling His people to
be gathered together in a new Pentecost for renewing
society and the nations. Or the Faith and Order movement
of Charles Brent who had gone out to the Philippines as
a missionary to the people there, who saw that the call
to mission was a call to unity in the Spirit. Or the
World Council of Christian Education (the World Sunday-
School Movement) in its sense of the education of children and grown-ups, was motivated by the conviction that
God gave his Spirit to each, and each must be allowed
and enabled to bring the fullness of his or her being
for the life of the Body of Christ and of the Holy Spirit.
And when the World Council of Churches was formed in
1948 (I was present - I even had the privilege of being

the leader of the youth delegation) that Assembly spoke
of God opening the gate into freedom and joy in the Holy
Spirit. I have to confess that the gift and presence
of the Holy Spirit was not very evident in the speeches
in Amsterdam in 1948 and we young people were very conscious of that. So that when I spoke on their behalf I
said that one of our first acts as young people on
assembling together was to read again the story of the
first Pentecost and the words of Joel about pouring the
Holy Spirit on all flesh. And I went on to say that
with these words we read the promise of God to us all,
even as we waited upon Him in prayer we listened to his
challenge to proclaim salvation to mankind. God has
called us to another Pentecost here, not as spectacular,
perhaps, as the first outpouring of His Spirit, but no
less real and powerful. We young people have been waiting upon God and have not ceased to make intercession
that God may use both you and us in His great desire for
His church in His world.

That was the sense in which we young people meeting at
that inauguration of the World Council of Churches, the
sense of the Holy Spirit was touching us and making a
new faith. And one of the functions of the World Council of Churches is to foster the renewal of the churches,
in unity, worship, mission and service. How did we get
to this? We found very soon in the life of the World
Council of Churches that the churches were made up of
99 and more percent of lay people. That they were the
frozen assets of the churches. Then renewal could only
come when the whole people of God was indeed participating in the life of the church. So in 1954 we set
up a Laity Department concerned about the laity and we
set up also a Division called "Ecumenical Action" and
at the heart of the Division of Ecumenical Action the
Youth, Women, Laity, and this place, the Ecumenical
Institute, was the renewal of the whole people of God
through the Holy Spirit. And so in 1971 we reformulated
the structure of the World Council of Churches and set
up a special unit on Education and Renewal, and after
the last Assembly, when there was tremendous accent not
only on spirituality but on the local expressions of
the whole life of the Church, we set up this sub-unit
on Renewal and Congregational Life.

Now one of the points in the subject given to me is
"how to see the theme of Charismatic Renewal in the

present concern of the World Council of Churches" and I want to do this very quickly in terms of the four major areas of concentration of our work in the World Council of Churches and to show that Charismatic Renewal is relevant to all these four.

The first one is the expression and communication of our faith in the Triune God. Note that phrase - the Triune God, that is to say, God the Father, Son and Holy Spirit. As I have said before, the World Council of Churches was very deeply influenced by the very reformed theology with the accent on the work of Christ. And indeed, a theology which was very Western. Western in the theological sense, that is to say, the Western church - Roman Catholic and the churches which came out of it - the whole Augustinian accent on Christ and his work, and sin, redemption, the cross of Christ, and so on. And it was interesting that it was the Orthodox who insisted that the basis of the World Council should be changed to have a Trinitarian orientation, because the basis of the World Council, in its beginning and up to 1961 was: the World Council of Churches is a fellowship of churches which confess the Lord Jesus Christ as God and Saviour. Now the attack came from two areas - from the Scandinavians, who said we ought to have the Scriptures somewhere, and from the Orthodox who said we ought to have the Trinity somewhere. And in typical ecumenical style we found a way of including all of them in the basis by saying that the World Council of Churches is a fellowship of churches which confess the Lord Jesus Christ as God and Saviour according to the Scriptures and seek to fulfill their common calling to the glory of God the Father, Son and Holy Spirit.

Now you can say this is typical ecumenical compromise in producing a statement. But it was much more than that. It was a recognition that if we are to express and communicate our faith it has to be in the fullness of the Trinity. When I look at the whole way in which the ecumenical movement expressed itself theologically, there has been a deep lack of the work of the Holy Spirit in our life, and what that means for the unity of the church and the unity of humankind. And with this question of the expression and communication of our faith in the Triune God goes the whole issue of our culture - our different cultures. We said in our conference at

Bangkok on World Mission and Evangelism that the voice
with which we respond to the voice of Christ must be
the voice of our own culture. And the only way in which
the gospel can be heard is when it is expressed in the
culture, the whole language and way of life of the people
to whom it is addressed. And that is a question of
diversity and here we get to the very heart of the Godhead because the Godhead is in itself a unity in revelation. The revelation of God the Father in the Son and
the Holy Spirit shows this sense of this tremendous
diversity of God's revelation.

The second major concern of the World Council of Churches
is about the unity of the church and its relation to
the unity of humankind. And here there are two points.
The Charismatic Renewal has certainly broken through the
more dogmatic approaches to the unity of the churches
and has thrown people together. The question which has
to be asked is: How far has that coming together broken
through our divisions as human beings in race, class and
all the rest of it that divides us? And how far is the
Charismatic Renewal a renewal about humanity both in
ourselves and in our relationships with each other?
But it is more than that, because the unity of the
church and the unity of humankind are related to God's
purpose to unite the whole of His creation. Romans 8
does not stop at our own life in the Spirit, calling
God as a Father, it goes immediately into taking on the
sufferings of Christ for His whole creation which is
groaning and travailling, waiting for the redeeming of
the children of God. The Charismatic Renewal is also
the renewal of the whole of creation and the whole of
creation means the whole of what creation is. My question therefore is how far is the Charismatic Renewal
opening us to the work of the renewal of the whole of
God's creation?

And related to that is the third major and more specific
concern of the World Council of Churches - the search
for a just, participatory, and sustainable society.
That of course makes more precise the issue of the unity
of humankind. It raises a very profound question for
us today, because the issue for us, whatever our stances
may be, is that we are living in a deeply disordered
world. A world in which the powers are engaged in the
preparation for the destruction of humanity. And this
is not just a matter of words, you know. I could give

you a lot of details about it, about the whole arma-
ments race, militarism and all the rest of it, plus the
millions of people who since World War II have died in
over a hundred conflicts in which the powers are engaged,
and so on and so forth. The fact that the gap between
the rich and the poor is greater than ever and that every
year more than fifty million people die and ten times
more live on the margin of life and death, the fact
that so many people participate in decision making and
in the life of their own community, the fact that we
are wasting God's creation in the most selfish way,
just to feed a minority in this world - these are not
matters that we can ignore. What is God's Spirit saying to us? What is the Charismatic Renewal saying?
That is the test of these years to come. So when people
say the World Council of Churches is socio-political,
what do you think about that?

The last thing is of course the major emphasis in the
search for education and renewal in the search for true
community. Of course there you are at ease because
that is what the Charismatic Renewal is about - education
and of course the sub-unit on Renewal and Congregational
Life. But I want to bring one or two other matters to
your attention. We have in the World Council of Churches a commission called the Christian Medical Commission.
Now that Commission is made up of very highly skilled
people, experienced in medical work of various kinds.
And they have been working on community health care,
because hospital health care only reaches about 7% of
the population, but if you engage the whole community in
health care there could be a revolution. What is more,
this Commission is engaged in the study of the churches
as a healing community and I can myself witness to this
because in the last eight months my own wife has been
in a position of being between life and death and what
I do know is the love, the prayer, the care of the
Christian community, not only here in Geneva but around
the world. It is the only thing that has sustained us
and enabled her and me to go on. So the question of
healing is not a kind of curious, eccentric thing. It
is a very deep concern of the renewal for community,
and one could give you many other examples in our work.

In view of this, what do we expect from this meeting?
I would say first of all that the member churches of the
World Council of Churches need the Charismatic Renewal

for their own renewal. And the fact that the Charismatic
Renewal has taken place makes it easier for conversation
between the three major traditions of the Christian community - that is, the Orthodox, the Roman Catholic and
the churches of the Reformation and their offshoots.
That is a very important contribution. The second one
is that the Charismatic Renewal gives us a new self-
understanding as the World Council of Churches. What
does authority really mean? According to the constitution of the World Council of Churches it has no authority except in the inherent truth and wisdom of what it
says and does. How, if you put the accent on the inherent truth and wisdom of what we do, we put ourselves
in the hands of the mercy of the Holy Spirit and therefore also at the discernment of it, and not in any fixed
tradition and moulds and criteria of judgment. And that
is a challenge, that is a part of the ecumenical challenge. And here the Charismatic Renewal is of importance.

Thirdly, the Charismatic Renewal is important for helping
the World Council of Churches to work at the aim which is
the unity of God's people and the unity of all the people
of the world - diversity in unity. And that is the work
of the Holy Spirit.

Now, I want to finish by reading the words of the Moderator of the sub-unit on Renewal and Congregational Life,
who is not here because he is boxed in by the structure
of his own church as a Patriarch, but at Uppsala he had
these words to say about the Holy Spirit, and these
words have been quoted by Michael Ramsay in his book
on the Holy Spirit. He said, in Uppsala, in 1968:
"Without the Holy Spirit God is far away, Christ stays
in the past, the gospel is simply an organisation, or
authority a matter of propaganda, validity no more than
an evolution, Christian loving a slave morality. But
in the Holy Spirit the cosmos, the created world is
resurrected and grows with the birth pangs of the Kingdom. The risen Christ is there, the gospel is a power
of life, the church shows forth the life of the Trinity,
authority is a liberating science, mission is a Pentecost, the liturgy is both renewal and anticipation,
human action is deified."

But of course I must end not with the words of a Metropolitan and Patriarch, but with the words of Scripture
which belong very much to the Orthodox tradition, in

II Corinthians, chapter 3, verses 17 to 18, because that
sums up the whole matter: "The Lord is the Spirit, and
where the Spirit of the Lord is, there is freedom. And
we all, with unveiled face, beholding the glory of the
Lord, are being changed into His likeness, from one
degree of glory to another; for this comes from the Lord
who is the Spirit." Amen.

B. SAINTS IN BIRMINGHAM

The story of a revival

Walter J. Hollenweger

As Mr Chips approached the city centre the taxi driver
pointed out the Rotunda, an elegant, thirty-storey
building which towered over the shopping centre. The
traffic came to a halt and the taxi stopped. Chips
saw the blue lights of police cars and ambulances and
heard their familiar siren. A police loudspeaker announced: "This is an emergency. Will all taxi drivers
please come to the Rotunda. They are urgently needed."
The taxi driver said, "Sorry!", and leaned back to open
the cab door. Before Chips realized what was happening
he found himself standing on the pavement in the cold.
Luckily he had just got time to grab his suitcase.

Bombs in Birmingham

He was sorry that he had never learned to curse properly.
Now, he thought, he could have used a few strong words -
but after all he was a well-educated man and a grammar
school teacher. He started to walk towards New Street
Station but a police cordon blocked the way. A police
constable ordered everyone to leave the area immediately
because a bomb had gone off in a very crowded pub. When
he looked round, Chips could see the broken windows.
He walked away but did not know where to go. It was
obviously going to be impossible to find a taxi as they
were all too busy assisting the ambulances to carry

the many injured to hospital. He decided to try and
phone his friend Shirley Delattre, a French nun, to
explain his predicament. He found a phone box and
looked for Shirley's number, but a big bang shook the
booth. Chips covered his ears with both hands. As
he jumped outside the booth he could see that another
bomb had exploded on the other side of the street. He
could hear the cries and moans of the wounded. Half the
street was littered with debris, and Chips could hardly
believe his eyes when he saw bruised and bleeding arms
and legs lying among the scattered furniture, bricks
and broken glass. He ran across the road and helped
a woman to get out of the ruins of the bombed building.

"Just like during the war, just like during the war",
he thought. "And we have learned nothing." Although
the woman was only slightly injured, her face was
gruesomely cut by the broken glass and she was covered
in blood. Chips gave her his handkerchief. Now the
police and the ambulance men who had been working at
clearing the pub where the first explosion had occurred
came running over to search for further victims. A
constable said politely but firmly to Chips, "Please
move along. There could be another bomb in store for
us." Chips looked at him. "Of course. If only I knew
where to go."

Somehow he found another taxi and the driver told him
that he had heard on local radio that over two hundred
people had been wounded and twenty had been killed.
"It's always these bloody Irish", he added and shook
his head.

"Just in time, just in time", said Shirley Delattre,
when Chips arrived at her home. "Tonight you are coming with me to an evening of spirituality at the home
of Mr Hellberg, a well-known orthopaedic surgeon."
"Wait a minute..." Chips grumbled. "No, there is no
time for waiting, you can explain everything on the
way". Before Chips realized what was happening, he
was in Chirley Dellatre's French "Ugly Duckling" and
off they went.

He cleared his throat and said, "You heavenly charismatics, you don't care a thing about the world. As
long as you have your religious parties, nothing else
matters. The world could go to pieces or starve to
death..."

"Oh, I see", the French nun smiled at him. "You know, my friend, when you come to the Hellberg's you will see for yourself that now is the time to pray and that prayer is more important than mourning and complaining."

Mrs Hellberg received them personally at the front door and introduced them to the other guests who had already arrived and who were sitting or standing in the big living room. Shirley Delattre told Chips about Mr Hellberg: He was regarded very highly for his professional skill, although he was looked on as a little bit odd. For instance it was told of him that he had introduced himself at an official banquet as a carpenter. A carpenter he was, so he said, because he repaired bones. He replaced them, put them together again just as a cabinet maker would repair a precious antique cupboard. In their house the Hellbergs had an old French medicine cabinet made in Napoleon's time. Chips would have loved to have seen it, but he did not have the courage to ask. After all he had been invited to an "evening of spirituality".

When Jesus comes...

For the moment, however, the atmosphere did not look spiritual to him. People were laughing and talking, and what did he see over there - the manager of the local bank had a whiskey in his hand. Chips greeted him with a nod of the head. Ah, yes, the Hellberg's eldest son was pouring out drinks for everyone. There was white wine, red wine, whiskey, beer and orange juice. Suddenly a young woman smiled at him and said with a marked Irish accent, "Good evening, Mr Chips. Don't you recognise me?"

Chips could not place her, until it dawned on him that this was the young woman who cleaned his classroom every evening. In her trousers, headscarf and apron, she looked very different. Now for the first time he could see her shining red hair and her brilliant eyes.

"My sister is with me", she said, and smiled teasingly. "She has never seen a real live grammar school teacher. Moira, come over here!" Moira came across and greeted Mr Chips. "So this is what a grammar school teacher looks like", she said. Embarrassed, Chips laughed un-

comfortably and thought, "And this is what a real Irish
revolutionary bride looks like." But, being an English-
man, he hid his thoughts.

Instead he said, "Nice to meet you. What are you
actually doing here?"

"For the past year we have come regularly to these
prayer meetings", she replied. "When we first came to
England, we were lost. The weather and the people seemed
so cold. The manager of the bank over there - I clean
his bank every Friday - invited us here. he is an
Anglican, but I am a Catholic. I wanted to ask our
priest if we should go, then he decided to come with
us and was astonished to find out that the hosts, the
Hellbergs, are Catholics too. English Catholics of
course. And what's more, we found quite a number of
sisters and monks from different orders here as well.
I like it here."

Nobody seemed to have heard about the bombs in the city
centre. Everybody was happy - Irish and English, Catholics and Protestants.

Mrs Hellberg lifted her guitar down from the wall and
began to sing some short simple songs which Mr Chips
had never heard before. "Spirit of the living God"
was one and another was the story of a man -

> Who sat alone beside the highway begging
> His eyes were blind, the light he could not see
> He clutched his rags and shivered in the shadows
> Then Jesus came and bade his darkness flee.
>
> When Jesus comes the tempter's power is broken
> When Jesus comes the tears are wiped away.
> He takes the gloom and fills the life with glory
> For all is changed when Jesus comes to stay.

Everyone joined in the chorus, "When Jesus comes...".
The two Irish women had unpacked their guitars and were
also playing, whilst a young black man accompanied the
singing with an original ostinato bass on his trombone.

The hippie from Athens

Then Mrs Hellberg began to recite a kind of litany. It
sounded very Catholic to Mr Chips's ears, and yet it

was not Catholic in the way that he expected it to be. The invocation of the saints began with the "bridegroom of poverty, our brother Francis, follower of Jesus and friend of creation". it included Gandhi, "apostle of non-violence, reproach to the churches", "Good Pope John, friend of the poor, who longed for the unity of all people", Athenagoras, "patriarch of love" and Simon Kimbangu, "prophet and prisoner of hope", the "peace-makers", Dag Hammerskjold and Albert Luthuli, Gautama Buddha, "masks of Christ", and "fountain of compassion", John of Patmos, "visionary and apostle, resister to the World Beast", Dante, Bunyan and Isaac Watts, "vis-ionaries and poets, pilgrims of the inner light", Mary Magdalene, "faithful harlot, first witness of new life", Bach, Mozart and Beethoven, "who speak the soul's lan-guage", Darwin and Teilhard de Chardin, "students of the earth, voyagers in the past and in the future", Einstein, Marx and Freud, "children of the synagogue", Menno Simmons and George Fox, "explorers of the gospel, generals in the warfare of the Lamb", and many others whom Chips did not know. Also included were the inno-cent victims of Coventry, Dresden and Hiroshima and the more recent ones in Londonderry, Belfast and Bir-mingham. ("So, had they heard of the bombs?" Chips asked himself.) Socrates was called "the hippie of Athens", much to the astonishment of Mr Chips who was after all an educated man.

Mrs Hellberg continued, remembering the "unwed mother, blessed Mary, wellspring of our liberation". The litany culminated in the praise of "our hero and leader, Jesus the manual labourer, root of our dignity, the prophet who resisted the Establishment, the Liberator, a king because first a servant, the poet who gave us a new form of expression, Jesus, the Son of God, bright corner-stone of our unity in a new Spirit".

Chips was profoundly astonished by this intercultural theology. The prayer meeting went on. Without embar-rassment they prayed for personal matters, for sickness, children, their work, the school (here Chips sighed slightly), the churches, their boys in the British Army and their boys in the Irish Republican Army. Again and again they prayed for the Holy Spirit.

"Come, Holy Spirit!", they sang.

A man, whom Chips did not know, prayed in tongues.
Chips turned his head in order to hear better, but he
could not understand a word. After the message in
tongues - silence. One of the Irish girls interpreted.
"How could she?" Chips asked himself. Her English
was simple and almost without fault, something which
Chips noticed with satisfaction. At least these prayer
meetings were good for the culture of the English language.

Chips kept his eyes open. Something tickled his nose.
The Catholic priest sitting on the floor next to him
was slowly smoking his pipe. "Well," thought Chips,
"is this a party or a prayer meeting?"

Party or prayer meeting?

Mrs Hellberg began to lead the small community in a
chorus and then asked: "Does anyone want to read a
Bible passage or ask a question?"

Chips would have liked to put his question, "Party or
Prayer Meeting?", but now a woman, a late-comer he had
so far not observed, stood up. She tried to talk but
she couldn't because her words were smothered by waves
of violent weeping. Chips was very embarrassed but he
was obviously the only one who was. At last the woman
began to speak.

"I have just lost my brother and my husband", she said.
"Blown to pieces by an Irish bomb." Silence. "I am a
Protestant and I would like to ask a Catholic and a
Protestant to pray together with me so that the bitterness in my heart does not take root. Please help me
to believe in God and to love his children." She sank
to her knees and broke down.

The Catholic priest came forward. "Which of the Protestants is going to pray with me?" he asked. Shirley
Delattre nudged Chips but he did not want to be part of
this public group-therapy scene. "No", he whispered.
Fortunately Mr Thoroughgood, a teacher whom he knew
by name, volunteered. What they prayed, Chips immediately forgot, because he just could not understand
how on earth a Catholic and a Protestant could pray
together in this situation for peace and reconciliation.

"They must be suffering from a mild form of religious madness", he told himself. Then they all sang the Lord's Prayer together and most of the guests left for home.

Chips wanted to leave and to say good-night to Mr Hellberg, but he could not find him. Mrs Hellberg explained that her husband had been called out to a patient during the meeting but that he was now in the kitchen drinking coffee. Chips knocked at the door and went in. Mr Hellberg was sitting at the kitchen table, his head buried in his hands. The coffee in his cup was cold. Chips would have liked to make his excuses and leave, but the doctor said, "Come in. Come and sit down. My coffee is cold. Let's make a fresh pot."

Chips said nothing and sat down.

"Something is very wrong with little Peter", the doctor continued, speaking his thoughts aloud to Mr Chips. "Something is very wrong and I have failed. True "when Jesus comes the tempter's power is broken". I have done my job and I have prayed too. But Peter's leg is not right. And way was it injured in the first place? Peter is not a politician, just a school boy. Why should he have been wounded? Now he will never be able to walk normally. Who has done a shoddy job here, Jesus or I, or both?"

Chips felt very uncomfortable. He had never expected to hear the famous doctor talk like this. Mrs Hellberg came in and joined them at the table in silence, for there was nothing to say. Embarrassed, Chips put his hand into his pocket and pulled out a tract which somebody had given him that evening. He read:

> If you will turn your faith loose tonight you can take heaven home with you.
> If there is going to be any healing for that body in that heaven, there is healing down here now.

"Such nonsense", Chips thought, and he decided to put the tract back in his pocket.

Then he realized that the doctor was still looking at him and waiting for an answer. "I cannot answer your question", Chips said abruptly. "But one thing I can tell you. What you have said to me tonight is more important for me than the whole evening of spirituality.

I too have my difficulties, but that a famous doctor
like you had his doubts, that has been a visitation of
the Holy Spirit for me."

On his way home Mr Chips sang quietly to himself, "When
Jesus comes the tempter's power is broken."

But he was slightly irritated by the song. Was it not
a little bit too unrealistic?

The memorial service

The following Sunday a great remembrance and memorial
service was held in the Cathedral under the auspices of
the Birmingham Council of Churches. In order not to
offend either the Protestants or the Catholics, it was
decided that John Adegoke, a leader of a black Christian
church, should preside. At least half the nave was
filled with black people who had come to mourn and pray
with the white congregation.

A long procession filed into the church: first a large
black choir, followed by the choir and the canons of the
Cathedral; then Sir Peter Scott, Chancellor of the University of Birmingham; behind him the Catholic Archbishop and the Anglican Bishop of Birmingham; following
them the chief shop steward of British Leyland and the
Conservative Mayor of the city; and finally John Adegoke,
Senior Apostle of the Cherubim and Seraphim Society.

A young Negro opened the service with a song. He sang
accompanied by a battery of drums and the cathedral
organ.

"When the Holy Ghost fills you
    you can smile
When you feel like the baptist"

and here he interrupted his singing and commented: "You
know, brothers and sisters, John the Baptist, the one
who had to eat locusts and wild honey. When you feel
like the baptist..." And most of the congregation -
although not the two bishops - joined him: "You can
smile."

"When your heart is full of mourning
    you can smile."

The black choir, dressed in long bright gowns took up the theme. "You can smile." The drummers took up the rhythm, first very softly: "You can, you can, yes, you can smile." The choir joined in with full harmony and strong syncopation. And the drummers made their sticks dance on their drums. "You can smile."

The soloist sang the next stanza:

"When they throw bombs at you"

And here he was not able to sing "You can smile". Only the drummers beat out the rhythm and the congregation remained silent.

"When they stare at you because you are black
    you can smile."

"Halleluja, you can smile." The choir began to move and, with short, rhythmical steps, they danced up the aisle into the church nave. Many in the congregation stood up and shouted and sang repeatedly, "Yes, Lord, you can smile."

"When the National Front throws stones at you
    you can smile.
When the Black Power people call you a coward
    you can smile."

John Adegoke stood up. "In the name of the Father, and of the Son, and of the Holy Spirit." The choirs and the congregation responded, "Amen."

"Here in the Cathedral of Birmingham we all meet as brothers in Christ and members in the Body of Christ. We greet the Anglican Bishop of Birmingham, the Roman Catholic Archbishop of Birmingham. We greet Catholic and Protestant Christians."

"And now with angels and archangels and all the glorious company of heaven, the saints of the past from Europe and Africa, including those saints who died this week, we laud and magnify thee."

"Amen", sang the choirs again.

"Let them rest in peace", said the Senior Apostle.

The black choir sang another hymn. It was one of those
famous spirituals about the final liberation of all
people. Superficially it was a hymn about heaven.
"I'm going to lay down my heavy load." Chips knew the
spiritual well. It came from Michael Tippett's oratorio
"A Child of Our Time". His wife had sung it to him
many times.

"What, brothers and sisters, shall we lay down?" asked
one of the singers. And in full harmony choir and congregation replied, "I'm going to lay down my heavy
load."

A well-endowed, elderly Negro woman sang the next stanza.
She did not only sing with her mouth, which she could
open unbelievably wide. Everything about her sang -
the well-upholstered hips, the thick legs, the strong
arms. Even the large, swaying breasts sang the rhythm
of the hymn:

"I know my robe's going to fit me well.
I've tried it on at the gates of hell."

And again the congregation joined in: "I'm going to
lay down my heavy load."

Chips couldn't help but think about the civil war which
was tearing his country apart, a war between catholics
and Protestants, between Irish and English, between the
left and the right. Unbidden a prayer rose in him:
"Thy Kingdom come."

When the hymn ended, John Adegoke greeted the few German
Lutherans who were also among the congregation. "You
know, Martin Luther, the great hero of faith, is their
church father", he explained, for he had learned something about Luther in the Theology Course which the
University of Birmingham had started for black church
leaders. To Chips's great astonishment, the congregation - first the black and then the white - broke
out into the hymn: "We shall overcome..."

Chips wondered whether they were not confusing Martin
Luther with Martin Luther King. Perhaps the two were
one and the same person to them. It seems that the

dimension of times does not exist for the black Christians. Nearness to them is neither temporal nor spatial. That which moves them is near.

"Yes, good people", the Catholic Archbishop took up the theme, "we shall wonder, wonder and marvel, when we overcome, when we all triumph over our own egoism, when all the saints are marching into the city of golden streets..." He had hardly finished when the trombone began to play - it was the same black trombonist whom Chips had met at the Hellbergs. The trombone played: "Oh, when the Saints..." The music now came from all sides in any number of variations. "Oh, when the saints, oh, when the saints, oh, when the saints come marching in." And the choir and some members of the congregation stood up and danced and marched through the church.

Then the Catholic Archbishop said aloud, "Amen" and everything was quiet again.

"Friends", it was now the turn of the Anglican Bishop to preach. "Friends", he said, "when the saints march into the new Jerusalem, do you think there will be Catholic saints, Lutheran saints, Anglican saints, Pentecostal saints?"

"No, no", the black Christians shouted and the white Christians looked around.

The Anglican Bishop was very surprised but he continued. "Will there be black saints and white saints, Irish saints and English saints?"

And the congregation shouted again, "No, no", and this time a number of the English and Irish joined in.

"No", the preacher continued. "No, there will only be saints. Saints who have dedicated their lives to Christ. But some of us will marvel. In heaven we will marvel even more than down here. You see, in heaven it will become clear, very clear indeed, what we worship. Whether we worship Jesus, the manual worker, Jesus our saviour, or whether we worship our own fear and our own prejudices. Yes, it will become clear whether we worship our own race, our money, our church, our culture, and our tradition, or whether we worship Jesus. I wouldn't be a bit surprised if, on the Day of Judgment, all white people stand confronted by a black Jesus..."

97

The preacher paused. There was dead silence in the church.

The Bishop continued. "Yes, I wouldn't be surprised in the least if all white people stand confronted by a black Jesus, and all black people by a white Jesus. Amen."

John Adegoke thanked the two preachers and added, "I wouldn't be a bit surprised if, on the last Judgment Day, all Irish stand confronted by an English Jesus, and all English by an Irish Jesus. Let us pray."

The prayer was a silent prayer. Nobody said a word. Only a few sighs were to be heard and some weeping. After the prayer the Cathedral choir sang one of its beautiful traditional hymns.

"Let us confess our sins", said John Adegoke. The Conservative Mayor of Birmingham, the chief shop steward from British Leyland and a black lady came forward. They prayed in turn, and in the intervals the choir sang "Lord have mercy".

"We first sought to win elections
and not the good of the people."

"Lord have mercy."

"We first sought to coerce people into trade unions
and did not seek the good of the people."

"Lord have mercy."

"We thought that first and foremost our people wanted
money and we did not realise that what they wanted
was honesty."

"Lord have mercy."

"We behaved like the churches.
We believed that we, the vicars of the Unions,
we believed that we, the pundits of the parties,
knew best what was good for the people.

"Lord have mercy."

"And now that our country is in ruins
   our youngsters laugh at us
   our neighbours shake their heads
We come humbly to thee, O Lord, and beseech thee,
to help us to become human,
human in our industrial negotiations
human in our political tactics."

"Lord have mercy."

After a long silence, the Chancellor of the University
of Birmingham, made the final announcements. He said,
"Let me ask you a question which puzzles me. Although
I am a Christian, I do not understand why it is that
we can mourn together but not act together. Why is
it that we can sing together but not celebrate the
eucharist together? Will you promise me that you will
think about this? It is a simple question of a layman."

With this benediction the congregation was dismissed
and Chips reflected: "A simple question of a layman,
certainly, but the most important question."

That was the beginning of a thorough process of re-think-
ing by the Christians in Birmingham. They pooled their
spiritual and intellectual resources - and occasionally
even their financial resources - and demonstrated that
Christians are different.

C.   MODELS OF CHRISTIAN COMMUNITY IN THE NEW TESTAMENT

James D.G. Dunn

The NT preserves several different models of Christian
community. Some were what actually happened; others
an ideal held before first century believers. In some
cases we have enough information to provide a reasonably clear picture (particularly Paul); in others we
must be content with hints and allusions.

1. Discipleship - following Jesus

Jesus called men (and women) to follow him. Among the
various characteristics of the life of discipleship we
may mention particularly the following.

a) It was eschatological. Jesus called for discipleship
in view of the coming kingdom (Mark 1:15; etc.). In one
sense discipleship was a celebration of the kingdom, of
the priority and power of God already manifested in and
through Jesus' ministry - particularly insofar as that
discipleship was characterized by Jesus' table-fellowship
(Mark 2:15f; Luke 15:1f), since there is a strong im-
plication that Jesus saw his table-fellowship as an
anticipation of the messianic banquet (Mark 2:17, 19;
Luke 6:21; 2:30; Mark 14:25; cf. Isa. 25:6; 65:13). In
another sense it was a preparation for the kingdom yet
to come in its fulness - not least insofar as those
who followed Jesus shared in his summons to Israel to
make ready for the coming kingdom (particularly Mark 6:
7-12/Luke 9:1-6).

b) It was discipleship - a matter of individuals following Jesus either literally (Mark 1:17; 2:14; 10:21;
Luke 9:57-62) or while they remained where they were
(Mark 5:19; Luke 19:8f). We can speak quite properly
of "circles of discipleship" round Jesus. Closest to
Jesus was "the beloved disciple" of the fourth gospel
(if in fact a historical individual rather than a symbol of discipleship), and the inner three (Peter, James
and John); then the twelve (Mark 3:14); then those who
went about with him (including the women mentioned in
Luke 8:2f); then those who were evidently close to Jesus
but did not leave home (e.g. Martha and Mary); then "whoever does the will of God" (Mark 3:34f) and "the poor"
(Luke 6:20; Matt. 25:31-46). It should not be inferred
that the various circles were distinct from each other.
On the contrary, they seem to have merged into each other
or overlapped (Mary was "closer" to Jesus than some of
the twelve).

c) It was open. It is not possible to draw a clear line
round one of these circles of discipleship and mark an
inside and an outside. In contrast to the Baptist Jesus
evidently did not practise baptism, neither as a rite of
preparation for the kingdom nor as a rite of entry into
discipleship (John 4:2). In contrast to the Pharisees

he laid no requirements of ritual purity on those who
ate with him (Mark 7:1-23). In contrast to the cove-
nanters of Qumran he welcomed to his table those who were
least acceptable on religious grounds (Luke 14:12-24;
Jeremias, Theology I p. 175). There was no ritual bar-
rier to surmount for the would-be disciple; no ritual
exclusiveness to mark off the disciple from others.
Jesus' discipleship was open to whoever was open to him -
be they Parisee or prostitute or tax collector (Matt.
11:19; Mark 12:28-34; Luke 7:36).

d) It focused on Jesus. There is no suggestion of communities existing apart from Jesus; everything depended
on Jesus himself. Indeed it is misleading to speak of
"community" at all when describing discipleship of Jesus.
Apart from what is implied in Luke 8:3 and John 12:6
there seems to have been no real internal structure of
responsibility, far less any hierarchy of authority.
Jesus alone was prophet and teacher (particularly Matt.
23:8); he was the only authority figure. Some enjoyed
a more intimate relation with him than others (above (b));
but any attempt to claim special authority or status was
severely rebuked (Mark 10:35-44). The fact that twelve
were chosen presumably implies that their discipleship
represented eschatological Israel, the coming kingdom
(cf. Matt. 19:28), but there is no indication that they
had some special role within the circles of disciples,
as e.g. "priests" to the others' "laity".

This model if discipleship of discipleship is too dependent on the particular circumstances of Jesus' earthly
ministry to provide a pattern for Christian community
today. But it should not be put aside as irrelevant.
If "discipleship of Jesus" still has any meaning for the
1980s (and it certainly has), then the character of that
discipleship, particularly of celebration and mission,
of openness and service, should be a constant challenge
to any ecclesiastical structure which does not positively
promote such discipleship. The church exists to enable
the same quality of discipleship as that to which Jesus
called his first followers.

2. The mother church - loyally conservative

The only first century church which we can view over a
lengthy period is the church in Jerusalem. Although
Luke's account in Acts (our principal source) is from a

particular perspective, we can gain a clear enough view
of the Jerusalem church at several points between 30 and
70 AD. What we see is a community in transition, particularly as regards its organization. The principal
factors in its development were three-fold: the initial
outpouring of the Spirit; reaction to the Hellenists
and the Gentile mission; and the pressure of Jewish (religious) nationalism which steadily increased throughout
this period.

a) Initially its chief feature was <u>enthusiasm</u>. The quo-
tation from Joel 2:28f characterizes it as a community
of prophets (Acts 2:17f) - the prophetic Spirit was not
confined to a few, and a principal mark of divine acceptance as the new movement subsequently spread was the
sharing of the same experience (8:15-7; 10:44-7; 19:6).
Such experiences of immediacy of inspiration evidently
were highly prized (4:8-31; 6:3; 11:24). Likewise
important shifts in policy were prompted and justified
by visions (9:10; 10:3-6; 10:6; 22:17f). In the beginning
at least there was also a spontaneity about their coming
together in each others' homes, whether for a meal or
for teaching (2:42-46; 5:42) - a continuation presumably,
in part at least, of the earlier life-style of discipleship.

b) The period was marked by an <u>evolving organization</u>.
Initially the twelve seem to have provided the focus,
symbolizing the self-consciousness of the new movement
as eschatological Judaism (Acts 1:6; 20:6; 6:2; Matt.
19:28; I Cor. 15:5), with the inner circle of three
apparently most prominent (Acts 2:5; 12:2). The seven
elected in the wake of Hellenist unrest over the administration of the common fund were probably the most prominent or most active of the Hellenists, as the subsequent
ministries of Stephen and Philip seem to indicate (6-8).
They were not particularly "subordinate" to the twelve,
despite 6:3, and to designate them "deacons" is mis-
leadingly anachronistic and presupposes a more developed
organization than was most probably the case. Subsequently, the two main developments were the emergence
of James, brother of Jesus, as the leader first of the
"pillar apostles", and then on his own (Ga. 2:9,12;
Acts 12:17; 15:13-21; 21:17); and the appearance of a
system of eldership round James (Acts 11:20; 21:18).
Converted priests and Parisees do not seem to have been

accorded any particular status within the church (6:7; 15:5), nor do we read of prophets (like Agabus) or teachers exercising a role of leadership, as they seem to have done at Antioch (Acts 13:1-3).

c) Perhaps most striking of all, particularly as the Gentile mission developed, was the degree to which the Jerusalem church identified with and remained loyal to the Judaism in the midst of which it dwelt. The leadership system of James and the elders was probably patterned on the Jewish synagogue (ruler of synagogue and elders of local community). Throughout the period the temple remained central in their worship, despite Stephen's attack on it (e.g. 2:46; 5:42; 21:26; 22:17; cf - Matt. 5:23f). And strong devotion to the law continued to characterize their life despite Paul (Acts 11:2f; 21:20; Gal. 2:12; cf - Matt. 23:2,23; 24:20). Very few Hellenists or practitioners of a law-free life style would remain long in Jerusalem after Stephen's martyrdom. Their practice of baptism and belief in Jesus as Messiah and risen from the dead would mark them off as a sect within Judaism (like the Parisees or Essenes) but not distinguish them from Judaism.

In all this the mother church is probably less of a model and more an example of how a church will tend to conform to its dominant environment. The ad hoc evolution of organization in the high period of enthusiasm gave way to a more stable and regular system patterned on the closest parallel structure already well established. Under growing pressure from the powerful political currents of religious nationalism the church was not able to hold the full range of the expanding Christian spectrum within itself. It became only one part, one end of the spectrum of Christian faith and lifestyle, a prime example of how difficult a church emerging from and living within a strong older religious tradition will find it to be anything other than conservative in its faith and life style.

3. The Pauline ideal - charismatic community

Paul's concept of community is determined by his understanding of the church as the body of Christ (see particularly I Cor. 12, Rom. 12 and Eph. 4). These passages are not descriptions of the historical reality of the Pauline churches, or not entirely so, but we can certainly say that they express the ideal which Paul held out before his churches and the principles he encouraged his converts to apply in their coming together and common life. To appreciate the force of Paul's concept of church we must note the following points.

a) The basis of community is the shared experience of the Spirit. "The koinonia of the Spirit" (II Cor. 13:13,14; Phil. 2:1) means primarily "participation in the Spirit", the common experience of the Spirit which was the other side of the coin from their common faith in Christ (e.g. Rom. 8:9; II Cor. 1:21f; Gal. 3:2-5); not the strong appeal to experience in Phil. 2:1f. It was this shared experience which drew them together and out of which their oneness grew: I Cor. 12:13 - one Spirit, therefore one body; Eph. 4:3f - the unity of the Spirit is something given, the oneness of their starting point as believers, not something they create, but something they can maintain. In short the unity of the Christian community for Paul is not primarily something structural, but rather the unifying power of a shared experience of grace inspiring a common gratitude and purpose.

b) The focus of community is the local church. In the earlier letters of Paul there are probably no instances of ekklesia meaning "the (universal) church"; it always seems to denote the Christians living or gathered in one place - hence the plural in Rom. 16:16, I Cor. 7:17; 16:1,19; etc., and its use of house-churches in Rom. 16:5; I Cor. 16:19 and Col. 4:15 (in Eph. it is different). So too "the body" in Rom. 12 and I Cor. 12 is not the universal church, but the church in Rome and the church in Corinth. It is particularly clear from the way Paul develops the metaphor in I Cor. 12 that the body referred to was the Corinthian body of believers: 12:27 - "you (Corinthians) are Christ's body". It is not clear how the (house) churches in a particular place functioned in relation to "the church" in that place; the descriptions in I Cor. 10-14 refer presumably to gatherings of the whole church of Corinth. The fact that smaller groups within the church in Rome are also called churches should not be ignored (Rom. 16:5).

c) The ongoing life of the (local) community is charismatic in character. As the shared experience of the Spirit is the beginning of community, so it is the continuing manifestations of the Spirit or gifts of the Spirit which constitute the life and growth of the community as the body of Christ. The "functions" of the body are precisely the charismata of the Spirit (Rom. 12:4) - charisma for Paul denoting any word or act which embodies or manifests grace (charis), which is a means of grace to another. Charismata (or charisms) thus understood are the living movements of the body (I Cor. 12:14-26; Eph. 4:16). Without them the body is dead. Christian community exists only in the living interplay of charismatic ministry, in the actual being and doing for others in word and deed.

d) It follows that to be a member of the body of Christ is by definition to be charismatic. There are no dead organs in the body of Christ; each has some function - "to each" is given some charisma or other (I Cor. 7:7; 12:7,11). To share in the Spirit means also being open for the Spirit to prompt some word or deed which will minister grace to the rest. At no time did Paul conceive of two kinds of Christian - those who have the spirit and those who do not, those who are charismatic and those who are not, those who minister to others and those who are ministered to. For example, although there were regular prophets (see (f) below) any might be moved to prophesy, and indeed all should seek and be open to this most valuable of charismata (I Cor. 12:10; 14:1,5,26,39; I Thess. 5:19f). There was certainly no concept of a monoministry or of a priestly office confined to a particular individual or group within the body.

e) The unity of the church is a function of its diversity. The members of the body have different functions, different ministries (Rom. 12:4; I Cor. 12:4ff) - otherwise the body would not be a body (I Cor. 12:17,19). Without the diversity of charismata there can be no unity, for without the Spirit's activity in and through each there is no unity and no body. The unity depends on the diversity functioning as such, and can be injured as much by one member taking too much to himself as by one member failing to respond to the Spirit's prompting (I Cor. 12:14-26; Rom. 12:3). The sharing in one loaf (as part of the common meal - only the cup is "after supper", I Cor. 11:25) is (or should have been) an expression of the oneness of the grace that knits the many together, not by eliminating their diversity or despite their diversity but in their diversity (I Cor. 10:17).

f) Within the diversity of ministries shared by all some evidently had more regular ministries. They "had" a

particular charisma, not in the sense that it was theirs
to use or not as they chose, but in the sense that the
Spirit regularly moved in and through them to express
some word or act which would benefit the community -
for only if the Spirit was behind and in any word or
act would it be a charisma, only if exercised in depen-
dence on grace and divine strength would it be a means
of grace to others (Rom. 12:6; cf. I Pet. 4:11). First
and foremost, and unique, was the role of apostle (I
Cor. 12:28). As founder of the church he had brought
the gospel that converted and the traditions about Jesus'
teaching and ministry (I Cor. 7:10; 9:14; 11:23-5; 15:1-3;
etc.). Second in importance were the prophets and teacher
(I Cor. 12:28), the one responsible to be open to new
revelation (14:6, 26, 30), the other to pass on and interpret the traditions of the faith (Gal. 6:6). There
were also a wide variety of other regular and overlapping
ministries in the Pauline churches - including preaching,
a wide range of services, administration and/or some
kinds of leadership (Rom. 12:7-8; 16:1,3,9,21; I Cor.
12:28; 16:15-8; etc.). Among them we see the first
use of the titles "bishops/overseers" (plural) and
"deacons" (Phil. 1:1), but what their functions were
at Philippi is not clear. None of these were yet
clearly defined, far less established offices. We
should also note that in Ephesians Paul's concept of
the local church as charismatic community is univer-
salized (either by Paul or by a close disciple), and
the ministries of apostles, prophets, evangelists,
pastors and teachers are presented as ministries of
the whole church (Eph. 4:11-6).

g) The authority of these various ministries lay primarily in the act of ministry itself. It was not something
given by another person, even the church's apostle(s).
Only the risen Christ appointed apostles (I Cor. 9:1;
15:7; Gal. 1:1,15f). And though Paul expected respect
for himself and his emissaries from his churches (e.g.
I Cor. 11:17, 34; 16:1; II Thess. 3:6-12), everything
he says strongly implies that he did not appoint prophets
or teachers or individuals to particular ministries.
There were those who like Stephanas (at the prompting
of the Spirit) acted to meet some need for the benefit
of the church (I Cor. 16:15 - literally "appointed
themselves to" their ministry). There were those who
"worked hard" at particular ministries (I Cor. 16:16;
I Thess. 5:12). That was the expression of their spiritua.
maturity and the community should recognize it (I Cor. 16:.
I Thess. 5:13; cf. Gal. 6:1-2). But where a community
was lacking leadership in various areas (over grave moral

issues, in the disorder of their gatherings for meals and for worship - I Cor. 5-6, 10-14) Paul did not vest authority in one individual or group. The authority of prophets and teachers was evidently limited to the sphere of their ministries; likewise, it would appear, the authority of Stephanas (just at the apostle's authority to his sphere of ministry - II Cor. 10:13-6, see NEB). Paul's hope evidently was that when the church came together the Spirit would give wisdom to some member of the community appropriate to the situation (I Cor. 6:5; cf. 12:8-28; 14:26).

h) The responsibility of the community itself should not be undervalued. It is clear from Paul's concept of the body of Christ that each member and all members together have a responsibility for the welfare of the whole (I Cor. 12:24-6). So we are not surprised when Paul exhorts all the members of different communities to teach, admonish, judge, comfort (Rom.15:14; I Cor. 5:4f; II Cor. 2:7; Col. 3:16; I Thess. 5:14), and encourages all to seek the most beneficial charisma (prophecy - see (d) above). Still more important, the community as a whole had the responsibility of testing all words and acts claiming the inspiration and authority of the Spirit (I Cor. 2:12,15; I Thess. 5:20f), even those of Paul himself (cf. I Cor. 7:25,40; 14:37). It was part of their responsibility to give assent, to say "Amen" to the inspired utterances (I Cor. 14:16), to recognize the authority of the Spirit in those ministries undertaken at his compulsion (I Cor. 16:18; I Thess. 5:12f); but also to evaluate and if necessary reject any word or deed, however inspired it might seem to be, which was counterfeit or did not benefit the community (I Cor. 2:15; 12:3; I Thess. 5:21f). Another way of putting this is that the gift is not complete until it has been evaluated and received (I Cor. 12:10; 14:27-9; I Thess. 5:19-22 NEB).

The Pauline concept of church differs from the discipleship of Jesus' ministry in that it was a concept of charismatic community, characterized by mutual interdependence, where each though he experiences the Spirit for himself must depend on his fellow members for a whole range of ministries. So too it differs from the pattern which evolved at Jerusalem in that it was essentially a concept of charismatic community, "of free fellowship, developing through the living interplay of spiritual gifts and ministries, without benefit of official authority or responsible "elder"" (von Campenhausen). Its challenge is exciting, but the defects are obvious too. (1) The model of the body focuses exclusively on the mutual internal relationships of the community. Paul himself was obviously committed to evangelism; but the other most relevant passage seems to envisage outreach happening only as a sort of by-product of the community's worship (I Cor. 14:23-5) - though we may assume that the "boundaries" of the church were still very fluid with "uninstructed and unbelievers" continually passing over them (both in and out); not also 10:27. (2) Within Paul's eschatological perspective (the imminence of the parousia I Thess. 4:13-8; I Cor. 7:29-31; the apostles the last act on stage before the final curtain - I Cor. 4:9), his churches did not require a structure that would endure. Charismatic community was a one generation ideal - nor is it finally clear whether his vision actually worked for any length of time in any particular church. On the other hand: (1) his concentration on the building up of the church was fully appropriate in that evangelistic situation, and underlines the importance of a spiritually sensitive supportive community for new converts; (2) perhaps we need to receive afresh the one-generation perspective lest we bestow on our successors the sort of entrenched structures and traditions which are so inhibiting for the present generation.

4.   The Pastoral Epistles - early Catholicism

The latest letters in the Pauline corpus (I Tim., II Tim., Tit.) reflect a significantly different concept of church and community. So much so that the question of authorship is virtually irrelevant here. If written by Paul or at his behest they show that Paul himself had abandoned his ideal of charismatic community and, looking into the next generation of Christianity, had accepted the need for a more carefully structured community, with authority more clearly and defined.

My own judgment is that the Pastorals reflect a second generation situation (c70-100 AD) when the organizational pattern of the Jewish churches (eldership - see 2b above; also Jas. 5:14f) had begun to merge with the evolving structure of the Pauline churches (overseers, and deacons - cf. Did. 15:1-2) - hence the near synonymity of "elders" and "overseers" in the Pastorals).

Either way the model given in the Pastorals is quite distinct from that presented in the earlier, undisputed Paulines.

a) Elders appear for the first and only time in the Pauline corpus (I Tim. 5:1f, 17:19; Tit. 1:5).

b) "Overseers" (bishops - I Tim. 3:1-7; Tit. 1:7ff), and deacons' (I Tim. 3:8-13) appear as descriptions of established offices (I Tim. 3:1 - "office of overseer"). The presentation of I Tim. 3 suggests that deacons were subordinate to overseers, though we cannot tell from this chapter what their respective functions were.

c) Timothy and Titus are not simply emissaries from Paul visiting one of his churches as his spokesman, as in earlier days (I Cor. 4:17; II Cor. 7:13f, etc.). Rather they are invisaged as having an authority which even Paul never exercised - an authority over the community much like that of a monarchical bishop. Theirs is the responsibility to keep the faith pure (I Tim. 1:3f; 4:6ff; 11:6; etc.), to order the life and relationships of the community (I Tim. 5:1-16; 6:2,17; Tit. 2:1-10,15), to exercise discipline and mete out justice not least in the case of elders (I Tim. 5:19ff), to lay on hands (I Tim. 5:22) and to appoint elders (Tit. 1:5).

d) The Pauline concept of charisma has been narrowed and regulated. It seems to be understood more as a single gift given once-for-all in the course of ordination, a gift which Timothy now possesses within himself and which equips him for his different responsibilities. From being an event (word or act) or series of events which carry their authority in themselves and must be evaluated by others, charisma has become the power and authority of office (I Tim. 4:14; II Tim. 1:6).

e) A concept approaching that of "apostolic succession" is beginning to emerge - Paul to Timothy to "faithful men" to "others", though whether the succession is yet conceived in formal terms, from office to office, is not clear (II Tim. 2:2).

f) The only general congregational activity mentioned is prayer (I Tim. 2:8).

In the Pastorals therefore we see Christian communities
girding themselves with an increasingly hierarchical
structure and authority to ensure continuance into
future generations. The Pauline vision of the body, of
a community of mutually interdependent ministries, has
been left behind. So too the important Pauline tension
between prophet and teacher, between (new) revelation
and (old) tradition. There is no question that the Pastorals' model can endure (it did!); the question rather
is whether it has lost something vital in the earlier
Pauline vision, not least the vision itself.

5.   The Lukan alternative - enthusiasm and catholicism

The striking feature about the Acts of the Apostles is
that it seems to be working with two models of Christian
community and trying to hold them together. How much is
straight history and how much history viewed from a one-
sided perspective, or history with a pattern impressed
upon it, is always a problem in interpreting Acts. But
some Lukan emphases and some significant silences give
us sufficient clues.

a) Luke not only presents the beginnings of Christianity
as enthusiastic in character, but he seems also deliberately to heighten the enthusiastic features. For Luke
the Spirit is most clearly seen in extraordinary and most
obviously supernatural phenomena, something tangible,
unmistakeable, whether inspired speech or manifest physical impact (Acts 2:3f, 17f, 33; 8:16-9; 10:44-6; 11:15f;
19:2,6). He seems to put great weight on the ecstatic
visions which guided the development of the young church
(9:10; 10:3-6, 10-6; 16:9f; 18:9; 22:17f, 26:19f) and
shows none of Paul's reservations on the abuse which
could and did arise from claims to authoritative revelation based on vision (cf. II Cor. 12:1ff; Col. 2:18).
He seems deliberately to heighten the importance of
miracles (particularly Acts 8:13; 19:11), and calls
them regularly "wonders and signs", whereas that phrase
is used more often elsewhere in a more negative sense
denoting something to be wary of (Mark 13:22/Matt. 24:24;
John 4:48; II Cor. 12:12; II Thess. 2:9). He seems to
imply that all inspired utterance can be taken at face
value as the work of the Spirit, making no attempt to
distinguish prophecy from glossolalia (2:4, 16:8; 10:46;
19:6; contrast I Cor. 14), and attributing contradictory
directives both to the Spirit without comment (Acts
20:22; 21:4).

b) On the other hand Luke presents a Christianity which shows more features of early catholicism than we would expect on the basis of historical analysis. The expectation of the imminent parousia which was still strong in Paul's time and which must have been if anything stronger at the beginning (Jesus' resurrection as the "first-fruits" = beginning of the final resurrection - Rom. 1:4; I Cor. 15:20-3; "Our Lord, come" - I Cor. 16:22) is only hinted at. Eschatology in Acts 10:42, 17:31, 24:25 is much more like "the doctrine of the last things" than the imminent expectation of Paul (and Jesus) - a second generation perspective. He passes over in silence the continuing tensions and significant differences within the early church between Paul and Jerusalem. (Gal. 2:11ff; II Cor. 10:13; Phil. 3), showing Jerusalem to be much more the authoritative centre of the whole mission (including the Gentile mission) than Paul would have accepted (particularly II Cor. 10:13-6 NEB), presenting a much narrower picture of apostleship (= the twelve) than Paul would have accepted (particularly I Cor. 15:7; Rom. 16:7; I Cor. 9:5f; Gal. 2:9), and depicting Paul as actually appointing elders in his churches from the beginning (Acts 14:23; cf. 20:17). It is difficult to avoid the conclusion that Luke is stamping his portrayal of early Christianity with a greater degree of homogeneity in self-understanding and uniformity of organization that was historically the case.

The boldness and challenge of Luke's presentation deserves more attention than it has been given. He attempts to present a church or churches in which enthusiasm and regular order coexist in harmonious interaction; and also an enthusiasm which does not go hand in hand with expectation of an imminent second coming, and which is therefore not dependent on it and not destroyed by the delay of the parousia. How difficult it is to hold these two together, enthusiasm and early catholicism, is evidenced by the fact that Acts has provided inspiration and authority for both enthusiasts and catholics, without each usually being aware of the support afforded to the other by the same document.

6. The Johannine alternative - pietism

The Gospel and Epistles of John seem to share with Acts a similarly altered eschatological perspective (cf. John

21). The future eschatological hope is by no means lacking (e.g. 5:27-9; 14:3f), but few would dispute that the
emphasis is on realized eschatology (particularly 3:8,
5:24, 11:25f; I John 3:14). The difference with Acts
is that whereas Acts shows a church whose organization
can withstand the delay of the parousia, John seems to
understand Christianity as much more an individual
affair, the immediacy of the disciple's relationship
with Christ through the Spirit ensuring his presence
(John 14:15-20; I John 3:24).

a) The individualism of the Fourth Gospel is one of the
most striking features of this remarkable document.
The sense of mutual interdependence in belonging to Christ
so strong in Paul is lacking in John: each sheep hears
the shepherd's voice for himself (John 10:3f, 16) each
branch is rooted directly in the vine (15:4-7); each
seems to eat and drink for himself (6:53-8; 7:37f);
the unity of believers is patterned on the unity of
Father and Son and depends on the individual's union
with Christ (17:20-3). Similarly in I John (e.g. 3:24;
4:13; 5:10-2).

b) The disciples closest to Jesus do not form any kind
of hierarchy, nor are they given any particular office.
They are never called "apostles" or "the twelve" and
presumably include (some of) the women who feature so
prominently in this gospel (4, 11, 20); they are simply
"the disciples", and John thus probably intends them to
represent all (including future) disciples in their common responsibility of mutual love and mission (14:16,
20:22). In particular "the beloved disciple" is probably
used by John to symbolize the individual believer in
the immediacy and closeness of his relationship to Jesus
(13:23-5; 20:2-8). The picture does not change in the
Johannine epistles. We may note especially I John 2:27,
where the anointing (of the Spirit) obviates the necessity of teachers - the Spirit indwelling each believer
is teacher enough. A specifically pastoral role however
is given to Peter in the epilogue to the gospel (John
21:15-7).

c) There is a very strong sense of "us" and "them" in the
Johannine writings. The Johannine Christians have passed
from darkness to light, from death to life (3:19-21;
5:24; 8:12). In I John in particular the distinction
between believer and unbeliever is clear-cut (I John

2:4,23; 3:6,9f, 14f, 4:5f). The frequent call for love
is for love of the brethren (John 13:34f; I John 3:10-
8,23f; 4:20f). Those who "went out" demonstrated thereby that they were never "in" (I John 2:19).

This understanding of Christian community has been ap-
propriately likened to conventicle Christianity, to the
pietistic Christianity of "conferences for the deepen-
ing of the spiritual life", where, though she/he seeks
to worship in Spirit and truth (John 4:24) in company
with others, it is the immediacy and growth of her/his
own spiritual life which the individual counts as of
greatest importance. The greater the love of brethren,
the greater apparently the divorce from the world, lack
of involvement with the world. This too is NT Christianity. And the influence of the Johannine writings on
countless generations of Christian spirituality shows
how important it has been - and continues to be - in a
world dominated by materialistic concerns and values.

7. The Matthean church - the law-abiding brotherhood

Matthew is generally thought to have been written about
AD 80, at a time when (in the aftermath of AD 70) rabbinic
Judaism was beginning to formulate its distinctive character, and when Jewish Christians (in Syria?) found themselves having to say to their fellow Jews, "We know and
keep the law better than you because we follow Jesus"
(see e.g. Matt. 5:17-20; 23:3,23). There are four passages which shed light on the concept and practice of
Christian community reflected in Matthew.

a) 7:15-23. Matthew's church seems to have suffered
somewhat from the ministry of wandering prophets - a
charismatic ministry which, in Matthew's view at least,
was wedded to antinomianism (7:22f; cf. 24:11,24).
Matthew does not reject such ministry (cf. 10:7f, 41;
17:20), but seeks to ensure that it is more closely integrated with a continuing loyalty to the law - not so
very different from Paul's emphasis in Gal. 5:13f, but
with greater stress on keeping the Jewish law.

b) 16:13-20. Peter is clearly the apostle most highly
regarded within this community. Principally because
(for them) he was the church founder par excellence
(16:18) - both as the one whose preaching called the
mother church of Jerusalem into existence (Acts 2), and

113

presumably as the apostle to the circumcised in general
(Gal. 2:7f) as of many Jewish Christian churches in particular (including Matthew's). But also because, in
Matthew's presentation, he is the typical disciple, representing both the insight and authority of faith (16:
17,19; cf. 18:18; 21:21f) and the weakness of "little
faith" discipleship (14:28-31; cf. 17:20).

c) 18:1-20. This "community rule" seems to envisage no
special leaders who can be distinguished from the ordinary church members. The passage speaks only on "these
little ones" - obviously the membership as a whole,
since to enter the kingdom of heaven each must become
such a one (18:1-6,10). The "rule" lays responsibility
on every one to find the lost sheep, to win back the
erring brother, to "bind and loose" (18:12-20).

d) 23:8-10 contain a solemn and quite explicit warning
to the Matthean church against conferring any rank or
title or special status on any individual member - God
alone is "father" and Jesus alone is "teacher" and
"master". The greatness to which they are all encouraged is, using Jesus' words, not that of executive power
and authority but that of humble service (20:25-7; 23:
11f).

The Matthean community is perhaps best described as a
brotherhood (5:22-4,47; 7:3-5; 18:15,21,35; 23:8) grouped
round the elder brother Jesus (12:49f; 18:20; 25:40;
28:10), striving to develop a form of outoging life and
all-member ministry amid Jewish hostility, and conscious
of the opposite dangers both of a hierarchical structure
which might inhibit the manifold ministry of the brotherhood and of a charismatic prophetism which divorces
miracle and revelation too sharply from a proper loyalty
to the law. In other words, we see reflected in Matthew
what seems to be an attempt to develop or maintain a
form of Pauline "churchmanship" within and more appropriate to a rabbinic Jewish context.

8. Fragmentary reflections elsewhere

a) I Peter shares the Pauline concept of charismatic
ministry (4:10f). The concept of a priestly ministry
is referred to the church as a whole (2:5,9); and the
title "pastor and overseer" is used only of Jesus (2:25).
The only prophets (including Christian prophets?) men-

tioned are spoken of in the past tense (1:10-2). A clearly defined circle of elders is addressed in 5:1-5, although "elder" here may simply mean "older" (5:5). If the community herein alluded to belongs within the spectrum sketched out above it could be characterized as a church (probably within the Pauline mission) which has already begun to integrate charismatic community with a system of eldership.

b) Hebrews mentions "leaders" who are clearly distinct from the rest of God's people (13:7,17,24). A ministry of teaching is spoken of in 5:11-6:8, but as with "the spiritual ones" in Paul (I Cor. 2:12-3:4; Gal. 6:1), it is a status of spiritual maturity and experience rather than of office which is envisaged. No other ministries are referred to individual members, and elsewhere responsibility for service and exhortation is laid on the whole membership (6:10; 10:25; 12:15). The most striking feature is the writer's focusing of all priestly ministry of Jesus in an exclusive and exhaustive way (2:17; 3:1; 4:14f; 5:1; etc.) so that there is no room or role left for any priestly intermediary within the Christian community. Such a priesthood belonged to the past, the era of shadow, but Christ has brought the reality thus foreshadowed to every believer (7-10), so that each can now "draw near" the very presence of God for himself without depending on other believers or any human intermediary (4:16; 6:19f; 10:19-22). In short, if I Peter falls somewhere between Paul and the Pastorals in ecclesiology, Hebrews seems to share more of John's individualistic pietism.

c) Revelation. Here the ecclesiology envisaged is too obscurely reflected to give a clear picture. Apostles belong to the founding era (21:14). All believers are priests (1:6; 5:10; 20:6). The elders in the heavenly throne room presumably represent the church as a whole (4:4,10; 5:8; etc.). Likewise the "angels" of the churches in 2-3 are most probably heavenly counterparts of the churches in question. Most prominent are prophets (e.g. 10:7; 11:18; 16:6) and witnesses (2:13; 11:3; 17:6), who are envisaged as particular individuals in 2:13,20 and 22:9. Whether they were clearly distinct ministries within any community, let alone formed a hierarchy within the churches, is not clear to us. But so far as a generalization can be ventured it would be that the church of Revelation is one which lives through and out of prophecy.

Conclusion

There is clearly no single model of Christian community
which emerges from the NT as the NT church. We see
different churches in different situations (inevitably?)
reflecting something of the dominant characteristics of
their environment - the church at Corinth mirrors the
libertarian abuses of Corinthian society, just as the
church in Jerusalem and the church of Matthew mirrors
the law-centredness of Jewish society. We see already,
both in Jerusalem and the Pauline churches, evidence of
the now familiar historical sequence - the transition
from first generation community, enthusiastic, loosely
structured, innovative, to a second generation community with developing hierarchical structure and growing
consciousness of tradition and the need to preserve
rather than to innovate. We see already what has become the most regular way of escape from a too rigid
institutionalization, in the pietism of John and probably
Hebrews. All these are what we might call sociological
truths, the facts of life and social relationships both
within the church and between the churches and their
environment, which we cannot ignore and must always
live with.

But we see also theological principles which must always
provide the motivating starting point from which we move
out to challenge merely sociological pressures, the yardstick by which we measure our quality of community, the
vision by which we live and which we refuse to conform
to the pattern of this world. Here the challenge of
Jesus' call to discipleship and Paul's visitation of
charismatic community should particularly be mentioned,
as being those models of community which show least influence of these same sociological pressures. Of the
various elements in these two may I mention not least
their eschatological character. That is to say, part
of what gave them their challenging quality was their
focus on the present and unconcern to organize for the
future. May it be that the model of Christian community
which emerges from the NT with most force today is the
one-generation model: the church which organizes for the
future may simply be ensuring that the future will be so
burdened with the past that it cannot bring to reality
Christian community in the present.

Nottingham, February 1980

116

D. A SURVEY OF THE WORLDWIDE CHARISMATIC MOVEMENT

Peter Hocken

I. Origins and development

Origins

Charismatic Renewal is usually traced back to the late
1950s, but reference should be made by way of background
to the Pentecostal movement at the start of the century.
The Pentecostal movement with its roots locally in
Topeka, Kansas, in 1901 and internationally in Azusa
Street, Los Angeles in 1906, was not a separatist movement in original intention, but was seen as a charismatic revival within the churches.[1] Most of these
"tongues-speakers" were driven out of their churches,
though one or two early Pentecostal leaders remained
in the denominations, though with increasing difficulty
and diminishing impact.[2]

The origins of Charismatic Renewal in the historic
churches are customarily placed at Van Nuys, California,
USA, where in 1959 the Episcopalian rector, Dennis Bennett,
and a good number of his parishioners had received the
baptism in the Spirit and gift of tongues. The crisis
occasioned by this outbreak, and particularly by the
attendant publicity,[3] helped to uncover evidence that
many Christians in the mainline churches had already
experienced this blessing of the Lord without seeking
or attracting publicity[4] and sometimes without much
understanding of what had happened. It was as the e-
vents at Van Nuys became known and were followed by
similar outbreaks in other places and denominations that
people became aware of a widespread movement of the Holy
Spirit.

This move of the Spirit spread rapidly beyond the Epis-
copalians to other denominations within the United States.
As early as 1961, David du Plessis saw these occurrences
as an inter-church phenomenon giving the first edition
of his book The Spirit Bade Me Go the sub-title "An
Astounding Move of God in the Denominational Churches".
The Full Gospel Business Men's Fellowship International
(FGBMFI) played an influential part in this expansion.[5]
FGBMFI published collections of testimonies of members
of historic churches receiving the baptism of the Spirit.

Booklets relating to Methodists, Baptists and Presbyterians all came out in 1963. At this stage, the movement was generally designated "neo-Pentecostalism", indicating a basic affinity to what now became known as "classical Pentecostalism", i.e. the Pentecostal denominations dating from the time of World War I.

The spread of Charismatic Renewal to other parts of the world was not long delayed. It is recorded among Anglicans in England in 1962, among Lutherans in West Germany by 1963, and in several churches in New Zealand during the early 1960s. There was an indigenous Charismatic Revival in parts of Indonesia in 1964. In the spring of 1967, the Van Nuys experience was in some ways repeated for a number of Roman Catholics at Duquesne and South Bend. Once again, the publicized event helped to reveal that other Catholics had already begun to receive this blessing. Charismatic Renewal has since appeared in Latin America and Asia, for example in Argentina by 1967, and Sri Lanka by 1969. Its arrival in Africa has generally been more recent.[6] In Europe the main flowering of charismatics in almost all countries came with the start of the 1970s.

While Charismatic Renewal is now found in virtually all churches and all continents, its influence and strength varies from country to country, and from church to church. Serious students of this movement recognize that reliable statistics for the incidence and impact of this renewal are almost impossible to obtain except on a very local basis.

<u>Unevenness of extent and impact</u>

In sheer terms of quantitative expansion there is some evidence that Charismatic Renewal is most evenly spread, in proportion to church membership, among <u>Anglicans</u> and <u>Catholics</u>, followed next by <u>Lutherans</u>. Among Lutherans, Charismatic Renewal appears to be more widespread in Scandinavia than in Germany, and more in Eastern Germany (DDR) than in Western Germany (BRD). Charismatic Renewal among <u>Baptists</u> is relatively strong in England[7] but disproportionately sparse in the USA which has the greatest concentration of Baptist Christians.[8] There is evidence that many Baptist groups in the Soviet Union are charismatic.[9] Charismatic Renewal is found throughout the <u>Reformed-Presbyterian</u> world, but its impact and growth seem to have been slower than in some other traditions, though many Presbyterian congregations in Latin America have been strongly influenced by Charismatic Renewal and put "Pentecostal" after their name. Though individual Methodists have exerted strong influence,[10] Charismatic Renewal does not seem to be firmly established in many Methodist congregations. Among the Orthodox, Charismatic Renewal is mostly restricted to the diaspora of the western world, primarily in Canada and USA, though unequally in the various jurisdictions. Charismatic Renewal is also reported among the Orthodox in Australia, Uganda and Lebanon. Mennonites, though numerically one of the smaller denominations, report extensive charismatic renewal, especially in the Americas. Two Christian groups, though not technically churches, the Quakers and the Salvation Army report charismatic activity in a few places.

Among blacks, two principal factors appear to affect the incidence of Charismatic Renewal. The first is the extent of the black presence in society with an evident difference between countries with a black majority and those where blacks form a minority of the population. The second is the presence or absence of black Pentecostal or Independent churches. Where there are rapidly growing Independent churches, as in the USA,[11] there is sometimes reluctance on the part of leaders in the mainline denominations to encourage Charismatic Renewal among blacks for fear of losing members to these other churches. This fear is accentuated where blacks are in a minority. In the minority situations black Christians when confronted by the challenge of Charismatic Renewal mostly tend to change to a Pentecostal church or reject the charismatic experience. However, while the presence of the independent churches in Africa acts as a brake factor for Charismatic Renewal,[12] Africans generally have a greater familiarity with spiritual phenomena and many aspects of Charismatic Renewal do not seem as strange to them as to Christians in the white western world. Charismatic Renewal appears to be having a particular impact in the Caribbean especially on those small islands where the historic churches are numerically strong.

Charismatic Renewal shows signs of having a particular impact in places of sharp political conflict and/or constant tension, where present insecurity and danger provide a definite incentive for seeking the face of God in repentance and humility. Instances include Finland,

Northern Ireland and Zimbabwe. In South Africa, where more church leaders are personally involved in this renewal than in other countries, there is evidence of a growing openness to Charismatic Renewal among the white population. From settings such as Northern Ireland and Lebanon there are reports of the power of Jesus Christ to reconcile people from opposite sides of warring factions but understandably these remain less publicized than other visibly impressive effects of Charismatic Renewal.

Another situation obtains in the officially atheist and socialist countries of Eastern Europe. There is definite evidence of the spread of Charismatic Renewal in these countries, probably stronger at this point among Protestant than among Catholic Christians, though Charismatic Renewal in Poland is spreading steadily among Catholics.[13] The close regulation of all religious activities by the State in such countries causes spontaneous religious movements to develop in distinctive ways, either leading to their being registered and recognized as a part of official church life or to being unrecognized and proscribed.

In Latin America, the Pentecostal churches have been growing much faster than the Protestant bodies, with both groupings recruting primarily from the ranks of nominal Catholics, "sacramentalized" but not evangelized. In this situation, where classical Pentecostals are much more numerous and successful than traditional Protestants, the latter are coming to be more influenced by the former. The term Renovacion is often used of Charismatic Renewal among Latin American Protestants. The loss of many nominal Catholics to Pentecostal churches does not seem to have discredited Charismatic Renewal in Catholic eyes, though Catholic leaders in this situation are particularly concerned to stress Catholic identity and particularities. The widespread existence of syncretistic forms of religious in Latin America and the Caribbean, especially in such countries as Brazil and Haiti, causes church authorities to be somewhat wary of spiritual phenomena and to be concerned lest gifts of the Spirit lend themselves to spiritualist appropriation. Such leaders have a similar caution in the Islands of Melanesia where there have been successive waves of cargo cults among the native population.

Some reasons for uneven spread

A variety of reasons can be advanced to account for the uneven distribution of Charismatic Renewal across the world and the churches.

a. US origins. Movements ordinarily start in one place and expand from there. Charismatic Renewal began in the USA. Hence it is not surprising that Charismatic Renewal is longer established and often more mature in the USA than in places at greater remove from the western hemisphere. Granted the wide range of attitudes to the USA found throughout the world, it is not surprising that suspicion of American influence is a factor affecting the development of Charismatic Renewal. In the Third World this can take the form of suspicion of American power and culture but in western Europe more often takes the form of the pride of the "old world" that is reluctant to learn anything from the "new".[14]

b. Acknowledged need for spiritual renewal. Charismatic Renewal seems to spread more rapidly where the need for spiritual renewal is more acutely felt and explicitly acknowledged. Churches that are successful by common standards, with attractive worship, popular preaching, growing numbers, flourishing programmes and vigorous social life, are often less open to Charismatic Renewal. This may be one reason why the numerically strong Baptist churches in the USA are not strongly represented in Charismatic Renewal, whereas the less flourishing Baptists in Great Britain have proved to be among the front runners in that country.

c. Evangelical opposition on doctrinal grounds. Some of the strongest Christian opposition to Charismatic Renewal comes from a section of evangelical Protestantism which sees in Pentecostalism and Charismatic Renewal a threat to the unique status of the Bible as the revealed word of God. Their objections generally focus on what they see as the threat to the objective revelation in the scriptures and its unique authority posed by the appeal to personal subjective experience and by regarding any contemporary utterances as authoritative words from the Lord.[15] This factor is important in understanding the hesitations in the Lutheran church - Missouri Synod.

d. Wider impact in liturgical-sacramental churches.
It would appear that Charismatic Renewal has had greater
impact in churches with liturgical-sacramental forms of
worship. One factor here is that such churches are less
tied in their theology of Christian initiation than
evangelical groups to affirming a particular pattern of
experience.

e. Role of church structure. In churches with a congregational form of government, in which local congregations voluntarily affiliate within a regional or national
union or federation, the widespread eruption of Charismatic Renewal often provokes greater tensions than
within churches of an episcopal type. Individual congregations are often faced by the need to declare themselves for or against Charismatic Renewal.[16]

Churches with an episcopal form of government (whether
or not their officers are called bishops) generally
allow for a greater variety in expressions of church
life at local level and this makes for greater tolerance
of distinctive groupings within the church. Churches
such as the Catholic and the Orthodox with a strong
tradition of monasticism and religious life have a
framework that allows for bodies that are not parochial
to be fully integrated into their church.

The Methodist circuit system may act as an inhibiting
factor to Charismatic Renewal in those countries where
there is a limited tenure in ministerial appointments
and where ministers are as much appointed to the circuit
as to one congregation. This structure can render effective renewal of a group more difficult.

Subsequent developments of significance

a. Formation of denominational charismatic bodies.
Particularly since the beginning of Charismatic Renewal
in the Roman Catholic Church there has been a growing
tendency in the USA to form denominational charismatic
offices and committees and to hold annual denominational
conferences for Charismatic Renewal. Among Catholics
the pattern for establishing National Service Committees
for Catholic Charismatic Renewal has now become standard
practice throughout the world.[17] The Anglicans held a
worldwide Anglican Charismatic Conference at Canterbury
immediately prior to the Lambeth Conference in 1978 and

the Baptists are considering something similar in association with the World Baptist Alliance meeting to be
held in Vancouver in 1980.

b. Adoption of designation "Charismatic Renewal". From
the early 1970s the terminology of "neo-Pentecostalism"
has steadily given way to that of "Charismatic Renewal".18
This terminology, which distinguishes the movement in
the mainline churches more clearly from classical Pentecostalism reflects a concern to reduce obstacles to its
acceptance within the churches.

Charismatic Renewal was chosen (i) because the recovery
of the charisms was seen as a central feature of what
God is doing in this movement and (ii) because renewal
suggests the revitalization of the entire life of the
churches, not just the conversion and sanctification of
individual Christians.

II. Salient features of Charismatic Renewal

As with the Pentecostal churches, Charismatic Renewal
is not adequately described by a listing of tenets believed. Its distinctiveness is only adequately conveyed
when its praxis and its less-articulated insights are
taken into account, for example the ways in which Pentecostals and charismatics express their faith in worship
of God (not just their theories about faith and God),
the ways in which the Word of God is received and believed (not just their theories about God, man and Satan),
the ways in which the church as the body of Christ is
built up and experienced (not just their theories about
the church). The more Charismatic Renewal is defined in
doctrinal and theological terms, the less will it be
seen as significantly different from Evangelical Protestantism; the more its praxis is noted, the more will it
be seen to exhibit variant patterns from historic Protestantism, some being more akin to aspects of Catholic
and Orthodox tradition. it is the distinctive praxis
that indicates the ethos of Charismatic Renewal, and
which is an important element in its distinct appeal.

a. Its spontaneous origins. There has been something
quite unpredictable about Charismatic Renewal. It does
not correspond to any human blueprint for the renewal
of the church. It cannot be traced to any one prestigious
figure, nor, despite the role of the places mentioned,
can the whole movement be traced back to any one human

source. Being part of this movement does not involve following any particular leader. The extraordinary way in which similar patterns of charismatic outbreak occurred in widely different places, without any obvious inter-action between them, is but one indication that this movement cannot be simply explained in human terms.

Charismatic Renewal has not been planned by the churches, and it is not the sort of renewal any church would willingly have chosen. The steadily more positive response of the churches to this phenomenon represents, not a predilection for this pattern of renewal, but a recognition that despite its surprising and puzzling elements it does carry many signs of being a work of the Spirit of God.

b. Lay initiative. While Pentecostal and charismatic tenets alone do not indicate the place given to lay initiative, this is a significant feature of Charismatic Renewal and part of its ethos. The strong element of congregational participation, not only in singing, is indicated by the characteristic layout at charismatic meetings, in which the customary square or circular arrangement provides for continuity between the leaders and the rest. Besides the general participatory character of charismatic worship, charismatic gatherings provide various opportunities for personal initiative in prophecy, in spontaneous reading of scripture and in personal witnessing and sharing. There is a direct link between lay initiative in charismatic gatherings and lay initiative in evangelism outside the prayer meetings.

c. Baptism in the Holy Spirit. At the heart of all charismatic testimonies is a witness to an interior revelation of who Jesus Christ is, in which the Holy Spirit is experienced. God's Spirit witnesses to our spirit that we are children of God (cf. Romans 8:16) and makes known His power for sanctification, evangelism and mission. This transforming experience is most frequently given the designation baptism in the Spirit.[19] In baptism in the Spirit there is a new awareness of the truth that God has first loved (I John 4:10) and a recognition that Jesus Christ is living Lord now. The fullness of this experience includes a decision to live in submission to His rule by the power of His Spirit. Through baptism in the Spriit, there is an added awareness of Jesus as, par excellence, the one filled with the Spirit. (Cf. Luke 4:1,14,18; 10:21; Acts 10:38).

An outdoor worship service during the Stony Point consultation

Photos: Wendy Goldsworthy
and Arnold Bittlinger

Walter
Hollenweger

WCC General Secretary Philip Potter,
with Arnold Bittlinger

Peter
Felber

Kilian
McDonnell

Two scenes from the Bossey consultation: above, a group meeting; below, the consultation participa

While much theological discussion of baptism in the Spirit focuses on whether or not there are two norma- tive stages in Christian initiation, this question is not decisive for an understanding of what is happening today when people are baptized in the Sprit. The more basic question is "what is normal Christian life accor- ding to the mind of Jesus Christ?" All charismatics[20] whatever their theology of baptism in the Spirit would agree that this decisive act of God is a grace for the restoration of normal Christian life among Christians and in churches which have become accustomed to regard as normal what is subnormal by apostolic standards (in regard to faith expectation, knowledge of God in Jesus Christ, the power of God for evangelism, healing and moral transformation).

d. A trinitarian movement. Christians baptized in the Spirit commonly come to a lived awareness of the distinc- tive persons of the Trinity, Father, Son and Holy Spirit so that the doctrine of the Trinity is experienced as living truth and not just as theological theorem. This is demonstrated by the way in which Charismatic Renewal is as much a Jesus Movement as it is a Holy Spirit move- ment. Whatever two stage accounts of Christian initia- tion may be advanced by charismatics, they do not see conversion as receiving Jesus without the Spirit and baptism in the Spirit as receiving the Spirit in addi- tion to Jesus. There is an awareness that the deeper life in the Spirit that is given through baptism in the Spirit is a deeper following of Jesus Christ through an annointing with the same Spirit that animated His min- istry and prompted His submission to the will of His Father that led Him to the cross of Calvary.

e. Praise and worship. Charismatic Renewal is every- where characterized by the praise of God and a deeper recognition of the worthiness of God and Jesus His Son to receive praise and glory and honor (Rev. 4:11; 5:9-10). Charismatic worship manifests the important truth that praise is first of all a corporate gift whereby God's people are empowered to proclaim His glory and to ex- perience the presence of God in the power set loose by vigorous praise. This sense of the importance of volume in praise, which is neither a sheer glorification of noise, nor a rejection of Paul's warnings against mere noisy gongs and clanging cymbals (cf. I Cor. 13:1), recognizes a wholesome and liberating quality about the

full-blooded praise of God that has overcome the timidity
of reticence and a one-sided equation of silence with
closeness to God. Charismatics have rediscovered the
concept of "ministry unto the Lord", which has priority
over all ministry to men.[21]

Many characteristics of praise in the Charismatic Renewal echo emphases found in the Psalms, in which praise
is so central. For example, the narration of the mighty
deeds of God does not end at some point in the past but
continues to the present day, in which the words of God
still provoke wonder and thanksgiving. The whole earth
is invited to "make a joyful noise to the Lord" (Ps.
98:4) and God's people to "shout for joy to the God of
Jacob" (Ps. 81:1).

f. The role of the Bible. Charismatic Renewal is evidently a movement that takes the Scriptures seriously
as the Word of God. Baptism in the Spirit commonly
leads to a new thirst for the Word of God, as well as
providing a new affinity between what is experienced
through the Holy spirit in one's life and what is read
in the inspired Word under the guidance of the same
Spirit.

Charismatic Renewal is leading to a deeper recognition
of the Scriptures as food for the Christian life. Although there are dangers that charismatics who rediscover
Scripture as the living Word will understand the text
in too literalist a manner, there are several influences
at work in Charismatic Renewal promoting a richer Christian
usage of the Bible.[22] So, for example, Charismatic Renewal is leading in some circles to a rediscovery of
the spiritual sense of the Scriptures (the sensus plenior)
centred on the Incarnation, that is illustrated by the
words of Jesus "If you believed Moses, you would believe
me, for he wrote of me." (John 5:46).

Charismatic Renewal also includes a new sense of the
authority of the scripture as God's Word. Because the
charismatic is convinced that God speaks today (see
section g below) the authority of God's word is not seen
within Charismatic Renewal simply in terms of the immu-
tability and universality of God's law. There is an
authority in the word that God speaks to the individual
believer and to a particular community. Potentially
the conviction that God speaks today through His Word

126

grounds a greater flexibility in the understanding of the authority of the Scriptures as the Word of God.

g. God speaks today. In Charismatic Renewal God is restoring to ordinary Christians an awareness that He speaks to each believer and to each Christian group as much today as in any previous era. God's word is sought and heard in many ways: the most important is generally through the text of the Scriptures whereby the Holy Spirit illumines the heart of the believer to see the relevance of a particular passage of scripture for his present life situation. It is in such usage that the charismatic particularly experiences the truth "the word of God is living and active, sharper than any two edged sword, piercing to the division of soul and spirit, of joints and marrow, discerning the thoughts and intentions of the heart." (Hebr. 4:12). God's word is also regularly heard in other ways through forms of inner locution, through the word of another, particularly through committed brothers and sisters (whether in prophecy spoken in the name of the Lord or in direct speech) and through external events.[23]

Charismatics are generally aware that not all inspiration and words come from the Holy Spirit and that there is need for discernment. There is danger of illusion as there is danger in ignoring such inspirations, but leaders in Charismatic Renewal see the way of countering this danger as teaching (i) the Christian to believe that God will speak to him and (ii) the need for what he hears to be discerned with other Christians of proven wisdom.

h. Rejection of dispensationalism. While few churches have adopted an explicitly dispensationalist position of maintaining that the endowments of power in the New Testament were intended only for the period of the church's foundation, most Christians assume this to have been the case. Charismatic Renewal challenges this mentality, affirming that what the Holy Spirit did in the first century, he can and does do in the twentieth. It thereby manifests a distinctive understanding of the relationship between the work of the Spirit in the one-and-for-all event of Jesus Christ (ephapax) and the work of the Spirit in making that salvation present and effective in the course of history. Charismatic convictions and expectations combine a subordination of the

post-apostolic (the power in the Word today, the experience of Pentecost today, the sacrifice of Christ today)
to the orginal event in Jesus Christ (the unique Word
then, the unique Pentecost then, the unique sacrifice
then) with a recognition that the Spirit is as active
now as then. This implies a distinctive understanding
of tradition in a way that is more creative than previous Protestant attitudes and more subordinate to the
original event than the received Catholic approach.[24]

i. Evangelism. Charismatic Renewal emphasizes that evangelism is a task imposed on each Christian. Baptism in
the Spirit gives the Christian that confidence in God's
love and His saving Power that he can witness effectively
to others about Jesus Christ.

With its recognition that Jesus Christ acts today as
Lord and Saviour in visible events Charismatic Renewal
follows a common biblical pattern of evangelism in which
the proclamation of Jesus Christ is given as the explanation for an event that has attracted the attention of
the public. Cf. Acts 3:12-26; 4:8-12; 8:5-8; 9:33-35;
16:25-34.

j. Spiritual gifts. Many people, both participants in
Charismatic Renewal and sympathetic observers, see the
rediscovery of the spiritual gifts and their restoration
to ordinary Christian life and ministry as the major
contribution of Charismatic Renewal. The spiritual
gifts listed by St. Paul in I Cor. 12:8-10 are: word of
wisdom; word of knowledge; faith; gifts of healing;
working of miracles; prophecy; discerning of spirits;
divers kinds of tongues; interpretation of tongues.

There is fairly general agreement within Charismatic
Renewal as to the meaning and purpose of healing, prophecy, discernment, tongues and interpretation of tongues.
Gifts of healing are given to members of the body of
Christ so that human diseases and disabilities of every
kind, organic and non-organic, psychological as well as
physical, can be healed through the direct action of
Jesus Christ and the ministry of the Christian. Prophecy
is a gift by which God speaks a message to an individual,
a group or an entire Christian community. It may or
may not be accompanied by an action illuminating the
spoken word. Discernment of spirits is that gift whereby
Christians are able to judge whether an event, a propo-

sal, an utterance is from the Holy Spirit of God, from the human spirit of man, or from evil spirits.

The gift of tongues is in most instances a gift of prayer for the individual Christian, whereby the recipient is enabled to praise God in a way that is more immediate than the prayer of ordinary language. The gift of interpretation, by which a hearer is enabled to receive the sense of an utterance in tongues (it is not a gift of translation) is used following an individual use of tongues in public.

As with many aspects of this movement, experience of spiritual reality often precedes adequate understanding, and so there is less unanimity over the other gifts in the list. Some charismatic commentators on I Corinthians 12-14 have tried to sub-divide the gifts into different categories. Some regard the list in I Cor. 12:8-10 as illustrative rather than as exhaustive, but stress that love is the context and the fruit of the gifts and is not itself called a gift (charisma) in the New Testament.[25] While most leaders recognize that, as charismatic groups mature, these gifts receive less explicit attention, they do not thereby become peripheral. These gifts all manifest ways in which God equips His People to do His work and they have played an important part in making Jesus Christ central in the lives of those experiencing them.

k. The Holy Spirit for the body of Christ. More than in classical Pentecostalism and previous Protestant revivals, Charismatic Renewal is developing an awareness that the outpouring of God's Spirit is for the sake of the body of Christ and leads to a renewed sense of what it is for the church, both local and universal, to be Christ's body.

"Is the primary work of the Holy Spirit to initiate, sustain, renew, and shape the lives of individual believers, so that the bestowal of shared life on the community is a happy by-product? Or is the primary work of the Holy Spirit to initiate, sustain, renew, and shape the shared life of the community, so that the bestowal of life on individual believers is instrumental to that end? I am solidly convinced that the latter is the case. Though it flies in the face of the individualism that so strongly marks

our Western culture, I believe that the Spirit's primary work is the bestowal of shared life on the community. I believe this to be the correct understanding of Scripture as a whole." A.C. Winn, "The Holy
Spirit and the Christian Life" Interpretation, January, 1979, p. 50.[26]

(i) Renewal of the parish/congregation. Many of those
baptized in the Spirit are seeking to promote parochial
or congregational renewal in their churches. Serious
attempts are being made to overcome the general dichotomy between an active clergy and a largely passive
laity, and to develop "every-member ministry" utilising
the charisms bestowed on all believers. (Cf. I Cor.
12:7; Eph. 4:7,12; I Peter 4:10). In parish renewal, a
more immediate opportunity is available for allowing
the whole liturgical life and the whole parochial programme of education, service and formation to be influenced by the characteristic graces of Charismatic Renewal. Parish renewal is, however, faced by the limitations of contemporary church structures. Not only
does parish renewal presuppose the personal renewal of
the clergy, but it is vulnerable to changes in parish
personnel, especially in traditions in which local
church members have no say in the appointment of new
ministers or priests.[27] Long-term transformation of
parochial/congregational life would appear to require
some form of effective eldership guaranteeing a continuity
in leadership. Though congregational-type churches for
the reasons stated may experience more difficulty when
first encountering Charismatic Renewal, their tradition
of lay elders or deacons could provide a firm basis for
the Holy Spirit to form a committed brotherhood over-
coming inherited divisions between ministers and people.

It remains a common situation for charismatic prayer
groups to meet on church premises without the regular
participation of any minister or priest. Such groups
often aspire to renew the parish, but have to wait in
hope and patience, recognizing that it is one thing to
have a parish or church prayer group and another to
renew the parish/congregation.

(ii) Covenant communities. In the Cahtolic Church which
has a long tradition of monastic and religious life existing independently of the parishes, Charismatic Renewal not surprisingly has given rise to committed fellow-

ships of charismatic believers. Such contemporary communities, unlike religious orders, are open to married
and single alike (often also to members of other Christian churches). Grounded in commitment to one another,
with leaders needing to be examples in commitment, such
communities are less vulnerable to sudden changes in
leadership. Besides the USA, countries with covenant
communities include France, Ireland, South Africa, Belgium, England, Philippines, Nicaragua and Australia.
In episcopal-type churches with a tradition of religious
life, such communities are in no way marginal just because they are not parochial.

Due to the depth of commitment that characterises covenant communities, they have had a profound impact on Charismatic Renewal well beyond their own membership,[28] and
particularly in their own locality where they exercise
a considerable influence on local parish life, often
greater than the effect of parochial prayer groups.
Covenant communities have also been responsible for the
emergency of a strong lay leadership, particularly among
the Catholics.

1. Holistic view of man. Charismatic Renewal while not
concerned to formulate any theory of human nature, in
fact assumes a holistic view of man. This holistic view
is expressed in: 1. The role of the body in charismatic
worship (the range of bodily postures, the use of arms
and hands in praise, the "bodiliness" of tongues, the
relationship between nusic and physical movement).
2. The role of the body in charismatic ministry (the place
given to the laying-on of hands, the attention given to
the bodily posture and reactions of those prayed for).
3. The place of creativity in Charismatic Renewal (in
bodily activity as in dance and in musical expression
both impromptu and composed). 4. The place of healing
in Charismatic Renewal which expresses a more integral
understanding of the relationship between sin and sickness, health and salvation.

2. Impact on the whole church. There are various indi-
cations that Charismatic Renewal is having an influence
on wider church life, even beyond the ranks of those
baptized in the Spirit and participating regularly in
charismatic groups. There is more recognition of the
need for and role of the Holy Spirit in worship, evangelism, spiritual growth and service. There is a greater

awareness of the place of celebration in worship, and
songs of charismatic origin are now widely used in the
congregational worship of many denominations.

III. The ecumenical dimension of Charismatic Renewal

The outline of the origins and development of Charismatic Renewal (above) indicates the ecumenical character
of this movement. Charismatic Renewal cannot rightly be
ascribed to any one church more than to others. It is
not a movement in one church that subsequently spread
to others. It is one movement touching many churches.
The salient features are common to Charismatic Renewal
in each church. In fact, it can reasonably be claimed
that Charismatic Renewal is affecting more people and
more churches on a wider scale than any previous movement of revival and renewal. While its size also reflects a more heavily populated world with a new rapid-
ity of travel and of communication, these factors alone
do not explain how Charismatic Renewal is found in all
continents and in almost every church tradition.

Significant new ecumenical features

By comparison with previous patterns of ecumenical relationship, Charismatic Renewal presents several significantly new ecumenical features:

a. Mass movement promoting regular fellowship. Charismatic Renewal is the first instance of a mass or popular
movement that spans all the churches in a way that is
not indifferent to God's call to organic unity. Not
only does Charismatic Renewal cross almost all church
boundaries, it also brings people from divided churches
into regular experiences of shared worship and prayer -
something that had not previously been achieved on any
scale, despite the important contribution of the Week
of Prayer for Christian Unity.

b. New way of prayer. When charismatics of different
churches come together, they are able, through their
baptism in the Spirit, to praise and glorify God in a
new way, thereby experiencing a real unity in the Spirit
of Christ. This represents a quite new pattern, different from the previous ecumenical experience of visiting
the services of others who were different and of "patch-
work" services incorporating disparate elements and which

no participant really experienced as his own worship. This is not denigrating our different worship traditions or the value of learning more about worship in other churches. It is saying God is giving something new that itself throws light on what Christians already have in separation.

c. Belonging to worldwide movement. Because it is a mass movement and leads to an experience of shared worship in the Spirit, Charismatic Renewal induces a sense of belonging to a worldwide movement of the Holy Spirit of God. At the heart of this sense, there is a call of God to unity, a call to which the Lord is asking those who hear to be loyal. This belonging is fundamental to the movement's ecumenical potential, and is not to be dismissed as emotional people getting caught up in the excitement of the crowd.

d. Unprecedented ecumenical spectrum. The range of Christians being touched by this renewal is wider than the ecumenical movement itself. Not only is it found in the member churches of the World Council, but it includes those who see the ecumenical movement as the work of Satan and who oppose God's (ecumenical) move of the Spirit to man's attempts to unite divided churches.

e. Fellowship with classical Pentecostals. Another important ecumenical feature is the fellowship enjoyed between charismatics in the historic churches and the classical Pentecostals. Although the spread of Charismatic Renewal to the Roman Catholic Church has severely tested the openness of the Pentecostals to test the fruits of the Lord's renewing work, it is remarkable how ready so many of them have been to revise their judgments in the light of the Lord's unexpected moves.

f. Bridges fundamentalist divide. Charismatic Renewal includes both fundamentalist readers of the Bible and those who are open to the findings of biblical criticism and the empirical sciences. It would be inaccurate to interpret this fact (and the point in section d. above) as signs that the charismatic movement is not really one and is hopelessly divided within itself. Rather this inclusion of opposites is possible because the heart of renewal is not identified in terms either of biblical interpretation or of ecumenism. However, it remains true that if the grace of brotherhood across such divides is not grasped then such unreconciled differences have a potential to divide the movement.

g. Changes in church allegiance. Because Charismatic Renewal is centred on God and on Jesus Christ, and is only as a result a force for unity, rather than being a movement consciously for unity, it has inevitably included many instances of people changing their church allegiance with or after baptism in the Spirit. This fact needs to be faced and is not simply an aberration on the part of the ecumenically ignorant and insensitive, but reflects the fact that the hungry will go where food is to be found. People changing church allegiance should be a challenge to the churches, not just a stick with which to beat Charismatic Renewal. The challenge is: "What is wrong with our churches that people are leaving?"

h. "Messianic Judaism". Another surprise of the Spirit is the rise, since the mid-1960s, of groups of what are often called "Messianic Jews" or "Completed Jews". While this is a sensitive subject it should be included within any survey of Charismatic Renewal as these groups of Jewish people who accept Jesus as Messiah, who wish to remain Jews and form their own Messianic synagogues are all charismatic.[29] At present they are strongest in the USA[30] with some presence in France and Israel.

Following pre-existing ecumenical patterns

There are other ways in which ecumenical experience within Charismatic Renewal is following patterns already found in the ecumenical movement:

a. Spiritual ecumenism. Charismatic experience endorses the teaching of the Second Vatican Council on the primacy of spiritual ecumenism. "This change of heart and holiness of life should be regarded as the soul of the whole ecumenical movement, and merits the name "spiritual ecumenism"." (Decree on Ecumenism, para. 8).

b. Deeper penetration of own tradition. Christians baptized in the Spirit are, for the most part, finding new life in their own churches. This includes both greater relevance in present practice and greater affinity with the past. Truths professed for many years take on new life and rites attended for years have new meaning and mediate Jesus Christ with a new power. Regularly charismatics discover how features highlighted in Charismatic Renewal are already part of their tradition as the centrality of praise in the eucharist.

Catholics discover prayer for healing in the rite of anointing of the sick, and Orthodox are led to new acquaintance with the Fathers of the church.

c. The relationship between official and informal ecumenism.

As with earlier phases of the ecumenical movement, Charismatic Renewal started as an informal and unofficial pattern of meetings and later began to receive official church recognition. As Charismatic Renewal achieves more church recognition, official church initiatives regarding Charismatic Renewal begin .to have an influence on the direction taken by this movement. All this is part of the normal pattern of interaction between official and unofficial Christian activities, whereby unofficial leads to the official, a process which must happen if any spontaneous movement is to have any effect on basic church life.

Ecumenical structures for Charismatic Renewal

There are various forms of ecumenical structure that have been set up to serve Charismatic Renewal. This variety reflects the uneven distribution of the various confessions around the world as well as the overall size of the Christian population, the concerns of particular churches (especially the Catholic), and a variety of objectives.

In some countries, one church is dominant in numbers. This inevitably influences the form taken by ecumenism in that nation (the Agape Fellowship, a charismatic body in Norway, is not surprisingly predominantly Lutheran). In many countries with a plurality of church traditions, there are inter-denominational agencies to promote Charismatic Renewal in all the churches. Catholic charismatics generally support the work of such agencies, but prefer to have their own service committees, mostly on a national basis, and these usually work closely with the ecumenical agencies serving other churches.

In some places, there are national charismatic committees that include the Catholics. This was true in the USA for the planning of the 1977 Kansas City Conference.[32] In Ireland, where the bitter divisions between Protestants and Catholics are a gaping wound in the body of

Christ, charismatic Christians have been concerned to maintain an inter-church framework. This has recently led to the formation of a charismatic committee for the whole island, within which denominational fellowships can continue to exist. In Northern Ireland there is a tendency for charismatics to break away from the main line churches to form "non-denominational" house churches.

Relationships between charismatics and classical Pentecostals vary in intensity and warmth from continent to continent. In the United States and New Zealand, Charismatic Renewal is generally seen as one over-all movement with the classical Pentecostals, and Pentecostal speakers and literature are fairly common at charismatic gatherings. In Scandinavia, the classical Pentecostals are the largest of the non-Lutheran bodies, and they have the appearance more of Free Churches than of sects, and their relations with other churches are more positive and ecumenical in tone. In Latin America, by contrast, where classical Pentecostals have been opposed, sometimes even persecuted, by Catholics, there is considerable suspicion of Catholic Charismatic Renewal among the Pentecostals, and fellowship is slow to develop. In some countries, such as West Germany, Spain, Lebanon, Ireland, where classical Pentecostals are few in number, there is less Catholic and Protestant awareness of their existence. In Holland an ecumenical body for renewal, Charismatisch Werkgemeenschap Nederland, includes the classical Pentecostals.

Ways of interpreting the ecumenical character of Charismatic Renewal

While virtually all charismatics recognize the transdenominational character of Charismatic Renewal there are different ways of interpreting this inter-church dimension:

a. Denominational against ecumenical background. There are many charismatics who, while seeing Charismatic Renewal as a move of God across the churches, understand this first as a call to denominational renewal and subsequently or consequently a grace for the unity of the churches. This understanding which sees Charismatic Renewal as primarily denominational but against an ecumenical background involves in practice a more immediate commitment to the renewal of one's own church than to the reconstituting of the unity of God's divided People. It leads to hesitations about attending forms of ecumenical fellowship as frequently as forms of denominational fellowship and looks to approved blueprints to determine the relationship between church renewal and ecumenical fellowhsip.

b. Non-denominational. There are those who see the charismatic movement as a work of God calling for a newly united People so that the real people of God are all those who from whatever background have responded to this call of God. For those who see this movement in this way the existing churches are seen as at best unimportant and largely irrelevant or at worst as apostate. Those who adopt this non-denominational understanding see the charismatic movement as God's ecumenical movement in contrast to what are seen as merely human efforts of reconciliation and unification in the ecumenical movement, particularly symbolized for them by the World Council of Churches.

c. Ecumenical, respecting denominations. There are many in Charismatic Renewal who do not fit into either category. Such people would see God bringing together the divided churches, thus rejecting non-denominationalism. However, they would see subordination of the ecumenical to the denominational as a denial of the ecumenical grace of the Charismatic Renewal. This position corresponds to the vision of such sympathetic Pentecostals as David du Plessis and Vinson Synan. This third position can be explained in various ways but it would be characterized by a firm commitment that, as historic churches open up to Charismatic Renewal, its ecumenical character must not be relegated to the background. In this view it would be wrong on a priori grounds to obstruct or cut back on the new channels of communications and new forms of fellowship between divided Christians that God has opened up through Charismatic Renewal.

IV. Summary of forms of charismatic fellowship and their relationship to the churches

Different kinds of charismatic fellowship

The forms taken by charismatic fellowship vary according to phases of growth and commitment and their relationship to the structures of the churches. The following list attempts a basic classification:

137

a. Prayer groups. These generally consist of a weekly prayer meeting with no regular functions or ministries outside that framework.

b. Covenanting prayer groups and fellowships.[33] These differ from category a. in having developed some forms of commitment to participation, and in having some activities and services in addition to a weekly prayer meeting. The limited participation in such a group is compatible with regular participation in other forms of Christian fellowship.

c. Charismatic parishes/congregations. These are those local churches that have corporately welcomed and identified themselves with Charismatic Renewal.

d. Covenant Communities. These are bodies of Christians who have made a commitment to God and to one another to live a common life-style, under the Lordship of Jesus Christ, by sharing in life, prayer and service.

The normal pattern of development is from category a. to category b. and from category b. to category c. or category d.[34]

Different ways in which these charismatic fellowships relate to the churches.

The main forms would appear to be:

a. Denominational groupings fully integrated into the life of their church. In this category, the charismatic group has become part of the structure of local church life and so has no authority or leadership independent from that of the local church. This would include charismatic parishes/congregations in category c. above, and some prayer groups (more from category b. than category a.).

b. Denominational groupings, formed informally but subsequently recognized by local church authority. These would be those groups (some in category b., many in category a.) which are wholly or predominantly of one denomination, which have developed their own leadership patterns and which have subsequently been recognized in some way by local church authority. As a result they clearly belong to a church but are not yet part of its basic structure.

c. Ecumenical bodies respecting church membership.
These are open to members of any Christian church and
both encourage and respect church membership and affil-
iation. They may or may not be recognized by local
church authorities as consistent with their vision of
ecumenism and denominational loyalty.

d. Non-denominational bodies. These are open to any
Christian but do not respect or encourage membership of
the historic churches.

e. Small prayer groups. Some prayer groups are so
small, sometimes not much more than eight or ten people,
that the question of how to relate to the churches and
church authorities hardly arises.

Any kind of assessment of the desirability of different
forms of charismatic fellowship and of the ways in which
they can relate to the churches must bear in mind that
they arise within churches organized on a very different
basis. As a recent WCC document states:

> "The various Christian World Communions differ from
> one another. They have different understandings of
> unity. They view differently the relationship be-
> tween the local church and the universal church
> and therefore in different ways give expression to
> the universality of the church."[35]

V. Pluriformity within Charismatic Renewal

It is a conviction of the most widely travelled leaders
in Charismatic Renewal that the salient features outlined
above are found in all parts of the world. Variations
in culture, differences of political system, the relative
degree of poverty or affluence and varying extent of
Christian presence do not appear to change fundamentally
any of the basic characteristics of this movement. They
can and do, however, affect the rate of expansion of
Charismatic Renewal and the patterns of its organization.
They also condition particular forms of expression and
emphasis.

This section on pluriformity within Charismatic Renewal
examines some variations caused by socio-cultural and
political factors, seeks to clarify the right criteria
for distinguishing the variety of the Spirit from the

variety of immaturity and sin, ending with some remarks
on plurality of theological understanding within Charismatic Renewal.

1. Variations related to socio-cultural and political
   factors

a. Medicine and healing. One of the points at which
modern western technology is in sharpest contrast to
traditional ways of life is in the area of medicine and
healing. In Africa the majority of the people still
do not have the dichotomy between body and spirit, with
all its consequences for the understanding of sickness
and sin, as people educated within the traditions of
Europe and North America. It would seem that a greater
knowledge of how readily African people link together
prayer for healing with the prescription of remedies
for sickness could help to challenge more effectively
Western man's inherited and rigid dichotomy between
scientific medicine and religious faith. For what is
challenged is in fact the received understanding of
both religion and medicine.

b. Familiarity with spiritual phenomena. In many parts
of the Third World people are more familiar with spiritual reality than in the highly urbanized and technological world of Europe and North America. This factor
has positive and negative aspects. Positively it means
that Charismatic Renewal does not initially appear as
a strange and "way out" phenomenon but immediately shows
correspondence with aspects of reality that are a part
of local culture. In traditional societies in Africa,
and to a lesser extent in Latin America, in which forms
of social communication are less cerebral and less in-
hibited, Charismatic Renewal with its lively sense of
religious ritual readily promotes a Christianization of
traditional forms of corporate movement as in dance and
rhythmic procession. In such cultures there are more
instances than in the white Western world of prophetic
drama in which a word of the Lord is accompanied by
dramatic action as recorded of some prophets in the
Bible. Negatively, familiarity with spiritual phenomena often means the presence of witchcraft, sorcery and
forms of the occult. In such places Charismatic Renewal
with its emphasis on the power of the Name of Jesus
Christ and His Spirit for deliverance from all forms of
evil has a potential for purifying pagan religious practices and incorporating their positive features in a
Christian framework.

c. Patterns of community life. The thrust of Charismatic Renewal for the upbuilding of the body of Christ
occurs in a variety of settings. In much of the western
world there has been a steady disintegration of traditional patterns of community life. In this situation
the renewing work of the Holy Spirit seriously challenges
the viability of the nuclear family as the basic unity
of society. In parts of the Third World there has been
serious disruption of social life through the migration
of people to the major cities, though there are also
many places where traditional forms of community and
society are still able to function. In Africa several
countries which have recently acquired political independence have given priority to development and communal
living at village level. Some spiritual movements in
Africa have led to the construction of community based
on the concept of the Holy City or the new Jerusalem.
The patterns of organization in community arising within
Charismatic Renewal are likely to reflect the degree of
breakdown of traditional forms of community and society
in that place and to follow some of the same traditional
patterns where there still remains some kind of natural
basis for Christian community.

d. Situations of restriction on church activities. In
many countries of the world (some countries with Marxist-
socialist governments, some Islamic states, some countries with "right-wing" dictatorships) churches and
Christians are restricted in their modes of action.
Restriction may be by legal prohibition, by legal requirements of permission and supervision or by other
forms of constraint. In such situations, new movements
that threaten the status quo are particularly suspect.
Section V. on forms of charismatic fellowship and the
ways they relate to the churches will be less fully
applicable in such countries with restricted Christian
activity.

2. Some criteria for the discernment of pluriformity

Much discussion of pluriformity within the churches takes
insufficient account of the place of immaturity and sin
in producing human variety. With its unleashing of unfamiliar spiritual powers in a far from mature world
and an impoverished church, Charismatic Renewal clearly
poses the constant need for discernment of spirits:
this applies to forms of variety as much as to anything

else. Charismatic Renewal is itself a protest against
that variety in faith and theology that represents a
weakened hold on basic Christian truths concerning the
divinity and resurrection of Jesus Christ, the reality
of sin, the power of the Holy Spirit in repentance and
moral transformation, the enduring validity of the Ten
Commandments and the possibility of miracles.

Other forms of variety that do not come from the Spirit
of God include:

a. The variety that comes from the desire to be different for the sake of being different.

b. The variety that comes from a refusal to learn from
others.

c. The variety that comes from an unpurified attachment
to national traditions and cultural heritage, an attitude generally accompanied by a lack of appreciation
for the traditions and cultures of other people.

There are also forms of variety that simply indicate
different levels of maturity. If this renewal is to
achieve its God-given purpose, it is essential that the
variety between charismatic groups that reflects different levels of maturity is not confused with the variety
that comes from the Holy Spirit which produces comple-
mentary rather than rivalry and opposition.

3. Theological pluriformity within Charismatic Renewal

Not surprisingly there is no one uniform theological
understanding of Charismatic Renewal. There is much
more agreement as to what is at the heart of this movement at the descriptive level as has been attempted in
the section of this paper treating the Salient Features
of Charismatic Renewal.

Differences in theological interpretation of Charismatic
Renewal have varied causes, for example, differences in
denominational, theological and philosophical background.
Such differences affect the understanding of baptism in
the Spirit, for example, theologians from liturgical
traditions generally have an overriding concern to relate
this event to the sacraments of initiation. They also
touch on the relationship between gifts of the Holy

Spirit and natural talents, the relationship between
charism and office and understanding of the miraculous,
as well as the understanding of the church with differences between an emphasis on the universal and emphasis
on the local.

These examples illustrate that the grounds for theological pluriformity within Charismatic Renewal are the
same as those for theological pluriformity in the church-
at-large. However, they also show that Charismatic Renewal throws important new light on the traditional
theological points of difference. This is another aspect of its ecumenical significance.

Footnotes

1. "It is also evident that from the beginning the
   Movement wanted to be interdenominational. It was
   not intended to establish a new denomination. The
   intention was to create a movement which could flow
   through all churches." Nils Bloch-Hoell, The Pentecostal Movement, Oslo, 1964, p.46. See also W.J.
   Hollenweger, The Pentecostals, London and Minneapolis, 1972, pp.505-506.

2. Alexander Boddy and Cecil Polhill always remained
   within the Church of England. "They were determined to keep the movement in the churches - while
   the churches were equally determined to keep it
   out." M. Harper, As at the beginning, London,
   1965, p.45.

3. Time Magazine, August 15, 1960, LXXVIII, p.55.

4. Since 1932 there has been a charismatic fellowship
   in France that remained within the French Reformed
   Church.

5. "In 1953, the Full Gospel Business Men's Fellowship
   was founded by Demos Shakarian in order to encourage people to be open to the Spirit while remaining
   loyal to their churches." E.D. O'Connor, The Pentecostal Movement in the Catholic Church, Notre
   Dame, 1971, p.24, note 16.

6. Charismatic Renewal is reported as arriving in 1975
   in Zaire and Mauritius.

7.   There is reportedly a marked charismatic growth among Baptists in Assam, India.

8.   It is said that many overseas missionaries sent out by the Southern Baptist Convention, the largest Baptist grouping in the USA, have been baptized in the Spirit.

9.   Apart from the difficulty in obtaining reliable statistics for church membership in the Soviet Union, the situation in Russia is more complex due to the union of many Pentecostals with the Baptists to form the "All-union Council of Evangelical Christians - Baptists" from the end of World War II. Cf. W.J. Hollenweger, The Pentecostals, p.272.

10. The late Leslie Davison in England was instrumental in stimulating high-level theological reflection on Charismatic Renewal. Oral Roberts, a leading Pentecostal healer-evangelist, became a Methodist in 1968.

11. The same situation is true though on a lesser scale among the black population of Great Britain and Canada.

12. Many of the African Independent Churches have features in common with Charismatic Renewal. Because they do not define themselves in doctrinal terms, they are not always easy to classify as Pentecostal or non-Pentecostal.

13. Charismatic Renewal in Poland has been helped by encouragement from leaders of the Oasis retreat movement for young people.

14. Many leaders in Charismatic Renewal continue to visit the USA showing particular interest in the covenant communities. Both Word of God, Ann Arbor, Michigan and Mother of God, Potomac, Maryland report having received many visitors from abroad.

15. This opposition is clearly expressed in J.F. Mac-Arthur, The Charismatics: A Doctrinal Perspective, Grand Rapids, 1978.

16. The options available appear to be: 1. to opt firmly
    to stay within their denominational affiliation
    (the percentage of these seems to be increasing with
    time, as the denominational leaders and head offi-
    ces are becoming less disturbed by this renewal);
    2. to stay affiliated, but in name only: so that the
    congregation effectively ceases to play any part in
    its denomination of affiliation and possibly ceases
    to think of itself in denominational terms; 3. to
    withdraw from the denominational fellowship, and to
    become an independent congregation.

17. At least forty-nine countries now have a National
    Service Committee for the Catholic Charismatic
    Renewal.

18. Some participants prefer the phrase "Spiritual
    renewal" but this can cause confusion as it fails
    to distinguish Charismatic Renewal sufficiently
    from other Christian movements of spiritual renewal.

19. The phrase "Baptism of the Spirit" is also used.
    French-speaking charismatics generally prefer the
    expression Effusion de l'Esprit. Orthodox charis-
    matics and some others refer to the "release of the
    Spirit".

20. While few people within Charismatic Renewal like
    the term "charismatic" applied to individual Christ-
    ians, it is used occasionally in this paper to avoid
    more clumsy forms of expression.

21. Cf. I Chron. 6:31-32 and the use of the phrase
    "Priests unto God" applied to all believers in
    Rev. 1:6 and 5:10.

22. Several noted Catholic scripture scholars are active
    participants in Charismatic Renewal.

23. Some forms of divine communication are more common
    in some cultures than others, e.g. the prominence
    of dreams in African religion.

24. Cf. P. Hocken, "The Significance and Potential of
    Pentecostalism" in New Heaven? New Earth?, London,
    1976, pp.24-26.

25. Cf. A. Bittlinger, <u>Gifts and Graces</u>, London and Grand Rapids, 1968, pp.74-75.

26. Winn's article in fact criticises Pentecostalism for being "unavoidably individualistic", p.56. Winn shows a certain unfamiliarity with the ways in which Charismatic Renewal is more open to a corporate understanding of the Spirit than the classical Pentecostal churches.

27. It seems that charismatic ministers are staying longer than average in particular pastoral posts.

28. The Life in the Spirit seminars published by the Word of God, Ann Arbor, USA, has had a wide influence, as has a book by a member of that community, Stephen B. Clark, <u>Building Christian Communities</u>, Notre Dame, 1972.

29. The inclusion of "Messianic Jews" within the ecumenical spectrum corresponds with the position of some leading ecumenical theologians that Christian-Jewish relations are an "intra-covenantal" issue and that the Jewish-Christian divide is a schism within the one people of God.

30. The "Messianic Jews" were among the sponsors of the Inter-Denominational Conference on Charismatic Renewal held at Kansas City in 1977. On Messianic Judaism, cf. M. Evans (ed.), <u>Young Lions of Judah</u>, Plainfield, 1974.

31. Examples are the Fountain Trust in England, Scottish Churches renewal in Scotland, The Temple Trust in Australia, Christian Advance Ministries in New Zealland, The Cornelius Fellowship in Malawi and the Christian Inter-Denominational Fellowship in South Africa.

32. This Planning Committee is still in existence.

33. Unlike the other sub-headings in this section this designation is not in common usage. However, it seems important to recognize the intermediate stages between mere prayer groups and charismatic congregations or covenant communities. Some groups in this category now call themselves prayer communities but this seems to be a confusing label.

34. Besides the four categories of local fellowship here listed, some supporting fellowships have been formed, often on a denominational basis, to bring together charismatics across regions or countries. Some of these fellowships are associated with charismatic service organizations and renewal centres.

35. Relationships between the World Council of Churches and World Confessional Families, WCC Exchange, March 1979, p.2.

E. 1. PRESENTATION BY REV. KILIAN MCDONNELL OF HIS PAPER ON "CHURCH REACTIONS TO THE CHARISMATIC RENEWAL"

I have 15 minutes - I do not intend to give a balanced critique of the statements issuing from the churches and of the Charismatic Renewal. Rather I plan on giving an unbalanced account.

I will give a mostly negative criticism of the churches as seen in their documents and then of the renewal.

A. Criticism of the churches

1. There is an excessive fear of an overblown, exaggerated doctrine of the Holy Spirit. Actually there is more danger that the renewal will develop into a Jesus cult than into a cult of the Spirit. The renewal is saying that a mutuality exists between Christ and the Spirit. Christ sends the Spirit from the Father, but it is only through the Spirit that one can say Jesus is Lord. There is no christological statement without its pneumatological counterpart. Also the renewal is saying that the Holy Spirit is constitutive of the church. In the West we build up the church in christological categories and then when it is an already constructed christological reality we then, in the second moment of her existence, add the Holy Spirit as a vivifier and animator. The second moment is already too late. The

Holy Spirit belongs to the first constitutive moment of
the church's existence. With Christ, in the same simultaneous moment, the Spirit constitutes the church. All
of this has strong implications for ecclesiology, liturgy, mission, private prayer, evangelization, social and
political engagement.

A criticism the churches could have made of the renewal
but failed to do so is that the renewal only gives dim-
inished attention to the Father. In this respect the
renewal represents a bi-theism (Son and the Spirit).
The rythmn of the church's life and that of the Christian
is from the Father to the Father: from the Father through
the Son in the Holy Spirit back through the Son to the
Father.

2. Churches have been slow to recognize that what the
renewal is saying about the charisms is that the whole
spectrum A-Z belongs to the ordinary life, the everyday
life, of the Christian community. Charisms are not
usually to be considered under the heading of extraordinary graces.

3. Churches have not understood that the emphasis on the
personal moment in faith is not necessarily to say that
faith or the relationship to Christ is private. The
opposite of personal is impersonal not private. What
the renewal seeks is a global adhesion to Christ which
involves the whole of the person. In that global adhesion the personal commitment plays an important role,
and in the future will play an even more important role.

If one looks at the global cultural patterns, at least
in the West, one sees that personal decision is of decisive importance. Karl Rohner, who is not a great
admirer of the Charismatic Renewal, has said that the
church of the future will be a voluntary association or
it will not exist at all. If the church of tomorrow is
to be built up from below in personal decision, then
the personal moment in faith is of increasing importance.
That means that baptized pagans will find less place in
our churches.

4. The churches have been slow to realize that the renewal is only interested in the whole gospel. The renewal is not a conventicle of enthusiasts speaking tongues
to each other, or prophesying to each other. Those things
have their place but the renewal is concerned for the

whole gospel. Within that gospel there is a hierarchy of truths and realities, there is the core of the gospel. Very much the renewal wants to recognize that some gospel truths are closer to the core than others, some truths are higher on the hierarchy than others.

Fatherhead of God, Jesus as Lord and Saviour, the Spirit as the Power of God, the Death and Resurrection of Jesus, the forgiveness of sins, the call to holiness, the role of the sacraments of initiation all belong to basic Christian message. The renewal does not want to obscure this basic message, this basic hierarchy of truths, by giving undue emphasis to secondary elements. Speaking in tongues or healing are not more important than the Fatherhead of God and the churches will look a long time to find any responsible person in the renewal who will suggest that they are.

5. The churches were slow to recognize that you cannot play off the gifts of the Spirit on the fruits of the Spirit. Or set up a kind of competition between charity and the gifts. Undoubtedly charity is of a more fundamental order than the gifts, belongs to a more primary level of Christian life. Charity and gifts belong to two different orders of religious reality the way the heart and the hands belong to different orders of physical reality. But it is a perversion of Paul's meaning if one makes it appear that one has to choose between charity and the gifts. One chooses them both. Charity is the absolutely essential context in which the gifts are exercised, without the presence of charity there are no charisms.

6. Only sporadically have the churches grasped the importance of community in the renewal. Here I do not speak of covenant communities, although of course I include them. I consider the development of covenant communities of major importance. Unless the role of community is grasped one has failed to understand what the renewal is saying. It seems to me that the primary consequences of the resurrection and Pentecost is not the exercise of the gifts but community formation. This points to the relational nature of Christianity. To be a Christian is to enter into relationship, into Koinonia with the Father, Son and Holy Spirit. But it is also to enter into deep communion with and commitment to each other. The charismatic community is one expression of this communion which is the church.

7. The churches have been too defensive about the ecumenical nature of renewal. It was de facto ecumenical
from the beginning and did not decide to become ecumenical
at some later date. The churches, it must be admitted,
were often faced with a kind of enthusiasm which said
"If we have Jesus and the Bible do we really need the
church?" If one goes down this road one arrives at a
churchless Christianity.

8. Some of the churches have, when faced with the renewal, had to abandon their sola scriptura stance. Several
of the more evangelical churches who look to the Bible
as the sole authority in matters of faith have turned
to tradition to outlaw the renewal. One church said that
what the renewal stood for differed from the historic
doctrine and practice of the church. This is an appeal
to tradition.

Major criticism of renewal: isolation

Isolation in World
          Church
          Theology

1. Charismatic Renewal relates to the world too exclusively in terms of judgment, too little in terms of incarnation. Renewal needs to look at doctrine of creation.
Theological concern for Lordship of Jesus is too exclusively Lordship over souls, a primatization and trivialization of his Lordship. Charismatic needs to go back
and look at the meaning of the Cosmic Lordship in whom
all things are restored and the relationship of that
Cosmic Lordship to the Father to whom Jesus hands over
the Kingdom. If that Cosmic Lordship is taken seriously
then we will see that such secular tasks as feeding the
hungry, liberating the oppressed are integral and constitutive of evangelization. Are we going to trivialize
evangelization and restrict it to evangelization of souls?
What about the evangelization of cultures, an evangelization which makes life fully human and open to the Cosmic
Christ?

B. Criticism of the Renewal

In this section I will structure my thoughts around
isolation from the world, from the church, from theology.

1. Isolation from the world

The Charismatic Renewal relates to the world too exclusively in terms of judgment, too little in terms of incarnation. To correct this, the renewal has to think through again the doctrine of creation. Also it has to re-examine the doctrine of the Lordship of Jesus which it sees too one-sidedly as a Lordship over souls. This is a privatization and trivialization of that Lordship. The renewal needs to go back and look at the meaning of the Cosmic Christ. If that Cosmic Christ is taken seriously then we will see that such secular tasks as feeding the hungry, liberating the oppressed, the restoration of justice are integral and constitutive of evangelization. Are we going to trivialize evangelization by restricting it to the evangelization of souls? What about the evangelization of cultures, an evangelization which makes life fully human and open to the Cosmic Christ?

In this context I would like to mention the problem of women's ministry. In some countries this is both a Catholic and Orthodox problem, but also to be found among certain Protestant evangelical groups. Without pretending to treat the problem adequately, I would like to mention that if a church excludes women from ordination, this does not necessarily exclude them from the exercise of spiritual authority.

2. Isolation from church

a. Though the renewal is generally understood as renewal in and of the church or, as Herbert Mühlen said "it is the church in movement", in fact the renewal exists on the margin of the church, on her periphery. In part this is because church has pushed renewal to the margin. But there is another side. Many in the renewal have no intention of leaving the church but have as a matter of fact given up on the church. At the pragmatic level many believe that the parishes are dead and hopeless and one should notwaste one's energies on them. So the prayer group or covenant community seems to be directed to the renewal of the whole church and instead becomes an alternate option as a life style within the church; the prayer group or covenant community tends to live alongside of and on the margin of the church. In some cases it can be turned inward, preoccupied with its own life, and becomes a charismatic ghetto. This is not to say that the groups do not help the local church. Many do service local parishes in outreach programmes but this is band-aid help without the vision of the renewal of the whole church. It is not a structural vision.

In this connection I would point to the Anglican work in England, as exemplified by Michael Harper, and the Catholic work in Germany, exemplified by Herbert Mühlen, Sister Lucida Schmieder and other places where the vision still is both theoretically and pragmatically directed to parish renewal and renewal of the whole church.

b. There is isolation from the church when there is a too one-sided emphasis on experience. One of the strengths of renewal is the New Testament. This is extremely important. But an impoverishment of experience takes place when it is seen in too restrictive terms. If one sees experience as excluding rational intellectual content or even propositional truths then, I think, one has an impoverished view of experience. A corollary to this is the view that doctrine divides and experience unites. I am not at all sure that experience deprived of intellectual content unites. It is more likely to divide.

c. There is an isolation from church through styles of prayer. The renewal has enriched the prayer life of the church through free prayer, singing in Spirit, tongues, exercise of charisms within the liturgy. The enthusiasm of charismatic prayers has been good for the church. As a Roman Catholic, I find that the best expressions of the prayer dimensions of the renewal are not the prayer meetings but the Eucharists, and this is in part due to the exercise of the charisms within the liturgy.

But over-enthusiastic, over-demonstrative forms of prayer in certain cultural contexts isolate the renewal from the church and ensure that it will remain on the periphery of her life. The church needs to be open to freer styles of prayer but in certain cultural contexts she will never accept the forms of prayer which are excessively enthusiastic. Loud shouting of the praises of the Lord in public services, especially liturgical ones, will guarantee that the renewal will have little impact on the church and will remain isolated from her life.

d. There is isolation from the church through absoluti-
zing the charismatic way.

Certain elements dear to the Charismatic Renewal are
non-negotiable. The charisms belong to the internal
structures of the church which is a body of mutually
dependent ministries. A church without charisms is a
non-church, if one takes Paul seriously. Seen as a
whole, charisms are non-negotiable. Some concept of
community is non-negotiable.

But how the charisms are exercised, whether healing is
best exercised in huge tent meetings of 10,000, is very
negotiable. Belong to prayer groups or covenant communities as we understand them is negotiable.

The way the renewal contributes to the ecumenical movement in these are all negotiable and the renewal isolates itself from the church if it absolutizes these.

e. There is isolation from the life of the church if
the model of spiritual leadership is too one-sidedly
authoritarian.

3. Isolation of the renewal from theology

a. In general the renewal represents a kind of Barthian
theology of the Word - more or less. contemporary theology is best typified as a theology of the world, such
as process theology, political theology, liberation
theology, anthropological theology or theology of existence. The renewal need not and should not give up
the witness it gives through its theology of the word,
but if the leaders (and I speak of leaders) have no
awareness or appreciation of these broad theological
streams of thought in the church, the renewal is impoverished and is isolated.

b. The East German document mentioned the tension which
arises when theological students in the renewal are ex-
posed to the historical-critical method of exegesis.
Without uncritically accepting everything which is presented as the historical-critical method, the renewal
isolates itself from the dominant exegetical tradition
if it rejects this method as inherently opposed to
the gospel.

c. There is isolation of the renewal through the sea of
charismatic-Pentecostal literature which is enthusiastic
theological fluff - theological fluff I would define
as pink hot air in printed form. Feeding charismatic
groups on this fluff and a fundamentalistic literature
alienates and isolates the renewal from the broad
healthy theological culture and from the life of the
church.

E. 2. CHURCH REACTIONS TO THE CHARISMATIC RENEWAL

an evaluation by Kilian McDonnell

Obviously I am not going to evaluate one hundred documents representing a wide variety of ecclesial types,
and from quite different geographical and cultural settings, Protestant and Catholic. From a methodological
point of view it would be folly to comment on the just-
ness of the documents' evaluation which would presuppose,
on my part, an intrinsic knowledge of the actual state
of the renewal in a great number of countries. To avoid
these methodological pitfalls I will restrict my comments
to the theological areas.

The comments I make here do not represent a full scientific exposition which would require a book. Rather,
my reflections will indicate the direction a critique
should take. These remarks are accompanied by a mini-
mum of scholarly apparatus.

Some of the early documents reflect the churches' stance
in the first years of the renewal's existence when it
was not without a certain theological immaturity. One
hastens to add that immaturity is not an exclusive
property of the renewal but is also reflected in the
churches' reaction to this new movement in their midst.
On the whole one would have to say that scrupulous
fairness generally typified the churches' attitude,
even when handing down negative judgments.

154

What accounts for the negativity of the churches, especially during the early years but perduring beyond
them? One theory is that the churches could not absorb
so much vitality, could not endure so much divine reality and the challenge to their own easy accommodations
to the styles of the day. In a word the churches were
confronted with a prophetic protest in the name of the
gospel and they reacted with predictable anger. Prophets
do not die outside of Jerusalem. My own conviction is
that this theory carries a grain of truth but that the
situation calls for a more discriminating judgment.
Spiritual insensitivity, a fussy propriety, a bloodless
indolence, and an ineffectual institutionalism on the
part of the church does not adequately account for the
tensions which were demonstrably present between church
and renewal. Often enough the churches were presented
with a theology of the renewal in categories which were
foreign to their theological traditions, supported by
an exegesis which would not sustain critical examination. Though it is doubtful whether any significant
number of trustworthy representatives of the renewal
ever conceived of it as a tongues movement, it still
appeared to the churches that the renewal's theological,
spiritual and pastoral visitation was truncated, sectarian
and given to a restrictive piety. What, for instance,
was the ecclesiology of the renewal? What were its
hermeneutical principles? How did it conceive salvation? What was its relation to culture? What were the
modalities of its involvement in social and political
processes? Did all of these have anything to do with
the gospel? In general the churches looked at the renewal and found it wanting in many of these areas, even
when it was not worthy of outright condemnation.

The maturing which went on in the various denominational
expressions of the renewal would not necessarily vindi-
cate this broad judgment in its entirety, but it does
suggest that the churches were not without some basis
for their reluctance to embrace the renewal as in every
respect a true witness to the gospel.

What is being judged?

What is a document judging when it is issued? The posi-
tions assumed by documents are determined by an a priori
decision: the level at which one is going to judge the
renewal. If a church commission interviews theologically

unsophisticated persons it can expect to obtain theologically unsophisticated expressions of what the renewal
stands for, elaborated with an exegesis which might, at
best, be fanciful. Or if one consults the sea of charismatic fluff which appears in pamphlets, books, tapes,
and now in video cassettes, one can easily justify a
very harsh judgment.

Or does one turn to those who are theologically trained
and those who have been through responsible programmes
of formation? If one chooses the course of judging the
renewal by its best theological expression then one still
has to make a further judgment, namely, is this more
theologically responsible segment really reflective of
the broad life of the movement? If the renewal is judged
at its most sophisticated, is the renewal at that level
ever realized at the pastoral level? Or is one merely
judging an idealized abstraction?

Only if one had detailed information on the actual state
of the renewal in different churches and countries, and
of the methodology of the commissions, could one single
out individual documents and say that the renewal had
been judged at the level of its most popular expression.
After working with the documents for an extended period
of time, one gets a feel for them. On the basis of that
theological intuition rather than because of verifiable
scientific evidence, I have come to the conclusion that
the documents tend to judge the renewal at the level of
its most popular expression. Some documents focus on
that unsophisticated level but take cognizance of the
more theological articulation of the renewal.

The renewal does have a lay character to it. This is
not to say it is a lay movement. In the various denominational expressions there are unnumbered ministers,
priests, bishops and even a Roman Catholic cardinal.
But the dominant character is lay, which is to say that
it has a crude, impatient, daring, simple, direct, personal approach to religious reality. To a large extent
that is the character also of New Testament witness.
When a church makes a judgment on the renewal it has to
both keep in mind this unrefined character, correct its
irregularities, suppress its abuses but also respect
its populist character. To some extent its power is
related to the rougher, blunter instruments with which
it recaptures the original experience of gospel meaning

and purpose. To domesticate and refine the renewal would
be to defuse it, like a theologically antiseptic New Testament devoid of all crudities, "mythological" formulations, strained exegesis of Old Testament passages,
and discordant inaccuracies. A corrected version of
the New Testament would be like pureed carrots, food
for toothless babies.

What I call a populist expression of New Testament witness, Krister Stendahl calls "high-voltage religion",
of which glossolalia is one facet. Anyone who looks at
the documents issuing from the churches, especially the
early ones, will readily understand my judgment that too
much ink has been spilled on this question, whether one
is for the renewal or against it. That so much attention has been given to it might be the fault of those in
the renewal who, especially in the early years, focused
on tongues. Clearly, tongues is not the issue in the
renewal, even if one is ready to admit that very likely
there would have been either a classical Pentecostal
movement or a Charismatic Renewal without it. If one
looks at these movements from the point of view of cultural anthropology that much seems clear.

To focus on tongues distorts not only the movements but
the gospel itself. Except for Mark 16:17 (which is canon-
ical but very likely not Markan) tongues nowhere appears
in the gospels. On this basis of Jesus' preaching alone
it would be difficult to attribute to tongues a place
of importance in the Christian life. In Acts there is
a pattern in which tongues is related to conversion
and initiation.

There is a composite of religious realities: faith,
repentance, conversion, baptism, reception of the Spirit,
a charismatic manifestation (tongues or prophecy). For
this reason one of the early Episcopal documents granted
that there was biblical precedent for tongues as part
of the initiatory process of entering the Christian community. But a pattern is a pattern, not a universal law.
If the churches have to re-evaluate this early pattern
positively and reassess its meaning for today, the Charismatic Renewal has to refrain from making laws for the
Spirit. The legalism of the church is dwarfed by the
restrictiveness and shackles which a Pentecostal-charismatic legalism imposes. The theological horizon of
this mentality is minuscule.

Apart from the relation of tongues to Christian initiation mentioned above, there is no Scriptural basis for
calling glossolalia "the gateway" to the full Christian
life. But there is evidence that many persons enter
into a deeper Christian life with tongues. This is to
argue not from scripture but from experience, from
personal spiritual history. No compelling reason exists
for denying the ample testimony to this development, as
one of the documents admitted.

Even if one were to grant this, does one want to tie
church renewal to tongues or to the other individual
"charismatic" gifts? The LCUSA (Lutheran Church in
America) document rejects the argument I proposed in
Malines Document I. There I suggested that the church
has to be open to the full spectrum of the gifts, sig-
nified by A-Z. In that span the gifts in the A-P section are those domestic unspectacular ministries so
important for the life of the church: nursing, teaching,
visiting those in prison, feeding the hungry, clothing
the naked, giving shelter to the homeless, etc. In the
P-Z section of the spectrum one finds such gifts as
prophecy, gifts of healing, tongues, interpretation.
The church should be open to the full spectrum of the
gifts as real possibilities for her ordinary daily life.
Here openness should extend also to those in the P-Z
section. All of these gifts belong to the nature of
the church. If one would allow a scholastic formulation
one would say that most of the gifts (one would exclude
at least apostleship and prophecy) are properties of
the church. They do not form part of her essence but
flow necessarily from that essence.

To this LCUSA answered: "When charismatics seek the renewal of the church through charismata (I Corinthians 12)
they ask for gifts which Lutherans traditionally have not
regarded as essential to the nature of the church."
Specifically LCUSA asked whether the spiritual gifts in
the A-P section are not more significant for the renewal of the church than the gifts in the P-Z section.
Furthermore, there seems to be no direct correlation
between the exercise of gifts, especially in the P-Z
section, and spiritual maturation in commitment and
life. For this reason Paul pled with the Corinthians
that they "seek a more excellent way", that of love.

One would want to grant that the presence of a specific gift, say tongues, found in one of Paul's lists of gifts is not necessary to the nature of the church, so that were this gift not present at any given moment, the church is un-churched, any more than that a man or woman born without arms is deprived of his or her humanity. It is theologically quite possible that a certain gift which was prominent in the life of the New Testament church may not be present at every moment of the church's history. Gifts are ministries and are timed to needs.

If, however, need is the point of departure then it has to be demonstrated that the church today does not need a specific gift. This is not the same as saying that one can properly isolate tongues and point to its re-introduction into the life of the church as the key to church renewal. My own understanding of classical Pente-costalism and the various denominational Charismatic Renewals prompts me to suggest that one would find very little support among them for such a narrow view. This is to misunderstand what these groups are saying. But can one really a priori rule out a whole section of the spectrum (P-Z) and declare that it is not significant for church renewal? That is a quite different proposi-tion and is a radical impoverishment. That Lutheran groups react against enthusiasm in their midst is under-standable in view of the bitter denunciations Luther hurled at the "Schwärmer". The excising of all of the prophetic gifts as lacking in significance for the re-newal of the church is a truly staggering assertion. If the church is founded on the apostles and prophets, can one so lightly dismiss the prophetic dimension as unimportant and non-essential? Is not a church deprived of her prophetic dimension (which is not always what those in the renewal think it is), a non-church? C.K. Barrett contends that a complete denial of all prophecy would mean the rejection of the life of the church it-self, a "blasphemy against the Spirit." Prophecy as a theological imperative, as part of the church's per-manent endowment, continued to be espoused despite the very serious threat which Montanist enthusiasm posed in the middle of the second century.

Krister Stendahl suggests that if proper Christians had not suppressed such phenomena as glossolalia, then the gifts of the Spirit - including tongues - would belong to "the common register of Christian experience." For

Paul it was simply a part of the common Christian experience, a wonderful and treasured gift, part of the
complete spectrum of Christian experience. "Opening up
the full spectrum of religious experience and expression
is badly needed in those churches that have suppressed
the charismatic dimension."

Also to be deplored is the playing off the gifts against
love or charity, with special appeal to Paul's exhortation that the Corinthians "seek a more excellent way"
(I Cor. 12:31). This is, as the Dutch Reformed Church
remarks, to speak of the gifts of the Spirit, including
those incorrectly (because exclusively) called the
"charismatic gifts", as something which should not be
seriously entertained by the church. Quite correctly
love or charity is given a priority. Love is of a more
primary order than are the gifts, and is constitutive of
the Christian life in a more radical way than is true
of any of the gifts, even the greatest. What Paul is
doing in I Cor. 13 is not opposing gifts to love.
Rather he is saying that love is the matrix, the context, the all-embracing framework within which the
gifts are to be exercised and without which the greatest
gifts are vanity and emptiness. To imply that one should
choose love instead of the gifts is a basic distortion
of Paul's thought. A Christian chooses them both. The
gifts are chosen not because they are supernatural happenings (which on occasion they might be), but because
they are signs of a renewed creation, and are ministries
and service. Participation in the Spirit is the first
characteristic of a Christian, or as St. Thomas would
put it, "the new law consists chiefly in the grace of
the Holy Spirit". "The most evident, and also the most
outward, effect of the Holy Spirit was the extraordinary
phenomenon of early Christianity, the appearance of charisms, and the revival of Old Testament prophecy." At
this stage the question should not be a theological one -
whether tongues is an authentic Christian expression -
but a pastoral question, namely, how can it be of benefit to the individual and to the church?

Objective norms and subjective experience

There is in the common consciousness of Christianity
the supposition that 1) God has a plan or economy of
salvation, 2) that the lines of such a plan have been
revealed, 3) that one may discover in revelation what

160

that plan is. When Christians of various ecclesial traditions refer to baptism in the Holy Spirit, they are referring to one element in that economy. But what the structure of that event or process is, how it is described theologically, where it is located in the unfolding of the Christian life, all of these are perceived differently in the various ecclesial traditions. However disparate these theologies of baptism in the Holy Spirit, they have in common experience related to conscious awareness of the presence of God, or new sources of power for service and of a call to praise. Commonly the event or process is experienced and described reciprocally in pneumatological and christological terms. The experience is both that of Christ and the Spirit, or more correctly, of Christ in the Spirit. In some traditions, the manifestation of tongues or of other gifts is looked upon as a necessary concomitant, in other traditions that necessity is not recognized, while still other traditions see the manifestation of some gifts to be a usual thought neither necessary nor normative occurrence.

When it comes to locating the baptism in the Holy Spirit as an event or process some either understand it as either simultaneous or identical with conversion, or assurance (witness of the Spirit), Entire Sanctification (Scriptural Holiness). Some traditions have a two-level doctrine of sanctification (conversion, baptism in the Holy Spirit), some a three-level (conversion, sanctification or second blessing, baptism in the Holy Spirit). Some propose a theology in which water baptism may not be efficacious until it is appropriated at a later time, which appropriation would be the baptism in the Holy Spirit. Still others locate it within Christian initiation (baptism, confirmation, Eucharist) as a reality given present and efficacious, but frequently breaking through to conscious awareness only at a later date. I personally hold to the latter view which for a variety of reasons I consider more consonant with the biblical witness of God's plan of salvation, and the total historic experience of the church.

Two reflections need to be made at this point. First, supposing that one has correctly assessed the data of revelation and that one's theology of baptism in the Holy Spirit is a true reflection of revealed truth, there can still be, because of the finite and subjective

nature of human consciousness and experience, a certain
disparity or chasm between that theology or doctrine
of baptism in the Holy Spirit and experience. The theology or doctrine is given from without. Inner faith
experience is proper to each individual and is given
from within. The two, one given from without, the
other experienced from within, may not be faithfully
reflecting the other, may not meet at every point, may
leave a glaring gap between them. "Human subjectivity,
raised by grace, only achieves a sufficiently objective
level when operating in the framework of the whole of
human history and the total process of salvation and
revelation. For this reason the individual is always
obliged, and justified, in referring himself to this
historical objectivity." (Karl Rahner, "The Foundation
of Belief Today," Theological Investigation, Seabury
Press, 1979, vol. 16, 10).

Because human subjectivity is finite, wounded and weak
what we experience may not always correspond to what
has been revealed about God, humankind and the way of
salvation. A gap might exist between them.

The plan of salvation is the original historical object
which norms experience. But having discovered that plan
and built a theology upon it, one has not necessarily
described other people's experience, or even one's own.
Objective norm and subjective experience do not always
fully coincide as ideally they should. No matter how
highly we esteem the objective norm (ultimately the plan
of salvation), as indeed we rightly should, no matter
how highly we esteem it as normative, as we ought, a
given experience which does not fall within its patterns
is not necessarily invalidated. It may still be authentic Christian experience, even transforming. If authentic experience and authentic Christian life were to be
found only there where there was an absolute congruence
and fidelity between objective revealed plan and subjective appropriation, we would all be in dire trouble.

Having said this one hastens to add that such a gap or
chasm is undesirable and can be dangerous. It is not
to be dismissed as unimportant. Not for nothing has
God revealed His will and purpose in history. Without
entering into details at this time one would have to
say that there is a limit to this discrepancy, beyond
which experience is indeed voided of Christian meaning

in the strictest sense. If experience repudiates all those elements which make up the core of the gospel, evidently the experience which is normed by the message and person of Christ is not Christian experience, whatever else it might be.

Second, once we have discovered the economy of salvation we, in that moment, create an obligation for ourselves. If, in that plan we discover that the sacrament of baptism has an important role, to some large degree a necessary role (though not absolutely necessary role) then, according to all the qualifications and restrictions stated or implied in the economy of salvation, we have to pattern our quest for God with this plan in mind. We are not free to set baptism aside if our reading of the plan of salvation is correct. Briefly, we are bound by God's economy.

To state that we are bound is not to state that God is bound. Our task would be clearer and cleaner and there would be less fuzziness in our perception of the Christian life if God would follow the pattern he has laid upon us. That is not to be. The Spirit blows when he wills, where he wills, and how he wills, including before, beyond and alongside his own plan of salvation, his own ordinances. In a word, God is not bound by his own economy.

Besides the vagaries of our own subjectivity accounting for the failure of experience to always be adequate to the norming economy, there is a second reason: the Spirit blows where he listeth or God is sovereign and free and is not bound by his own decrees.

This should make us wary of easy judgments on the experience of others, especially those who read revelation differently than we do. The theology of the baptism in the Holy Spirit should be in accord with the plan of salvation and the whole history of God's education of His people. But if a given tradition only appropriates elements of that plan, or misplaces the primary emphasis, this does not by itself vitiate their experience, though it may make it less full. It does not dispense with either a theological or spiritual discernment of experience but makes those tasks both more necessary and demanding.

High-voltage religion and mysticism for the masses

What I call a populist expression of new Testament witness Krister Stendahl calls "high-voltage religion",
and Karl Rahner, "mysticism for the masses". This is
certainly characteristic of many expressions of the renewal which are enthusiastic, pre-occupied with religious experience, focused on the charisma, eager for
wonders, miracles and demonstrations of power, conceiv-
ing of the Christian life as a progress from peak experience to peak experience, from mountain top to
mountain top. The documents issuing from the churches
take full cognizance of this stream, sometimes mistakenly
making high-voltage Christianity co-terminus with
Charismatic Renewal. The cautions, structures, caveats,
rebukes and condemnations are sometimes fully justified.
In a broad popular movement where everyone is a partici-
pator, everyone has a scripture passage to read, a
message to give, a song to sing, a prophecy to proclaim,
it would be strange were careful balance, impeccable
propriety, theological precision, and exegetical exacti-
tude always in evidence. This high-voltage enthusiasm
is, as Stendahl rightly observes, "an important part
of the total Christian community in any time or place.
Of course, such enthusiasm has its risks - everything
has."

Some, if not total, defence of this high-voltage Christianity is in place. Having made it one would have to
add that many denominational expressions of the Charismatic Renewal (as well as of classical Pentecostalism)
would be more repressive in their cautions, structures,
caveats, rebukes and condemnations of high-voltage
Christianity than the churches have been. For this
kind of criticism one does not have to go outside the
renewal. No mature expression of the renewal conceives
of the Chrsitian life dominantly in experiential terms.
Growth in Christ through the Spirit is not character-
istically a series of transforming experiences. That
would be to return to the sensualism of religious senti-
mentalism which is essentially a pagan conception.
Nor is the panting after wonders, miracles, and demonstrations of power any less an impoverishment of the gospel
than their total pragmatic exclusion from Christian
witness. "The development of stereotypes of language,
understandings, and experiences; a preoccupation with the
gifts of the Spirit; the failure to appreciate the broad

and richly diverse ways in which the Spirit works in corporate and personal experience, a concentration on inner religious feelings and experience to the neglect of interest in practical aspects of Christian disciple-ship and social concerns," are, as the Mennonites point out, weaknesses in some expressions of the renewal. Essentially this is a trivialization of the gospel, a caricature which reduces the proclamation of the cru-cified and risen Saviour to religious confetti, which transforms the Pentecost event into tinsel. Psychic revivalism is a dead end. All of this is acknowledged in the self-criticism which goes on in the denominational renewals, though often enough it is not found in printed materials.

A prophetic movement should be allowed to be prophetic and confront the church with the gospel. The remedy to the excesses of that prophetic protest is not the denial of prophecy. The antidote to misuse is not non-use but right use. And the only viable place for the prophet to be is within the church. Outside of the church he or she is a non-prophet. With the church the prophet can only have a lover's quarrel, which never compromises the basic and radical commitment to the body of Christ.

If the church needs prophets, they need the church. The documents recognize the tendency of the renewal to substitute experience for doctrine and to isolate them-selves so that they are no longer rooted in a tradition which can sustain them. When such movements remain "in the full, rich, balanced life of the historic church," they are brought into that comprehensive history which represents the total experience of church, which is the best safeguard against "self-righteousness, divisiveness, one-sidedness and exaggeration." In a document from West Germany it was clearly seen that religious individualism is best avoided by commitment to the community.

Experience - resurrection and the cross

There is in the Charismatic Renewal an ambivalence with regard to religious experience. The various expressions of the renewal would want to claim what academic theol-ogy has long recognized, namely, the central role of the experience of the Spirit! Schweitzer - "Long before the Spirit was a theme of doctrine, he was a fact in the

experience of the community."   Barrett - "The church
would have had no doctrine of the Spirit if it had not
in the first place received an experience of the Spirit."
Lampe - "Experience of the Spirit is not merely one
aspect of the new life of the believing community; it
is the principle of it. It is that in which the new
life consists." Ebeling - "First there is the fact that
in early Christianity, as it understands itself, the
experience of the Holy Spirit was the very signature of
its existence... If a Christian were asked what was
really new in Christianity, he would not have spoken of
a new teaching, but he would have pointed to the new
reality of the Holy Spirit." Gunkel - "The root of
Paul's teaching on the Spirit lies in the experience
of the apostle... Paul believes in the divine Spirit
because he has experienced it/him."

While wishing to appropriate this doctrine into the
structure of the self by a knowledge of connaturality
which experience gives, the Charismatic Renewal knows
that a kind of infantilism and doll-like Christian life
can develop if there is a preoccupation with experience.
Classical Pentecostalism also recognized the danger.
What is acknowledged in some expressions of the renewal,
but by no means in all, is that the appeal of the renewal to New Testament witness is greatly compromised if
experience is conceived individualistic.   What St. Paul
is speaking about is shared experience, experience in
the Christian community. Only rarely does he speak of
the Spirit in individual terms.

In this context the question of healing, redemptive suffering and the cross needs to be raised. The renewal
has done a service in raising the question of healing
and the churches should re-evaluate it in the light of
the biblical testimony. It is true that the past twenty
years have seen a resurgence of interest in the resurrection, a needed correction in some traditions. Both
classical Pentecostalism and Charismatic Renewals have
been dominated by resurrection theology (classical Pentecostals had this in their history before academic
theology turned with such interest to the theme). It
is the risen Christ who sends the Spirit at Pentecost.
The documents which have issued from the churches are
rightly concerned lest the centrality of the cross be
lost in a resurrection - Pentecost enthusiasm. The experience is not that of charisms but of the exalted

risen Lord who is present in power through the Spirit. To experience the exalted Christ is to experience not merely new life, but new life through death, out of death. "As soon as the exalted Christ is separated from the crucified Jesus, the charismatic experience loses its distinctive Christian yardstick." For Paul this was more than a theoretical position. Paul's understanding of the cross derives from his personal experience of suffering, something which he thought was not peculiarly apostolic but belonged to the nature of the Christian life. Paul turns the illogical cross against the early Corinthian enthusiasts (I Cor. 18) who being filled with the Holy Spirit forgot that their lives are still governed by the concrete cross of Christ. Mark wrote his gospel for the Roman church which was being persecuted, probably by Nero. This church had experienced the presence of the Spirit in praise, deliverance, healings and miracles. But the ultimate test of discipleship was knowing how to die. The experience of the Spirit was not an escape from physical death, and the disciple could not expect deliverance from that pain any more than the master did. "Jesus is unlike other charismatics in that the Spirit is given to lead him to martyrdom, not miracles." The Spirit-given experience should focus on the heart of the gospel, namely, the cross of Christ and justification by faith alone (Romans 3:21-28)." Experience in the Spirit includes the experience of the cross. A charismatic triumphalism is untrue to the full biblical witness.

In restoring a much needed balance one would not want to fall into a mechanistic quantification of faith and experience as there was a tendency to do in reaction to Protestant pietism. This reaction proceeded from the assumption that what is given to experience is taken away from faith, so that any positive acknowledgement of the experiential is an attack on faith.

Experience however does not dominate those in the renewal so that every time one prays in tongues or exercises the gift of prophecy one is grasped by the presence and power of God. Perhaps the swiftness with which Isaiah experienced the presence is paradigmatic. He seems to have lived most of his adult life on the strength of that initial experience as a prophet. Those who are exercising a charism live, like all God's people, in the valleys of routine and everydayness.

Instant contemplation; instant maturity

Repeatedly the documents refer to the love of prayer
which seems to be present in the renewal. Several Catholic theologians have suggested that some are given high
graces of prayer: "I am convinced that some grace of
infused contemplation has been given to quite a number
of these people. This is what explains the joy with
which they pray, and the fact that with little or no
previous training in mental prayer, many of them suddenly find themselves able to pray for extended periods
of time simply by placing themselves in the presence
of God and abiding there quietly, wordlessly, lovingly..."
Perhaps with greater precision, Josephine M. Ford suggests the transitory nature of these contemplative
gifts received at baptism in the Holy Spirit. "In Catholic terminology perhaps we should say that this experience is a touch - but not the state - of infused contemplation... What had taken place after years of
discipline and practice has sometimes appeared to be
well nigh instantaneous and people who were living an
active life now appear to be able to combine an almost
contemplative life and the active life... The recipients have not arrived at the contemplative state, and
indeed many may not be called to do so. But God has
given them a taste of contemplative prayer, and this
taste should urge them to pursue a more generous, orderly, yet flexible spiritual life..."

All of this does not suggest that the recipients have
been endowed, in one moment of glory, with the spiritual
maturity which is the fruit of years of responding to
graces in struggle, pain, mortification, discipline,
and aridity. On the contrary they remain spiritual
infants. Before them still lie trials and disappoint-
ments which spiritual growth entails. Still some of
them have been touched by a transitory contemplative
gift not corresponding to the spiritual immaturity
which defines their present state and condition. Theologians of spiritual theology acknowledge that this
kind of pre-emptive transitory action of God does occur.
The experience does not exempt one from a life of discipline but is a call to it.

168

Inwardness and the political prophet

The Scottish Presbyterian Church reminds its constituents
that the charism of prophecy can be turned in upon itself
for the edification of the church, or it can be turned
out towards the world. This latter dimension, typified
by the Old Testament prophets, seems to be missing in
the prophetic understanding of the renewal.

Both the early nebi'im and the classical prophets were
involved in the political life of the nation and gave
politically loaded prophecies. The prophets who threatened Ahab for his treaty with Ban-hadad (I K. 20:35-42)
and who had predicted victory for Ahab at Ramoth-gilead
(I K. 22:6-12) were passionately attached to the political and military fortunes of their nation, and by their
predictions of victory they encouraged war. They were
concerned with injustice, oppression and liberation.
Care must be taken not to cast the Old Testament prophets
in a false mold. For all their passion for reform and
social virtues, they were not social reformers. They
had neither a political nor economic theory. Though
they constantly denounced the abuse of wealth and power,
they never attempted to transform the economic and political structures of Israel and Judah. In this sense they
lacked radicality. To suggest that they should have
these ideals is to read back into earlier history possibilities of which they could not have been aware.
But they did have a kind of religious sociology which
sprung from religious faith, namely, the human and social
values integral to Yahwism. One of the distinguishing
characteristics of prophecy in Israel was its astonishing ability to live on in ever new forms.

The documents point to what they perceive as a quite
restricted view of prophecy, lacking even the modest
social and political goals of the Old Testament prophets.
To this could be added the inability to find new forms
of prophetic protest which go beyond the limits of self-
interest and have social relevance. "The Charismatic
Renewal must take an active part in the church's involvement with the world, cooperating with Christ in the liberation and integral development of people."

Not sufficient research has been done in order to refute
the charge that the various denominational renewals are
really deficient in this matter. Some research has been

done among the Catholic laity in the renewal in the
United States by the sociologist Joseph H. Fichter.
His research showed that the laity in the renewal ex-
hibited "fairly favourable social attitudes, especially
on the major issues of the day." Though the renewal
tends to withdraw members from the struggle for social
justice and to blunt their zeal for social reform, the
low record of active involvement in social action movements is "probably typical of American Catholic laity."
In other words low involvement is not a specifically
charismatic characteristic but is typical of lay Catholic life.

Other Catholic leaders in the renewal in the United
States have independently expressed their concern.
Bishop Joseph McKinney continues to "look for signs
that it (the renewal) inflames its members to engage
in genuine social action." Francis McNutt is convinced
that "there is justice to the claim that pentecostal
people as a group have not distinguished themselves in
the overall quest for social justice," an issue "not
touched in charismatic circles." The Malines Document
III by Cardinal Suenens and Helder Camara is another
indication from within the renewal that this dimension
is lacking.

One could easily list a number of social action programs
in which various communities are engaged (e.g. the activities of the El Paso prayer group with those dump dwellers
in Juarez, Mexico through which food, clothing and housing are supplied). Or one could point to the beginnings
of the renewal in Mexico which grew out of the Social
Action department of the diocese among persons who were
already living in the barrios. At the Latin American
meetings of charismatic leaders (called ECCLA) it is
evident that a new social approach is developing.
Before their involvement in the renewal these leaders
consciously or unconsciously communicated to the poor
their hatred of the rich oppressors. After their involvement they taught the poor to love and pray for
those who denied them their basic rights even while
protesting and fighting against them. This is not a
small change.

But there is a prior difficulty: the relation of the
Christ to culture. In my own judgment this is the most
serious and enduring problem facing the various denominational renewals.

170

To borrow categories from H. Richard Niebuhr, while modifying them to fit my more modest purpose in this section of the essay one could speak of two typologies which describe the relation of Christ to culture. In this context culture could be a synonym for civilization that artificial secondary environment which we super- impose on nature: language, habits, ideas, customs, social organization, inherited artifacts, technical processes. In this framework culture is a human achieve- ment with a pattern and hierarchy of values understood to be good for humanity because they, through the tem- poral and material realization of a plurality of values, make life more human and open.

The first answer of the relationship of Christ (and his gospel) to culture is found in the typology of Christ in judgment over culture. This typology does not postulate a radical opposition between Christ and culture but in- jects a systematic suspicion that much of it flows from concupiscence. Culture in this sense is not sin but the occasion of sin: temptation, invitation, allurement. Culture is not world in the sense of "all that is opposed to God" and therefore sin. Rather culture is radically tainted by hatred, sensuality, superficiality, material- ism and egoism. Though not itself idolatrous, it lures to idolatry. A Christian is forced to live in a state of belligerent armistice with culture even when taking full advantage of many of the possibilities it offers: modern housing, up to date appliances, elegant clothes, travel, books, automobiles, the decorative arts, enter- tainment and television. The ambivalence of his atti- tude is determined by the judgment under which Christ brings culture. Habitual suspicion that one is unfaith- ful to that judgment over culture is the mark on the forehead of the true believer.

The second typology is Christ in culture. This is essen- tially an incarnational view, or more precisely, a view based on the cosmic Christ which is rooted especially in the Prologue to John's gospel and in a series of Pauline texts. The post-biblical development saw the cosmic Christ's relation to creation and redemption as the basis of all culture, and therefore it has a cer- tain ordination to his Lordship and to the Father to whom Christ will hand over the kingdom (I Cor. 15:24). Culture cannot be essentially opposed to that kingdom, nor can the "world" as culture be seen in simplistic

terms as the kingdom of godlessness even when the
presence of sin is recognized. The world as creation is
a kind of revelation (being made through the Word).
The world as culture continues to exist only through
that continuing sustaining power of the creator. If
one were looking for a statement of this cosmic, incarnational view of culture it can be found in the "Pastoral
Constitution on the Church in the Modern World," especially chapter II, articles 53-62.

Though the Charismatic Renewal is extremely diverse in
its many geographical and denominational expressions -
and therefore it is hazardous to make broad judgments -
the general stance seems to be typified as Christ in
judgment over culture. Some defence should be given
for this position. No mature Christianity is possible
if persons and institutions are not able to stand back
from the patterns of their environment and make judgments.
The procedures of this factory, to give an example, are
exploitive and degrading and contrary to the gospel.
The foreign policy of this nation is destructive of the
economic independence of that nation and is contrary
to the gospel. The lack of respect for human life in
this family development programme is opposed to the broad
patterns of the biblical witness. The ability to separate oneself out from the dominant values and procedures,
to recognize sin where it exists, to make jusgments in
the light of the gospel all belong to Christian maturity.
The infant cannot do this. The gospel is often not
heard by Christians because it is filtered to them
through the prism of attitudes and values contrary to
the message of Jesus. In order to form one's own prior-
ities by the gospel one has to examine the filter. This
is a task of some sensitivity.

No viable Christianity is possible unless this kind of
questioning of the total cultural environment, accepted
by almost all and held up as a national ideal, is part
of the on-going process. The ability to bring culture
under judgment is not always carried out with sensitivity
by charismatic groups. Indeed many of the attempts are
uninformed, crude and based on an unacceptable exaggerated super-naturalism. Aside from these miscarriages
one would have to say that the witness to culture under
judgment as a gospel value is one of the strengths of
the renewal. It belongs integrally to the mature Christian life.

Nonetheless an approach to the world which is dominated
by Christ in judgment over culture easily slips into
sectarianism. This is not to suggest that the various
expressions of the renewal are in danger of cutting themselves off from their denominational allegiances and
forming new churches. Here sectarianism is used to indicate a state of mind which is suspicious of literature
and the arts, indifferent to evils which are not immediately personal in nature, whose ethical preoccupations
are privatistic, whose passions are for a one-sided in-
wardness, whose instincts predispose for isolation
rather than involvement.

One could argue that a renewal movement might have a
special vocation within the total Christian community
to witness to the necessity of cultural discernment and
judgment. Further one could add that prophets are capable of discriminating but do not have refined, subtle,
balanced, wholistic judgments and neither does
a prophetic movement. These two rejoinders have some
validity. The renewal must be aware that Christ in judgment over culture is witnessing only to a partial truth
and that Christ in culture also belongs to the total
Christian experience. Without a conviction that Christ
is incarnate in culture the patterns of life are removed
from the absolute Lordship of Jesus, they are cut off
from the transforming power of the gospel, and the church
is isolated and confined to rubrics and denatured cere-
monial.

Prophetic protest also belongs integrally to the gospel.
It emphasizes the discontinuities: the new thing that
God is doing today; the faithful remnant that has not
bowed the knee to Baal; the bulwark the Lord wishes to
erect against infidelity and hardness of heart. No one
can rightly object to this prophetic language as long
as it is spoken in the context of the church in whose
total experience and history are supplied the continu-
ities: the new thing God has wrought for centuries; the
great cloud of witnesses who by faith and blood still
speak with assurance of their hope in a righteous God;
the mutuality of charisms, a church which is wholly ministerial, in which each member is called to service and
witness. The discontinuities of prophetic protest are
sectarian only when they are isolated from the contin-
uities of the church's total life. Within the broad
historic experience of the church's history that protest
has a necessary function without which the church is
impoverished.

1. What the Spirit is Doing in Our Day

The evenings of the Bossey Consultation were reserved for reports from different countries and cultures. There was also a film on the Kansas City Conference (see section e., below).

A. REPORTS FROM AFRICA

(1) The Charismatic Movement in African Israel Church
     Nineveh (Kenya)

Henry Asige AJEGA, General Secretary, African Israel
Church Nineveh

The African Israel Church Nineveh was formed on the
principles of the charismatic movement. When the word
of God was brought across the ocean from Europe the
idea of the working of the Holy Spirit remained a mystery to the church. In 1921 the Spirit of the Lord was
revealed at Kaimosi in Western Kenya. This was a new
and different experience for the church in Kenya. Many
people wondered what had happened to the church. Some
said that this new experience was madness and others
said that it was a group of poor confused people. The
saved group, as they were referred to, found themselves
rejected by the church. They could not mix freely with
other members of the congregation. This led to the
formation of the so-called Kenya Independent Churches
and of being referred to here as the Charismatic Renewal.

In 1932 the founder of A.I.C.N., the late M.P.D. Kwuti,
who also used to despise the work of the Holy Spirit,
received this power. This is the description of his
conversion, in his own words, as quoted by F.B. Welbourn:

"On 12th February I received the Spirit. As I was singing
in my house something lifted me and threw me to the ground.
Everything became dark and I was temporarily blind. That
night I began to speak in tongues like the apostles of
the New Testament. The whole house was filled with light.

174

For the next seventeen days I was blind and I heard a voice as of thunder. For twelve days I could eat nothing, and during this period God commanded me not to shave my beard and to take the name of Paul. Then I stayed in my house, praying, night and day.

"When I recovered I had lost interest in my professional job (teaching). I wanted to preach the word of God. So I began going from village to village, singing and converting people. The power of God filled me. I began praying for the sick and they were healed. I also prayed for barren women and they got children. People began to come to my house, so that I might pray for them. Usually they would come on Thursday evening and I prayed with them till morning when we held a big meeting. The Kellers (white missionaries) supported me, but many members of the Pentecostal church disliked me because I urged them to confess their sins. They wouldn't let me preach in their churches."

From the above example we can see that once you have received the power of the Holy spirit you are completely changed and you become a new person. Your old friends wonder and keep away from you and think you are confused and emotional, if not mad. It becomes extremely difficult to understand your new change.

You cannot receive the power of the Holy Spirit if you do not repent sincerely. You have first to accept that Jesus Christ is the Son of God and that he came to the world to redeem us from our sins. You have to see and feel spiritually the suffering of Jesus Christ on the cross. You have to sympathize with his precious blood which was shed on the cross for our sins.

Charismatic Renewal is not something which can be imposed. It is the will and work of God. It is a complete change. Paul said in his letters "you have to put off the old man in order to become a Christian". We believe and have experienced that the Holy Spirit works in you as long as you keep to the commands of the Lord. People see a new change in you as the gifts of the Spirit are manifested.

The members of this church have come to believe and discover that once you have the Holy Spirit the Lord can use you in many ways. The church has expanded all over the country due to these supernatural powers of the Holy Spirit. Some of the experiences of the work of the Holy Spirit include:

- healing the sick;

- through prayer water came out of a dry stone at Givavei hill during a drought and people were able to drink;

- rain has fallen as a result of prayer and meditation;

- members of the church can move and dance spiritually without getting tired;

- many prophecies have come true;

- many tribes have been united, regardless of tribe, race, language, colour or strength;

- the love of God has been manifested amongst the members;

- people have learned how to share what they have and help the needy or those in trouble;

- we have got a deeper thinking and understanding about God and his purpose to mankind through Jesus Christ;

- we have managed to minister to other churches which did not know or understand the work of the Holy Spirit and we have been able to spread this Charismatic Renewal to them.

I am very pleased that the Lord has made it possible for us to talk and discuss the Charismatic Renewal and united us in the Spirit at such an international meeting. I am very happy because the prophecy has come true and all mankind is now seeking to be renewed in the Spirit. It makes me very proud here to see the work of the Lord being accomplished. It is my prayer and hope that we all get renewed and united in the Spirit at this consultation, so as to manifest the work of the Holy Spirit and the reality of God. We are nevertheless bound to witness to others our new discovery of the Holy Spirit after this consultation. Thank you very much for listening to me. May God bless you and give you a deeper understanding of the charismatic movement than just as a theological or sociological issue.

(2) Renewal in Local Congregations in South Africa

Bill Barnett, Archbishop of Cape Town

I want to make it clear that I am speaking about renewal
in the local congregation and not simply renewal of church
structures, or liturgical renewal or renewal in general
terms whatever that may mean. I arrived late at the
Bossey Consultation because I was engaged in an evangelistic and pastoral counselling ministry in a congregation
in Johannesburg. I was assisted by my Chaplain and two
lay people in this ministry. Church people themselves
often need to be evangelized if they are to benefit from
the ministry of the Word and Sacraments and be motivated
to care for those who live around them. The purpose of
the Week of Renewal was to enable people of the parish
to appropriate their baptismal life. Each night $\pm$20-30
people came up to the altar rail to do this and were
ministered to by lay people trained in the parish for
this ministry and the four persons from Cape Town already mentioned. During the week both morning and
afternoons were used to counsel people on spiritual and
moral problems and in helping to heal spoiled marriage
and family relationships. It was a special joy to minister to a young man who had come into the church by
chance and who was brought to faith by the Holy Spirit
from a position of paganism. A joyful demonstration
that Jesus, the Lord, is among us.

Renewal in the Holy Spirit has taken place as a result
of retreats for clergy and they have more fully appropriated the grace of their baptism and ordination and
been empowered to communicate the gospel among their
people more effectively in the power of the Holy Spirit.
In addition, lay people have organized retreats at
weekends and invited other lay folk and retreat conduc-
tors to minister to them. As a result of these and of
"weeks of renewal" and of the many prayer groups and
parish house churches which have grown up, a number of
parishes have experienced a new spiritual vitality.
This is reflected in the acceptance of what St. Paul
called in Romans 15 "the obedience of faith". This is
seen in more joyful and more fully shared worship,
greatly improved giving of money for God's work, and in
some instances a greater social responsibility. During
times of trouble such as the 1976 riots in Cape Town and

the destruction of squatters' shacks a few years later, the parishes concerned with renewal were those which took some action, e.g. a parish with well developed "house churches" acted during the 1976 riots to take care of some families where bread-winners were in prison and to help in various ways where some had been shot. When shacks were bulldozed certain parishes put up tents in church grounds and tried to find other accommodation for destitute families.

A feature of congregational renewal of this kind has been a very significant increase in lay ministry in terms of evangelism in the work situation and elsewhere, in the ability to give simple pastoral counselling and in an ability to teach the meaning of faith. This has led to an increase in ordinands. Another feature seems to be a natural development of parishes involving team minis- tries. This means that gifts of the Spirit among both priests and lay people can be more widely shared for the building up of the people of God in a number of parishes. We have now reached the point where "weeks of renewal" requested in the diocese can be prepared for by both the laity and clergy in neighbouring parishes and some of the initial follow up can be done by them also. In this way congregations begin to be used by God to bring one another to new life in the Holy Spirit.

The Holy Spirit has also produced a new ecumenical cli- mate. The Spirit destroys barriers between people whether these are created by different church traditions or by ideologies and fears and resentments. He sets Whites free from fear and Blacks from the imprisonment of re- sentments so that they have a new freedom to communicate. Thus also ecumenical meetings and some very large con- ferences have resulted in new and deep relationships with Afrikaners who have become involved in the movement of the Holy Spirit. This is a new experience for many of us in the land and could have some significant con- sequences.

A new outward "look" is evident also. The Holy Spirit makes evangelists of us. Thus one of our parishes responded to a request from the Bishop of Mauritius to send priests to minister to his people. It sent a racially united team and financed the whole project itself.

In the same way, Bishop Lawrence Zulu and I responded
to an invitation to minister in Australia for a month
last year. The purpose of that visit was the renewal
of the local congregation in the power of the Holy Spirit.

B. CHARISMATIC RENEWAL IN PAPUA-NEW GUINEA

Ben Lenturut

I come from an area where God has been visiting his
people in a wonderful way. When God began to bless
his dead church in Papua New Guinea (PNG) we were dead
indeed: Evangelical, Biblical, but very dead. Of course
there were sparks of life here and there - there always
are, and praise God for that, for it means that he is
alive. If all the sparks went out we should be dealing
with a dead God.

When God moved in my area he began among the young people.
In 1976 I was speaking to a group of people in a mass
crusade of about 2,000 people. We finished without
calling upon them to make any outward sign of repentence,
but about one thousand seven hundred boys and girls
came forward and gave their lives to the Lord. The
church members, uncommitted, were sitting down. They
should have got up and gone forward, but they were too
proud of their religious life.

God moves in mysterious ways. Just as he moved in PNG
and other parts of the world. Brothers and Sisters, let
us not make the mistake which God's people so often make,
of scratching our heads and waiting for God to move,
when he is moving already. God has already moved; all
we have to do is to move with him. That is why I am
here, to know what this Consultation is going to say
about the Charismatic Renewal for the churches, for I
believe that Charismatic Renewal is for unity to fulfil
the prayer of our Lord: "That they may be one, just as
you and I are one".

Praise the Lord.

Some thoughts on the Charismatic Renewal.

In scripture it says that in the last days people will hold to forms of religion but will deny the power (II Timothy 3:5).

This is how I saw the church in PNG (on New Ireland) before the Charismatic Renewal and I was included. We faithfully went to church every Sunday, sang hymns, said prayer, heard preaching and gave our offerings. However, this "form of religion" did nothing to change lives and to meet people's needs.

Add to this picture the cultural things of PNG society which in fact displayed power - e.g. magic for healing, to attract women, to influence people for pay back, in gardens and so on. People within the church were involved in these things to a large extent. In fact I don't think they were ever challenged, even in early missionary days. Why were they involved? Because they could see the power that was there and the church was doing nothing to either challenge or replace these things. In most circles the types of things being done were not even recognized as evil and yet people were held in fear by the men and women able to use this magic.

Another problem was the rapid change in society which a lifeless church was not able to talk about. Such things as marriage, divorce, drinking, social nights and so on.

As I look back I remember the large emphasis placed on teaching about God the Father and Jesus his Son being our Saviour. That was fine, but the third person of the Trinity, i.e. Holy Spirit, was largely ignored and unknown. Yet Jesus had said quite clearly that the power we need will come from the Holy Spirit when he (Jesus) returned to the Father.

So we had a picture of a lifeless church faced with problems of magic and social ills but not drawing on the power available to do anything about these problems.

Then we saw God moving in ways we had not seen before. People actually started to get to know the Holy Spirit without the outside or Europeans, and as the Spirit

180

touched lives then new life was injected into the church.
We have seen ministries of Healing and true Deliverance,
we have seen a greater respect for God's word with
people studying it and then putting it into practice,
e.g. Tithing, Marriage, Dancing and so on. A clearer
line seems to have been drawn between what is acceptable
Christian practice and what is not, e.g. social nights,
magic, drinking. Many pecple who were church goers
through habit have dropped away and are going after their
real desires. Many people within the church are spending
more time in prayer, Bible study, fasting and fellowship.
The work of evangelism has grown and spread like fire
while the follow up is seen as a major need.

To draw conclusions about the meaning of this Charismatic
Renewal for the churches is difficult. Firstly I would
say that we neglect the Holy Spirit at our own peril -
this leads to stagnation, lifelessness, compromise.
Secondly, we need to ask why we are not like the churches
as described in Acts? My conclusion is that we do not
have the full measure of the power available to us
through the Holy Spirit. Why? Because we put limits
on Him through our own expectations and traditions.

Thirdly, it forces us to get away from reliance on man's
ways and get down to finding God's ways. An example
here - we often felt we should do something like hold a
camp or send someone somewhere for ministry, but then
would not go ahead because we could not see where fi-
nance would come from. But we must ascertain what God
wants us to do, then go ahead in faith believing that
all needs will be met.

Fourth, the church must be prepared to change in ways
that God wants it to change. Church traditions are all
very well, but if they hinder the work of God then we
must be prepared to change them, e.g. too rigid order
of service is but a small example.

Responses of the churches in PNG to the Charismatic Renewal:

1. Some people feel threatened because God is moving in
    new ways and this is not how it was done before.
    Here we need to clearly discern if something is of
    God or not.

2. We have to be prepared to admit that, at times, we have been wrong. After admitting that, we have to be prepared to change our ways.

3. Ordained ministers must see that God does not give his gifts to only them. The church is a body and must act together. Some ministers appear to resent a dynamic outpouring of God's gift on a layman and therefore they tend to deny his ministry. Thankfully this has not been evident on New Ireland where I come from, but it is evident elsewhere.

4. Church traditions have already been mentioned.

5. Scripture admonishes us to test all things to see if they are of God. Unfortunately the test has often been: is it noisy or emotional, does it meet needs, are people being helped, is God working?

6. God has shown that if the leaders of the church will not feed their flock then He (God) will provide Shepherds who will feed the sheep. We have not been honest enough to say that our past methods/services/ministries are no longer feeding the flock. If God required different pasture of grasses then who are we to argue that yesterday's pastures grasses were fine.

In summary, I would say that the Charismatic Renewal has had the following effects:

1. A more balanced approach to the Trinity where the Holy Spirit is not a neglected member.

2. A greater reverence for scripture.

3. An awakening of gifts within the church.

4. Ministries, long neglected being revived.

5. New life in a church that did not often reflect God's glory.

6. Real worship and praise insead of formal lifeless orders of service.

Praise God. May He bless you richly.

182

C. REPORTS FROM EUROPE

(1) The Charismatic Renewal in Ireland

Gordon Gray

I speak primarily as an observer of the Charismatic Renewal who has participated in and been blessed through
several small charismatic events.

I speak also as one who is deeply concerned at the political conflict in Ireland, including the division between
Northern Ireland and the Republic of Ireland; at the
religious division between the Protestant and Roman
Catholic churches and communities and at tension within
some denominations, for instance between "evangelical"
and "ecumenical" wings.

In this situation during the 1970s there has been a quite
sudden eruption of a new "movement", stressing praise,
prayer and personal religious experience, leaping over
historic barriers, and promoting reconciliation from a
particular perspective.

Local prayer groups of Protestants and Roman Catholics,
renewal events in congregations, major rallies and evangelistic mission events, and a Renewal Centre are among
the signs and expressions of this renewal.

An emphasis on correct belief, order and "conversion"
according to a specific formula is giving way to love,
and joy, variety and freedom in the Spirit. This renewal has produced many stories of Christian lives enhanced
and corrupt lives changed.

Nevertheless I personally - for I can speak only personally - have some lingering questions which I hope this
Consultation can in part answer:

- Does the Charismatic Renewal raise the threat of a
  new separatism, for instance in "communities"?

- Will there be in fact not one renewal, but two (Roman
  Catholic and Protestant)?

- Will the churches recognise what is really happening,
  or freeze it out by officially ignoring it?

- Why is there such suspicion towards the Charismatic Renewal from "evangelical" sources?

- To what extent is the Charismatic Renewal capable of and concerned to engage the endemic political problem?

I am assured by some of its key leaders that they see the Charismatic Renewal as the main, even the only hope of reconciliation in Ireland. But I remain unconvinced that the hard questions of social and political reform are being taken seriously enough.

Nevertheless, I affirm that the Holy Spirit is freeing people to dream new dreams, to think and speak new thoughts, and to envision a quite new future. So I close by offering you the hope which is expressed in a scripture passage often quoted by leaders of the Charismatic Renewal:

"...if my people who are called by my name humble themselves, and pray and seek my face, and turn from their wicked ways, then I will hear from heaven, and will forgive their sin and heal their land" (II Chronicles 7:14).

(Translated from the German - WCC Language Service)

(2) Charismatic Awakening Among Young People in the GDR

Ursula Mösender

The beginnings

"There was a kind of spiritual explosion at the New Year of 1972/1973..." That is how Pastor Christoph Richter of the GDR described the beginnings of the Charismatic Renewal among young people in the GDR. About a hundred young people had been invited to that memorable turn of the year celebration, reports Richter, who is pastor at Grosshartmannsdorf, destined to become one of the three important centres of Charismatic Renewal in the GDR, the other two being Buckow and Schniewindhaus.

"When we have our days of preparation, we work a lot with the Bible, indeed, almost exclusively...and always with an emphasis on pastoral care. We invited guests from Holland to conduct our Bible studies. The theme was...Holy Spirit. ...In a brief closing session for goodwishes at the end of the retreat, it was not possible to speak individually with everyone as we would have wished. The only thing we could do was to invite the young people into the church... But we wanted at least to pray with them a little longer! And it was in the course of these prayers that these young people had some very definite spiritual experiences which they wrote about or reported when they returned..."

Youth meeting

It was clear to Richter that it was essential to offer these young people pastoral care and a biblical ground-ing. He therefore invited them to monthly youth meet-ings at Grosshartmannsdorf. The response to this in-vitation exceeded all expectations. In the autumn the numbers had already risen to 1,200 and then to 1,700. Grosshartmannsdorf became in consequence a meeting point for young people. Similar gatherings were subsequently held in Dresden and Leipzig. But contacts between the different centres are close; in the piety of all of them there is a strong emotional element. To this day it has remained very Jesus-centred. Its gospel is simple and uncomplicated. The young people are not afraid to express their feelings, to talk of their experiences of Jesus. They sing enthusiastically, clapping hands in accompaniment. The movement has produced a great many new hymns.

Personal relationship with Jesus often finds expression in charismatic experiences. The main influence notice-able here is that of the Dutch Pentecostalists who have "popularized" the charisms among the young people by their quite unselfconscious way of speaking of and moving into these spiritual experiences. It is the gift of speaking in tongues which most frequently ap-pears, often conveyed through a prayer of blessing with the imposition of hands. A prophetic speech throwing light on the concrete situation of the individual is often also decisive in the spiritual growth of the young people. But this practice of the charisms, espec-ially the speaking in tongues, is by no means unchallenged. While some are very strongly in favour of it, others view it with considerable reserve.

Almost without exception, the young people set great store by fellowship. They come to the large gatherings and to the preparation meetings with great eagerness. They create local prayer groups which often exist as ginger groups alongside the youth fellowships in congregations. The work of the Saxony "Service of Christ" and other centres has had a formative influence here. In congregations influenced by the people's mission movement, the young people have quite often been welcomed too, in existing prayer circles. In some cases young people lead their own groups. But the quest for a spiritual authority to give allegiance to is much mcre characteristic... What has been especially noteworthy is the evangelistic fervour of the young pecple. This stemmed from their enthusiasm for Jesus and an uncomplicated piety. They took to the streets to invite people to evangelistic rallies or to engage in unrehearsed person-to-person evangelism by personal testimony. In this way they even reached young people with very little church connection. In some places the young people started "tea bars".

For a time, especially in the early years, the movement developed spontaneously and uncontrollably. Even the pastoral centres could hardly take it all in. ... Thanks however to the leaders of the movement and their desire for integration, it increasingly found its place within the church's youth work. The pastoral centres felt themselves especially responsible and followed up the different groups which had sprung up, brought key people from them together and continued to provide pastoral care by means of retreats and preparation days.

Since 1974 a new centre has emerged in the charismatic youth mcvement, this time at Niesky-See. With the cooperation of ecumenical guests (for example, a Dutch evangelist), Pastor Hartmann, who has very close contacts with Schniewind House, has organized the annual Church Weeks' at Niesky-See in the second week of August, which have attracted as many as 300 full-time participants and, at the evening meetings, up to 600 young people. The work which radiates from this centre has a marked charismatic emphasis.

It was through the youth evangelisation work that the movement also reached out to countless young people with no church connection. According to one full-time youth worker, there is at present a great demand for youth evangelization. Special mention needs to be made here of the evangelistic work of Dr. Theo Lehmann who has been engaged in full-time work of this kind for about two years. Dr. Lehmann had already accomplished remarkable work among young people in Karl Marx City in the sixties, with monthly services attracting as many as 2,000 young people. In recent years he has carried out evangelistic campaigns in many places in the area, supported by intensive preparatory and follow up work on the part of the local pastors and church workers... Grosshartmannsdorf no longer has the magnetism it once had. The spontaneous movement has subsided but the charismatic movement continues in local groups and parishes. A great many young people have been inspired by the youth revival to enter church educational institutions. For example, the tiny congregation of Forchheim in the Erzgebirge has in recent years produced as many as fifteen persons who have taken this step. The result has been the creation of prayer circles in these educational institutions: for example, in the Deacons Institute at Neinstadt, the Paul Gerhard Foundation in Wittenberg, the Pfeiffer Institute in Magdeburg, Bodelschwingh House at Wolmirstedt, the Deaconess Institute in Lehnin, Oberlin House at Babelsberg. At the beginning of the seventies a prayer circle was also started in the Leipzig Theological Seminary. This led to the formation of a student fellowship centred on a manse in the suburbs of Leipzig...

In the different educational centres, the prayer circles are not only a challenge to other students to examine seriously their own piety, religious commitment and life-style. They also put a question mark against habits and traditions and usually influence fruitfully the spiritual life of the community and the work of the educational institutions.

On the other hand, problems have frequently arisen, especially when there have been tensions with the distinctive local type of piety or when members of a prayer circle have made very specific criticisms of the behaviour or religious commitment of their fellow students. Difficulties have sometimes arisen in theological education centres, because of reservations often found in the circles in respect of academic theological studies.

World and politics

The world is hastening to its end - that is the view of
the charismatic groups. The world is essentially hostile to God and beyond redemption. With this as their
basic position, many show little understanding of or
sympathy for the concern to improve the world... Certainly life with Christ and witness to Christ includes
social solidarity. One group, for example, established
for itself the principle: "We set ourselves fairly and
squarely in the world". Socialism and Marxism are
usually regarded as normal secular phenomena... Government, too, is plainly a penultimate phenomenon... It
is constantly stressed, for example, that one should
adopt a loyal attitude to the local agencies of government, that there should be mutual respect and, where
possible, cooperation, and that there is no call to
overdramatize the problems. But in personal pastoral
care, the questions discussed are those which confront
the individual; for to the young people in the charismatic movement this movement is usually seen as a clear
alternative to superficial and even committed cooperation in social organizations.

The situation of the so-called "charismatic movement"
in the GDR is distinctive to the extent that it has
collected the initiatives for renewal together, whereas
in other countries it has tended to find expression in
a variety of religious forms (e.g. youth religions).

Since in the GDR context a religious revival movement
can only find a home within the church, there is also
a greater pluralism than elsewhere. The church connection which is consciously sought and emphasized is to
this extent also a necessity arising out of the situation.

(Translated from the German - WCC Language Service)

D. CHARISMATIC RENEWAL AND THE SLUMS OF LATIN AMERICA

In the city of Rio de Janeiro with its million inhabitants
stands a huge statue of Christ, thirty-eight meters high,
on one of the domeshaped hills. The figure of Christ
faces towards the city and his arms are outstretched as
if it was his desire to embrace all the people within
it - poor and rich, old and young, sick and well, black
and white... But in the immediate neighbourhood of this
statue of Christ are slum districts in which the poorest
of the poor are living, and there are a great many of
these in South America. The outstretched arms of Jesus,
it seemed to me therefore, were embracing first and
foremost these poorest of the poor, as if it was to them
in particular that he was saying: "Come unto me all you
who labour and are heavy laden and I will give you rest".

But Christ does not act directly in the contemporary
world but only in the measure that Christians allow him
to work through them. I want, therefore, to select
three examples to show how Christ is working today
through his Christians in the slum districts of South
America.

First example: Here is a huge slum district on the edge
of a city with a million inhabitants. There are endless
stretches of miserable ramshackle do-it-yourself shacks
in which men, women and hordes of children are living
huddled together in unimaginable conditions of confine-
ment. I spoke to one woman with thirteen children, all
of them with different fathers and among them some very
endearing children, a little black lad, for example, and
a lad with golden curls. For the latter she receives
about three US dollars a month from the father, but for
the others she gets nothing, since the fathers are un-
traceable. Some of the children had been found foster-
parents; the rest live with her in the tiny hut. How
do the people here earn a living? The men look for
casual work though they seldom find it. Women, too, are
casual workers but often earn money from prostitution
or begging. Many of them scour the garbage bins for
edible scraps or else steal.

For some years now, a group of Christians from the city
has regularly visited this slum area. They sing at the

square in the midst of the huts or in a primitive make-
shift hall - and they proclaim the Good News. And what
good does that do? Well, for one thing, quite a number
of the people have become Christians, including that
woman with thirteen children. Some of these Christians
are themselves spreading the Good News around in these
slums. Statistically the results are not spectacular
but certainly this slum congregation is growing and the
social situation of these people is being improved.

In a neighbouring district I was able to see how such
Christians are doing after a few years. Gradually they
had built stone walls around their huts and a roof over
them. When this work was completed they cleared the old
ramshackle huts out through the door. They also built
for themselves a church hall of their own where they now
hold regular services. Here they stand or sit on the
floor, simply but colourfully dressed and barefoot. I
have attended such a service and it moved me greatly.
The singing was clear and vigorous, sometimes in harmony.
They prayed still more strongly and all of them joined
in interpreting the Bible. Anyone with something to
say contributed. It was astonishing to see how much
these simple people knew. They had also established a
small common library. They read and studied biblical
commentaries with special enthusiasm.

Second example: What happens when people in these slum
areas fall sick? Many of them were ill because the sani-
tary arrangements are so unbelievably bad. Slums are
usually sited on hill slopes so that the rain can wash
away the filth or beside streams which are quickly turned
into cesspools. I think of one particular slum area.
Nearby stands an ugly concrete building with innumerable
windows. This is the poor people's hospital where the
sick from the slums are treated free. But in what
fashion? There are no doctors but only medical students
using the most primitive of methods. I was told by the
superior of a sisterhood who accompanied me on my visit
of inspection how during a recent flood the whole of the
slum area had become a hopeless sea of mud. One man -
barefooted - had trodden on a rusty nail. His foot became hugely swollen. Yet the hospital was too full for
him to be admitted. The foot got worse and worse. When
the superior discovered this, she acted energetically
and managed finally to see that the man received treatment. But what kind of treatment? The man's hands and

feet were held secure while a medical student "operated"
with a razor blade - unsterilized! The man yelled ter-
ribly but could thank his lucky stars that he was being
treated at all.

What happens to those who cannot be admitted to hospital?
The answer is that they lie in their huts without medical
attention and often enough die. A few years ago a Christian nurse named Alexandra was so affected by this dis-
tressing situation that with the help of a few slum-
dwellers she built a hut and took these sick people into
it to await admission to hospital. The numbers who came
were so great that it was necessary to keep on extending
the hut. It has room now for fifty patients. Food is
delivered there from the barracks; it consists of the
leftovers from the soldiers' meals. But Sister Alexandra
says it is good and nourishing food. She spends the
whole day long with the patients but at nighttime the
patients have a self-help programme. For some time now,
a Christian doctor has been coming once a week to give
these sick people free treatment. I have visited these
people, some of whom look dreadful and yet they were so
grateful for this temporary lodging. Some of them have
become Christians during this waiting period.

Third example: The conditions in the cancer "hospital"
for the poorest people who are unable to pay for treatment are appalling. The wooden shanties were completely
dilapidated outside and within. Medical attention was
practically non-existent. Medicaments were supplied by
the city authorities but only seldom reached the sick.
Long before that, these supplies ended up elsewhere. The
sick people lay there groaning (and shrieking) until they
died.

The wife of a medical professor learned of these appalling
conditions, saw the distress for herself and realized
she had to do something about it. She called together
her friends and acquaintances and together they discussed
what should be done. It was finally decided to request
the city authorities to entrust the care of the hospital
to them. Thanks to the good connections this woman's
acquaintances had with the authorities, the latter acceded
to the request. That was in 1972. Seven years later I
visited this hospital. It had changed out of all recognition. Indefatigably, the "charismatics" had renovated
the premises completely inside and out and completely

restored some of the buildings. They had also managed
to persuade the leading cancer specialists at the university that care of this hospital would be a rewarding
task for a doctor who was just on the point of retiring.
Five other doctors accompanied the specialist as his
assistants. Operating rooms were installed and furnished
with the basic equipment. A nursing school was established and a qualified nursing sister recruited to provide the training.

I went through the sick wards, simple rooms which contained
from ten to a dozen beds each, but were clean and inviting.
Each morning an ecumenical team of "charismatics" came to
visit the sick. The conversations and prayers helped
many to find eternal salvation. And again and again it
happens that sick people recover their health. "Because
of the good medical care", opines the head doctor. "Because of prayer", adds another doctor. Meanwhile the
group of friends has expanded. In 70 places in the close
and the distant neighbourhood of the hospital, the "charismatics" have established institutions for the study
of preventive measures.

Who finances all this? The "charismatics", in some cases
well-to-do, have decided to adopt a simple lifestyle themselves, and contribute substantial sums. But they are
planning to build a new hospital, a larger one, in which
30% of the patients will be paying for treatment and paying enough to make it possible for the remaining 70% to
be treated free (since the treatment provided by these
top specialists is eagerly sought after!).

Those are my three examples, then. The question arises,
of course: "Isn't this merely dropping a pebble into the
ocean? Surely it is essential to alter social conditions
so that there are no longer any such slum areas?" Of
course, this must be done! Charismatics like Ernesto
Cardenal and Dom Helder Camara are passionate advocates
of such change. In the meanwhile, however, something
must also be done - even if it is only like dropping a
pebble into the ocean!

E.   REPORT FROM NORTH AMERICA: THE KANSAS CITY CONFERENCE

John Blattner

The keynote was unity.

Kevin Ranaghan, chairman of the planning committee for
the 1977 Conference on Charismatic Renewal in the Christian Churches, told the opening session of the conference,
"The Spirit is saying that in the renewal, through the
renewal, there will be Christian unity. I believe that
God has spoken this conference as a living prophecy, in
the church and to the world, that he has decided to have
one people, one bride."

Dr. Ranaghan said the conference represented "the largest
grass-roots ecumenical movement that Christianity has
known in the last 800 years," and his assessment seemed
to be borne out by the size and composition of the conference. More than 50,000 men, women, and children,
from more than a dozen denominations, found their way
to Kansas City July 20-24 to join in proclaiming the conference theme, "Jesus Is Lord."

The opening session, Wednesday night, had unity as its
theme, and the array of speakers amply illustrated both
the unity and the diversity of the participants. The
session was co-emceed by two classical Pentecostals:
Bishop Samuel Green, of the predominantly black Church
of God in Christ, and Dr. Howard Courtney, vice-president
of the International Church of the Foursquare Gospel.

Dr. Vinson Synan, general secretary of the Pentecostal-
Holiness Church, presented a brief history of the Pentecostal and charismatic movements. He then introduced
speakers from several segments of the present-day movement, who described how the Spirit has worked in their
churches and traditions. Among them was Pauline Parham,
daughter-in-law of Rev. Charles Fox Parham, whose Bible
school in Topeka, Kansas - not far from the site of the
conference - was the setting for what was, in the mind
of many historians, the birth of the Pentecostal movement at the turn of the century.

Rev. Dennis Bennett, a pioneer in the Charismatic Renewal
among Protestants, described three streams of Christianity
which, he said, were flowing together in the Charismatic
Renewal. The Catholic stream, he said, brought an aware-

ness of the history and tradition of the Christian people. The evangelical stream focused on the word of God, both in Scripture and in teaching. The Pentecostal stream centered on the immediate experience of God. All those in the Charismatic Renewal, Rev. Bennett said, share a common spiritual heritage, are solidly grounded in Scripture and doctrine, and have experienced God through being baptized in the Holy Spirit.

The main address was given by Kevin Ranaghan. He discussed the unusual spectacle of Christians from widely divergent - and sometimes antagonistic - backgrounds coming together to proclaim their oneness: "We don't exactly have a reputation for mutual love, unity, and brotherhood. We're known to think differently, to act differently, to pray differently, to sing differently, to dress differently. Frankly, we have tended over the years to hold some very firm opinions about and against one another... Yet on all of us, in spite of our divisions and separation, God has poured out his Holy Spirit."

He ended by relating a prophecy received by the planning committee, in which the Lord promised to protect the conference from a spirit of divisiveness. Dr. Ranaghan then led the crowd in prayer, rebuking any work of Satan to divide the participants, and encouraging the crowd to approach the coming four days in a spirit of love and service.

The planning committee responsible for the conference was itself a sign of unity. Composed of representatives of each of the denominations participating in the conference, the committee began meeting more than three years ago to conceive and realize the conference. The degree of brotherhood and cooperation on the committee was, to many of its members, one of the most noteworthy aspects of the conference.

The structure of the conference also reflected its ecumenical nature. Actually, it was several conferences within a conference: ten different denominational and non-denominational groups held sessions and workshops during the day on Thursday, Friday, and Saturday. General sessions for all participants were held in the evenings at Kansas City's Arrowhead Stadium, home of the Kansas Chiefs of the National Football League.

The morning sessions in downtown Kansas City gave each
group a chance to express its unique identity. The afternoon workshops, sponsored by the various denominations
but open to all conferees, enabled participants to experience the life and worship of Christians from other backgrounds - an opportunity which many participants seized
eagerly.

The conference was a time, however, not only for increasing unity among the different groups, but also for increasing unity within them. Leaders of the Charismatic
Renewal in the American Baptist and Southern Baptist
Churches met to investigate the possibility of forming
a unified service committee for Charismatic Renewal among
Baptists. Methodists began to explore the possibility
of establishing an official church office to oversee
the Charismatic Renewal in that church. Three new service committees were established during the conference:
Pentecostal, United Church of Christ, and Holiness/
Wesleyan/Nazarene. Leaders of several messianic Jewish
groups acknowledged their need to enter into deeper,
more loving relationships at a dramatic foot-washing
ceremony held spontaneously during an afternoon workshop.

One of the most impressive aspects of the conference was
that so large and diverse an undertaking was able to
proceed in so remarkably organized and peaceful a manner.
It was the largest conference ever held in the Charismatic Renewal, and was also the largest conference that
Kansas City - known as a convention town - had ever hosted.

- Dozens of arenas, auditoriums, convention halls, and
conference rooms were used to house the bewildering array
of morning sessions and afternoon workshops.

- More than 13,000 hotel rooms within 50 miles of the
city were occupied by conference participants.

- Local restaurants were swamped, even though thousands
took advantage of catered box lunches and dinners served
at conference sites. Ice cream parlors did a particularly
brisk business in the hot humid weather.

- Traffic snarled each afternoon at 4 p.m. as streets
were lined for blocks with yellow-and-black school buses,
standing two and three deep, waiting to transport participants to evening sessions at Arrowhead Stadium.

Yet, through the heat and the crowds, the conference proceeded smoothly. Meals got served, buses appeared on time, complex public address and tape recording equipment functioned, and talks scheduled months in advance were given at the right time and in the right place.

Participants had been urged to present a good witness to their host city, and it soon became clear that they had succeeded. The politeness and tidiness of the crowds earned them a front-page accolade from the Kansas City Times, which cited numerous examples of their exemplary behavior and concluded, "Downtown has been filled for the last three days with genuinely nice people."

The evening general sessions at Arrowhead Stadium were the focus of the conference. It was the largest non-football crowd ever to use the stadium; nearly two-thirds of the 78,000 red, yellow, and orange seats were filled each of the four nights.

An enormous, computerized scoreboard, towering over the northwest end of the stadium, made both a practical and an entertaining contribution to evening activities. The scoreboard was used to announce songs, make special announcements, and introduce the speakers. As each major speaker stepped to the podium, the scoreboard beamed a remarkably realistic photograph-like image of him or her. Some speakers arranged to have outlines of their talks or illustrative Scripture passages displayed for their hearers' reference. A number of phrases, such as "Alleluia," "God Is Our Refuge and Strength," and "Jesus Is Lord," flashed on and off throughout the sessions.

Each of the three-hour-long sessions was packed with activity. In addition to the three main speakers each evening, there was time for praise and worship, for singing, for prophecy, and for a selection of personal sharings from leaders and participants in the Charismatic Renewal.

Music was one of the most notable aspects of the worship at the conference, as well as an expression of the unity among the participants. The music group was composed of members of The Word of God, an ecumenical Christian community in Ann Arbor, Michigan, and members of the St. John's Church of God in Christ young adult choir, from Newport News, Virginia.

Enthusiastically led by Dick Mishler, a coordinator of
The Word of God, the group covered the spectrum of Christian music. Traditional hymns and familiar songs of the
Catholic Charismatic Renewal alternated with favorites
from other streams - "Hevenu Shalom Aleikem" (messianic
Jewish) and "To the Utmost, Jesus Saves" (black Pentecostal) became especially popular.

Wholeness was the theme of Thursday evening's session.
Fr. Francis MacNutt, a Catholic priest known for his
work in the healing ministry, urged church leaders to
follow Jesus' example of personal ministry to the sick
and injured among his followers. It is not enough, Fr.
MacNutt said, merely to talk in the abstract about God's
healing power. "Somehow," he said, "we have to let the
church and the churches know that this really does take
place. God's power is made manifest among his people."

Mrs. Ruth Carter Stapleton, president of Behold, Inc.,
described her work involving inner healing. Relating a
number of her experiences of praying with people to overcome the bad effects of past events, she said, "Our inheritance in Jesus is wholeness: wholeness of body,
wholeness of mind and emotions, and wholeness of spirit."

The evening's main speaker was Rev. Larry Christenson,
chairman of the Lutheran Charismatic Renewal Service
Committee. Rev. Christenson urged all the Christian
churches to open themselves to the renewal of the Spirit.
"One of the problems God has with his church," Rev.
Christenson explained, "is that she has memorized his
yesterday-words so well, and chants them so loudly, that
she doesn't hear Christ's today-word." That "today-word,"
he said, is the Charismatic Renewal and the restoration
of the gifts of the Spirit.

Rev. Christenson defended the Charismatic Renewal against
church leaders and theologians who question the necessity
of the charisms. "You have looked upon these gifts as
though we had chosen them on our own initiative," he said.
"We did not choose these gifts; the Lord Jesus has chosen
to come knocking at these doors, and we have responded
to his knocking. Your controversy, if you have one, is
not with us but with him.

"The issue is not spiritual gifts. The issue is the lordship of Christ. This is his work, his initiative, his

renewal. He will welcome you into it, but he will not account to you for it, nor trim it to fit your theological prescriptions. He is Lord, to do in his church as he pleases."

Rev. Christenson also urged the Charismatic Renewal to continue, and further, its ecumenical stance: "A number of people have observed that where the Charismatic Renewal loses its ecumenical character, it tends to shrivel up. Yet there are some who want to cultivate a nice, cozy, well-insulated Episcopalian or Lutheran renewal. But the Lord has not brought this renewal to prop up and bless the status quo. He has brought it to advance his program, which is to make us one as he and the Father are one."

Friday evening's session was devoted to the theme of holiness. Speakers stressed that a wholehearted surrender to Jesus was necessary to serve the Lord effectively and to bring about unity in his body.

Bishop J.O. Patterson, presiding bishop of the Church of God in Christ, began the session with an introduction to the theology and practice of the holiness movement, a descendant of Methodism and precursor of Pentecostalism which began in the late 1800's.

"The Holy spirit is a person," Bishop Patterson intoned, "who dwells in the cleansed temple of the believer. We must allow the Holy Ghost to have absolute and complete control. That is why I call it "Pente-cost." Pentecost is costly. It cost God something. It will cost us more than just the lifting of our hands and the praising of God upon stringed instruments. It is going to cost us our lives."

Cardinal Leo Joseph Suenens, of Malines-Brussels, Belgium, further advanced the theme of holiness as complete surrender to God. "Christians," the cardinal said, "need eyes to see, ears to hear, a face full of love, hands to reach out, a heart to embrace, and feet to go forth and spread the good news."

Impressing on his hearers the importance of dedicating their lives to God's service, Cardinal Suenens said, "The world is dying because it doesn't know the name of its Savior, Jesus Christ. We have to be Christianized again, in depth, so that the world will see something of the Lord shining through us."

The main address Friday evening was an exuberant depiction of "The Beauty of Holiness," by Rev. Bob Mumford, a non-denominational evangelist and teacher. Welcoming the 45,000 participants to what he called "our little cell group," Rev. Mumford described a number of "helps and hindrances to holiness."

At one point, urging his hearers to abandon what he called a "seige mentality" and become victory minded, he opened his Bible to the book of Revelation and cried, "If you take a sneak look at the back of the book, Jesus wins!" At that, the huge crowd launched into a sustained period of exultant praise and worship. For almost ten minutes they shouted and sang and danced and waved their arms. "Whew!" Rev. Mumford exclaimed when the crowd finally settled down. "You just had a Holy Ghost Breakdown!"

He also stressed the importance of unity: "The Bible says the body of Christ does not fuction in all its power until all parts are together."

Saturday night's main address was given by Dr. James Forbes, associate professor of homiletics at Union Theological Seminary in New York. Dr. Forbes said Christians must have both the "fire" of the Holy Spirit and the "focus" of active concern for all God's creation. Repeatedly returning to his central theme - "See Me, saith the Lord" - Dr. Forbes urged his listeners to look beyond their own interests and problems and seek the coming of the kingdom of God.

It was on Saturday night that the Lord's word of unity came forth most clearly. During a time of prayer early in the session, the Lord spoke in prophecy and called his people - and especially the leaders of his people - to repentance and mourning for the divided condition of his body. It was a theme that had been sounded before during the conference, and this night the leaders of several denominational groups led the entire conference crowd in prayer, repenting of bitterness, prejudice, and hardness of heart, and interceding for the unity of God's people.

Fr. Michael Scanlan, president of the Catholic Charisma-
tic Renewal's National Service Committee, summed up the
Lord's prophetic word: "We know that we are called to
be one body. We know that a spirit of unity - the Holy
Spirit of God - has been given to us, and that the
Spirit won't rest until we are one."

In his talk, Fr. Scanlan referred to an incident recorded
in the Acts of the Apostles that had already made a deep
impact on many denominational leaders and planning committee members: Peter's vision that paved the way for
the opening of the early church to the gentiles (Acts
10:9-16). "Corporately," Fr. Scanlan said, "we are
Peter, sent to bring about the unity of God's people.
We have a mission. We have to be true to the word that
we've heard: that we are to be one, and that there's no
other way."

Confronting the magnitude of the task of reuniting the
separated churches, Fr. Scanlan said, "The Lord wants
us to know that as big as this problem is, as difficult
as it looks, it's not too difficult for him, and he's
solved bigger problems before."

The prophetic word, as well as the talks, served to send
forth the conference participants to spread the Lord's
call to unity, and to echo the words of Kevin Ranaghan
on the opening night of the conference: "From this night
onward, no matter where we go or what we do, even if we
have our own separate activities in our own separate
churches, we will always be together in the Spirit. By
the grace of God, we will be one people."

2. Report of the Consultation on the Significance of the Charismatic Renewal for the Churches

Bossey, 8-13 March, 1980

<u>Background</u>

The World Council of Churches' sub-unit on Renewal and Congregational Life, formed after the Vth Assembly at Nairobi, 1975, has produced various documents formulating its understanding of "renewal" and "the congregation".

One of the dimensions of renewal in which the sub-unit has been taking increasing interest has been "the Charismatic Renewal". This Consultation is the result of several earlier informal conversations and many contacts.

It was called with the following aim:

"The purpose of this encounter will be to <u>clarify understanding</u> of the Charismatic Renewal and its <u>meaning for the churches</u>, and to <u>study the responses of the churches</u> to the Charismatic Renewal.

"Through and beyond the quest for understanding, participants will be seeking a clearer picture of that renewal in faith and obedience to which Christ is calling his church."

The participants, numbering over 50, were drawn from member and non-member churches and the Roman Catholic Church and represented a number of dimensions of the Charismatic Renewal. The members of the sub-unit's working group also participated throughout.

While the Consultation did not attempt to define either "charismatic" or "renewal", being more concerned to <u>describe</u>, the following statement, adopted by the sub-unit at its meeting at Stony Point, New York, 1978, is the framework of its study and action on renewal.

"Certain characteristics seem common to all forms of genuine renewal.

   i)   Renewal is the gift of the Holy Spirit, and therefore requires in those who look and work for it <u>an attitude of dependent expectation</u> (anamone) towards the One who said, "Behold I make all things new". Therein lies the ground of the strange hope which inspires God's people in their search for renewal.

ii) Renewal requires <u>an attitude of creative faithfulness</u> towards authentic tradition as well as towards the concrete situation in which faith is lived out. It is therefore not necessarily experienced as "something new" but can be given through the revitalizing of the old. No actual expression of renewal is final, since renewal has its focus in the future (eschaton) towards which God is always leading His people.

iii) Renewal which is of the Spirit will lead to struggle in <u>terms of the personal, social, political and economic realities</u> which are the daily life of individuals and communities. The pattern of this renewal is to be found in the Lord Jesus Christ. God became flesh, taking on our nature, our condition, and thus transforming it. Any true "sign of renewal" will express this same mystical reality of the fusion of the human divine.

iv) The renewing activity of the Triune God is always marked by a loving <u>dynamism which radiates outwards</u> growing, expanding, always opening persons toward their neighbours and creating communities open to the world.

v) <u>Worship is clearly central</u> to all renewal. From it our visions are received, and hope is stirred. In it our failure is confessed and we are emboldened to offer again our schemes, programmes and endeavours. Through worship we are delivered both from that despair and from that presumption, which are perhaps the greatest barriers to that renewal to which God is ever seeking to call His people."

"What does this mean?" (Acts 2:12)

In story, statement, praise and prayer, with body, mind and spirit, we have shared some aspects of the Charismatic Renewal here at Bossey. What we have enjoyed the written word alone cannot contain. In the experience of our sis-

202

ters and brothers, in the echoing silence of our own hearts and in talking with each other we have been moved to wonder at this new thing that is happening across the world in our day.

Life with God, the Father, through the Son in the Holy Spirit is the context of this report.

A.   What does this mean?

For some of us our wonder has been a question - or a series of questions, as this report will show. For others of us our wonder is a prayer of thanksgiving for the gift we are sure we have received. Together we have asked: "What does this mean...?"

I.   "...for the churches?"

That this is of great significance for the churches is attested by our encounter here. It is affirmed by the unprecedented number of replies received by the General Secretary to his letter to the member churches of the World Council of Churches, inviting reactions. We recognize that the geographical and ecclesiastical extent of the Charismatic Renewal is far wider than has been commonly thought within the churches.

a) Together with the responses of the churches we affirm that the gift and gifts of the Holy Spirit are promised and given to the whole body of Christ. But this should not preclude the church becoming aware of the need to examine its life to determine whether her ministers and people are receiving the gift and gifts of the Spirit given them by God.

The Charismatic Renewal offers encouraging evidence of Jesus' promise of the Spirit's presence in the church, and we give thanks for the new hope we have discerned of "A Church Renewed and United".

Some of the elements are:

- a new awareness of the saving power and effective Lordship of Jesus;

- spiritual renewal, in a day of world crisis;

203

- the revitalization of the church not least at congregational level - a deep concern of many participants in the Charismatic Renewal;

- the creation of a new sense of community;

- spontaneity, sincerity, freedom and joy in praise and worship;

- renewed interest in the Bible "come alive" as God's living word;

- a deeper sense of the reality, holiness and transcendence of God;

- a deeper interest in and awareness of fundamental doctrines such as the Trinity, the divinity of Christ, the death and resurrection through experiential confirmation;

- renewal of the ministry of healing;

- an opportunity for the emergence of lay leadership;

- a greater concern for evangelism, mission and witness through the members of the church released and empowered.

B. However, together with the responding churches we recognize that the emergence of this renewal in the life of many churches is sometimes a source of tension and anxiety.

- spiritual elitism among some participants of the Charismatic Renewal, failing to recognize that all Christians stand on the same level of grace;

- judgmental reaction by other Christians who have not shared their experience, leading to tension and division in the congregation and the church;

- problems of authority and order (over e.g. intercommunion - though the question arises first from outside of the Charismatic Renewal);

- the danger of confusing mere exuberance and energy with the power of the Holy Spirit and of losing the transcendence of God;

- the danger of seeing experience as opposed to or excluding rational doctrinal content, as exemplified by the phrase, "doctrine divides and experience unites".

We praise God for the spirit of trust, openness and charity which has marked our discussions on such matters.

We believe that the church at large can be encouraged to welcome the tensions and strains accompanying this renewal, as birth-pangs of the church being renewed in pain and joy.

II. ...for the ecumenical movement?

a) There was a spirit of rejoicing in the consultation at the experience of Christian unity in the Charismatic Renewal, which offers inspiration and hope for tired ecumenists.

- Unity is not merely a calling but an experienced gift of the Spirit. Disunity becomes intolerable, a tremendous pressure is experienced to break through barriers that separate Christian from Christian. So the Charismatic Renewal is both a question and a spur to architects of structural unity.

- Nevertheless the consultation recognizes the gifts of diversity both within the New Testament church and the church of today.

- A new sense of community binds together people of multiple denominations, transcending historic divisions and demonstrating the urgency of the quest for the unity of the church.

The Charismatic Renewal has added new and significant ecumenical experience to the people of God, and that must be taken very, very seriously. It also puts pressure on church leaders to move more forcefully on unity concerns.

It suggests, however, that unity is essentially a matter of heart and spirit, a fruit of rather than a means to renewal.

We note the comment of one church correspondent: "There is a tension between the ecumenical vision and the churches. Because it is not integrated into the life of the churches the ecumenical movement tends to develop a life of its own and gets institutionalized. The Charismatic Renewal has gained strength at this juncture. It is challenging the churches in their self-understanding. It is challenging them as they participate in the ecumenical movement. What can they learn from the Charismatic Renewal for the fulfilment of their tasks in the ecumenical movement? How can the Charismatic Renewal remain a Charismatic Renewal and avoid becoming an organized institutionalized movement?"

b) Yet we also warn against some divisive tendencies, the danger of a new sectarianism, leading people to leave their churches.

c) We also encourage the renewal to bring to full fruition its reconciliatory potential, for example in Ireland. The confessional organizations of the renewal should promote reconciliation everywhere.

Yet we bear witness to the sense of community that has developed in our consultation - melting reserve, destroying superiority, banishing fear, each esteeming the other better than oneself, not for reasons of intellect, but for faith and favour.

Together we proclaim the unity of the church to be the Holy Spirit's gift and calling. Together we look to the World Council of Churches through its sub-unit on Renewal and Congregational Life to foster what has begun at this consultation; to receive that which the Charismatic Renewal can offer in the service of its aims; and to offer to the renewal its resources of contact, dialogue, expertise and prayer.

III.   ...for the world?

Perhaps the chief area of difference between us lies in our assessment of the meaning of the Charismatic Renewal for the world.

- While the consultation was pleased to note that in certain cases the Charismatic Renewal has led to a deeper commitment for socio-political action, we still ask what place does the Charismatic Renewal give to social and political concerns. "Faith without works is dead".

- In contrast we also recognize the danger of commitment to social and political action becoming detached from the sources of spiritual renewal.

"If I sell all my goods to feed the poor and have not love..."

Lord, help us to cast the beam out of our own eyes before troubling about the mote in our brother's eye.

B. What do these mean? - Some issues for further study and consultation:

Naturally the issues mentioned below can best be discussed by both the World Council of Churches and the Charismatic Renewal, though we here designate where we feel the priority interest should be.

I. Primarily as regards the Charismatic Renewal

a) How necessary is the prevailing terminology, e.g. "baptism of the Holy Spirit"? Is it only a language, or does it represent experiences that other Christians might know by a different name?

b) What are the safeguards against emotionalism, mass hysteria and manipulation? (On the other hand, it should be noted, emotion is often present in repressed negative forms such as anger, frustration, bitterness, in typical church business meetings!)

c) Are those in the renewal open to sociological and psychological understandings of the movement, or does the insistence on the activity of the Holy Spirit preclude this?

d) Do those in the renewal recognize sufficiently the ambiguity of charismatic manifestations, and the need for them to be tested and validated (I Thess. 5:10-22)?

e) What is the contribution of the Charismatic Renewal to the changing role of women in the churches and the world?

f) Do those in the renewal understand themselves called to a positive relation to the world and the evangelisation of cultures, which has to do with the transformation of social patterns?

g) Is there one Charismatic Renewal or "many", varying in different cultures and churches?

h) Do those in the renewal place enough emphasis on the Christ of the Cross, crucified for sinners, and on the suffering of Christians involved in the struggle against their old natures, and, finally, on the suffering of the poor and oppressed? (Matt. 25)

i) Would the leaders of the Charismatic Renewal generally welcome interest and initiatives on the part of the World Council of Churches in the future?

II. Primarily by the World Council of Churches (and the churches)

a) Ecclesiology in relation to the Holy Spirit.

b) Pneumatology - "A careful and Spirit-led study of the scriptures about the Holy Ghost and the appropriation of His Gifts." (Ghana Baptist Convention). How does the Holy Spirit differ from the "life force" or creative spirit?

c) Methodology - How can the method of "telling the story", a mode of communication often more authentic to African, Asian and other cultures, be extended within World Council of Churches activity?

d) How can there be held in proper biblical tension, within the concept of the body of Christ, local community, universal church and cosmic Christ? Are the "gifts" for the church only, or for the world?

e) Evil - what is an adequate understanding of the "evil one" and the principalities and powers? What is the demonic element that corrupts all human structures, often destroying those who enter them with vision and commitments?

f) Is there an "economy of God" whereby He calls movements into existence and leads them through different phases (as cf. monasticism) so that it may be wrong to ask for certain manifestations at a too early stage?

g) The prophetic nature of the Charismatic Renewal and of the World Council of Churches have an important convergence and urgency in dealing with the future. This convergence calls for reconsidering our eschatology.

h) The pastoral responsibilities of the churches vis-à-vis the Charismatic Renewal and ways of communication of the charismatic experiences to the churches and congregations at large need thorough consideration.

i) Noting the forthcoming World Council of Churches Commission on World Mission and Evangelism at Melbourne 1980, we recommend a study on the theme of "The Holy Spirit and the Kingdom of God".

We pray for God's Spirit to enliven the minds, inspire the imagination, and inflame the hearts of all who think, reflect and study.

C.   Some Contrasts

We have been discussing the Charismatic Renewal and the churches and noted the following contrasts:

- two structures	- the WCC and a "structured" Charismatic Renewal
- two movements	- the ecumenical movement and the charismatic "movement"
- two emphases	- structural church, order and authority; and free forms, of liturgy, relations, behaving
- two approaches to renewal	- planning, strategies of change, organization; prayer and dependence on God
- two foci of Christian life	- the world; the community of believers
- two understandings of faith	- ethical action based on beliefs; awareness of the living reality of God.

D.   Where do we go from here?

Some suggestions of directions or strategies for the sub-unit:

a) WCC form teams within nations to visit significant charismatic events already planned or scheduled by

on-going charismatic groups, perhaps scheduling con-
sultations afterwards and the writing of papers,
multi-media productions, etc.

b) Include persons with Charismatic Renewal experience
in team visits, and organise some visits specifically
of this character.

c) Consider the possibility of an international and ecumenical "Festival of Faith" culminating in a "Pilgrim-
age of Unity".

d) Have charismatic dimension actively present in Vancouver Assembly of the WCC worship (1983).

e) Do studies of different kinds of Charismatic Renewal
events and publish descriptions of what happened.

f) Do in-parish studies of impact of Charismatic Renewal.

g) Build up shared experiences of renewal and unity by
encouraging regional/local celebrations of Pentecost
involving both participants in Charismatic Renewal
and member churches of the WCC, with multi-media
expression.

h) Develop grass-root study programmes for theologians
and laity.

i) Collect and disseminate to member churches existing
materials pertinent to pastoral issues raised under
B. II. h.).

j) We recommend the publication in a "Consultation Book"
of the main papers, plus photographs, materials from
the worship etc., as well as this report.

k) The results of the consultation should not only be
distributed to the member churches but also to national and international leaders and organizations serving
the Charismatic Renewal.

l) We call attention to the international ecumenical col-
lection of 100 documents from the churches on the sub-
ject of the Charismatic Renewal (K. McDonnell (ed.),
Presence, Power, Praise: Documents on the Charismatic
Renewal. Collegeville, Minn., 56321 USA, Liturgical
Press, 1980, 3 vols.).

"You shall receive the gift of the Holy Spirit.
For the promise is to you and to your children
and to all that are far off, every one whom the
Lord calls to him."

E. Hopes for the Future

1. We hope that the World Council of Chruches will spon-
    sor future consultations and that its action in call-
    ing this consltation will encourage the churches to
    react more positively to the Charismatic Renewal.
    In future consultations there should be more times
    for worship, prayer, and sharing in personal encounter.

2. In order to bring the main Charismatic Renewal of
    the Third World into proper focus, we also hope that
    in future consultations Latin American Pentecostal
    churches, North American Black Pentecostal churches,
    African Independent churches, and Asian Pentecostal
    churches (member and non-member churches of the World
    Council of Churches) can be more adequately repre-
    sented.

3. We also hope that both the world Council of Churches
    and the Charismatic Renewal will be inspired to make
    certain that increased financial resources are avail-
    able.

A postscript. Nowhere have we described "the Charismatic
Renewal". Have you noticed? The point it "it" has to
be experienced. And, as for definition, each individual
can only give his or her own description. So here are
the individual statements on the Charismatic Renewal by
the individual members of one group at the consultation:

a) "something worked by the Holy Spirit, now expressed
    amongst other ways in the forms of life and gestalt
    of the charismatic movement."

b) "at heart a rediscovery of the Holy Spirit as exper-
    ienced, the forms of life which the living experience
    takes."

c) "the Charismatic Renewal leads to evangelism, this
    leads to mutual help of Christians for a personal
    encounter with Jesus Christ; this leads to conver-
    sion; to acceptance of initiation sacraments and to
    fulfilment."

d) "brings emotional and spiritual elements into intellectually dominated churches, brings power of healing to society in which spiritual needs are increasing, opens dimensions of faith for the experiences of transcendence for which there is a new yearning."

e) "expression of new life after being born again."

f) "enabling God's people to do God's purpose."

g) "outpouring of the Holy Spirit on the people of God, which leads to an infusion of power and divine life in the people of God, expressed in various charisms within the body of Christ, which at the same time is exalting Christ."

h) "the work of the Holy Spirit is more comprehensive than the Charismatic Renewal, and Charismatic Renewal is more comprehensive than what is happening in the charismatic movement today."

i) "restoration of parts of the church to a normal life, a counter culture to so-called power and efficiency of established churches, grace fulfilled in weakness."

j) "an outpouring of the Holy Spirit on God's people, this leads to experience of the Lordship of Jesus, this leads to living brotherhood, affirming basic faith of each church, calling them into full unity."

k) "renewal of the basic experience common to all Christians (see c., above) including adoration of the Father, the Lordship of Jesus and the Holy Spirit as the "between" between people, the Holy Spirit "as the social or interpersonal God experience" - it is no particular movement in the sociological sense."

l) "it is not less than the whole gospel and mission of the church, but emphasis for neglected areas like personal moment in faith and charisms."

IV.
After the Consultation

(translated from the German - WCC Language Service)

A. A CRITICAL PARTICIPANT LOOKS BACK TO THE BOSSEY CONSULTATION

Ingrid Reimer

The invitation came from the World Council of Churches in Geneva. I was asked to take part in a consultation on the significance of the Charismatic Renewal for the churches. Since I had already studied this worldwide renewal movement and followed its course with some scepticism, I went to the meeting at Bossey near Geneva eager to learn still more about it.

In the train on the way home again, I try to sort out my impressions of the five days in Bossey. The many different voices are still with me, mostly in English though often with a foreign accent. Certainly I had not got to know all the sixty participants individually. But the different personalities were still vivid, very much so. Alongside the Europeans from both east and west, and the Americans, it was the Africans and Asians who left the deepest impression on me.

The reception at the very beginning of the conference was already astonishing to me. It was no surprise, of course, to find a number of well-known names on the list of participants, people familiar to me because of their outstanding publications. Nor did the variety of churches represented come as any surprise. I was rather astonished, however, at the group of young African women who accompanied the opening service with their strong singing of African songs. What were they doing here at an "official" conference? On this first afternoon it was not yet possible for me to realize how important the presence of this group was to be for the whole consultation. Just because their way of expressing their religion was so strange and unfamiliar, this group was a constant reminder throughout the conference of the meeting between different cultural traditions. And in retrospect the encounter between the different confessional forms appeared a most memorable experience.

Now I begin to ask myself how all these addresses, discussions and conversations, and other impressions, can be digested and absorbed into my habitual ways of thinking.

There had been theological themes, of course, and most of the participants were theologians. Yet I still cannot fit all that I experienced into a single pattern. I recall the Swiss professor from Birmingham. All he did was tell a story. And just as we were saying to our-selves: "ah, yes, now he'll begin his real address", his contribution was already over. That really vexed me. I had, of course, already heard of Professor Hollenweger's narrative style of presentation, known as "intercultural theology". But it took me some time to realize just how this narrative form makes it pos-sible to do justice to the intricacy of a theme. I now had a similar experience with the consultation as a whole.

I was particularly impressed by the fact that Dr. Philip Potter, the General Secretary of the World Council of Churches, actually participated in the whole conference. This made me realize the importance attached to the con-sultation. In a notable address, Potter identified a number of basic concerns which unite the charismatic movement and the ecumenical movement. Both movements are seeking to bring people of different communities together and to give expression to the diversity of the whole church of Christ. Both saw themselves as renewal movements looking to the power of the Holy Spirit and based on the event of Pentecost. This suggested impor-tant themes which were picked up again and again in our conversations and discussions. For the representatives of the Charismatic Renewal movement, with their starting point primarily in the personal life of the individual Christian, the idea of salvation for the world was a special challenge.

For me the big question at first was how the Charismatic Renewal movement could create unity. Up to now I had heard again and again of problems and tensions in the congregations. But perhaps this was a difficulty pe-culiar to my own country.

Over against this, I was very impressed with the film of a charismatic conference in Kansas City attended by 50,000 people from twelve different denominations. Al-though put off by the American style of presentation and inclined to react strongly against mass enthusiasm, I nevertheless was able to enter sympathetically into the vigorous experience of religious unity in this gigantic stadium.

We also worked hard at the conference, of course. After the daily service, we went into small groups to study Bible passages chosen to highlight quite different aspects of the operation of the Holy Spirit. There was thorough discussion of a whole dossier of working papers. And finally the findings of the discussions were brought together in a report which was also thoroughly discussed by all the participants.

It was all very tiring. I tried to relax a little in the fresh air. I looked up at the snow-covered mountains. The morning worship came back to me again. We had prayed - quite spontaneously and personally. Even though I could not always understand the words in the various mother tongues, I was still able to make the prayers silently my own. I remembered how hard I often find the preparation of my prayers for public worship. I found the music, too, extremely beautiful. Suddenly I found I had composed a chord from a melody and this was then used by the individuals praying in song. It was most melodious and certainly had nothing to do with enthusiasm or even ecstasy, as if often asserted.

In our small study group we had tried to explain what we mean by Charismatic Renewal. We had decided not to give a definition but each to try individually to describe in a few words what Charismatic Renewal means to them personally. The power of the Holy Spirit was mentioned, personal experiences, renewal and a deeper dimension to church practices and activities. And I thought again of my own congregation, of the handful of people on whom I can really count and of the many who keep their distance.

"Towards a Church Renewed and United in the Spirit" - that was the consultation theme as given in the letters of invitation. And it had often sounded as if the renewal and unity of the whole church was really possible. A beautiful vision! But how remote from reality! But these people seemed to be convinced. They commit everything to the Holy Spirit. "Certainly we ourselves cannot do it", said one participant...

Perhaps we must become much more open and sensitive to what God purposes to accomplish in his church.

B. REPORT ON THE WORK OF THE WCC CONSULTANT ON CHARIS-
MATIC RENEWAL

Arnold Bittlinger

Dear Friends,

I was asked to give a report on my work as consultant on
Charismatic Renewal. Let me start with my personal prehistory.

As director of Evangelism and Stewardship (United Church,
FRG) I travelled through the USA in 1962 in order to
study evangelism, stewardship and congregational life.
Unexpectedly I ran into the beginnings of the Charismatic
Renewal (CR) in some Lutheran, Reformed and Episcopal
churches. I was impressed by the positive effects which
this renewal had in the realm which I was supposed to
study. I had the impression that under the influence
of the Holy Spirit many things were performed less
organized but more organically.

In the following years I studied practically and theoretically the significance of the charismata for congregational renewal. I organized many conferences (among
others I founded together with Rod Williams in 1972 the
European Charismatic Leaders conference) and published
numerous books and articles some of which got translated
into several languages.

My contacts with the World Council of Churches began in
1965 when I was invited to a Faith and Order consultation
in Geneva on "Ministry and Ministries". In 1966 I was
asked to serve as a Consultant of the WCC at a consultation in Gunten between the WCC and European Pentecostal
Churches. In the following years I spoke at numerous
ecumenical conferences and helped to organize charismatic meetings in connection with the Nairobi Assembly
in 1975. I also took part in encounters between representatives of the WCC and CR leaders in Rome (1975),
London (1976) and Rostrevor (1977).

After preliminary talks with WCC representatives in Geneva
(January 1977) and Bossey (March 1977), David Gill invited
me to attend the first meeting of the Renewal and Congregational Life (RCL) Working Group (Geneva, July 1977)
where I was asked to serve as a part-time WCC Consultant
on Charismatic Renewal.

In this capacity I tried to fulfil a threefold task:

I.   To interpret to the <u>churches</u> the significance of
     the Charismatic Renewal.

II. To interpret to <u>Charismatic Renewal groups</u> the
     significance of the churches and of the WCC.

III. To develop models of integration.

The following report is an attempt to describe how I
tried to fulfil this threefold task.

I.   <u>Interpreting to the Churches the Significance of
     the Charismatic Renewal</u>

1.   <u>To whom did I speak?</u>

a) At the ecumenical conferences which I attended (meetings of RCL Working Groups Geneva 1977 and Stony Point
1978; Pastors course Bossey 1978; CMC course Bossey 1979;
Mission Conference Burgos 1979; CEC Conference Crete
1979; CWME Conference Melbourne 1980) my task was to
describe the significance of the CR for the churches and
to help that this renewal found adequate expression in
the reports of these conferences.

b) I accepted numerous invitations to speak at conferences organized by regional or local churches (e.g. in
France: Conference of Lutheran and Reformed Pastors of
Alsace Lorraine at Strasbourg and conference organized
by the French Fédération Protestante at Versailles; in
the FRG: Ecumenical Conference of the Church of Baden
at Burg Liebenzell; in Switzerland: Pastors conference
of the Methodist Church in Hasliberg and of the Reformed
Church Schaffhausen and Basle; in Australia pastors'
conferences at Sydney, Newcastle and Sutherland).   I
also had conversations with church leaders from many
countries and denominations.

c) I also was asked to write articles for church papers
and magazines. Sometimes these articles were translated
and published in other languages. In 1978 my book on
the Ecumenical Relevance of the Roman Catholic/Pente-
costal dialogue was published.

2. What were the main problems?

a) Christians from the Evangelical Fundamentalist wing
of the churches in the USA and Europe expressed sometimes
the opinion that charismatic experiences had their place
only in the apostolic time. But when the canon of the
New Testament was finished the charismata passed away
(the New Testament canon is considered to be "The perfect"
of I Cor. 13:10). If charismata are appearing in our
time today they therefore cannot be from the Spirit of
God. Those groups have the same opinion of the World
Council of Churches, they think that for our time there
will be no visible unity; if there is visible unity it
cannot be from God. Evangelical fundamentalist Christians of the Third World apply these teachings only if
they are under the dictatorship of a Western Evangelical
Mission Society.

b) Church representatives with no dogmatic opposition
against charismata have sometimes had negative experiences with individual so-called "charismatics". I encountered objections like those which are listed in the
Bossey Report under A. I. b) and questions are asked
loke those which are mentioned in the Bossey Report
under B. I. a) to h).

Church people often find it difficult to accept that there
should be two kinds of Christians, those "baptised in
the Spirit" and those "not baptised in the Spirit". This
is a serious objection since many so-called "charismatics" make this distinction and many so-called "charismatic" books teach this.

c) In the Third World phenomena, which are extraordinary
to Western people like exorcism, faith healing, glossal-
alia and so on belong to the normal religious sphere
especially in non-Christian cults and religions. These
phenomena are therefore sometimes considered as "heathen"
and some of them are therefore not accepted in Christian
worship.

3. How did I react?

a) In talking with Christians of the Evangelical fundamentalist wing I tried to point out the large variety
of charismata, which are not limited to the list in I
Cor. 12. I also tried to explain that charismata are

manifestations of God's grace. Rejecting charismata therefore would mean to reject God's grace which is working through Christians. The alternative then would be pure human activity.

However, my success with Evangelical Fundamentalists were not very great. Sometimes those people accepted what I said but only as long as I talked to them privately. As soon as they were back in their clan they no longer dared to offer an opinion which was different from those of their leaders or their tradition.

Normally Evangelical Fundamentalists get only convinced if they get existentially involved in Charismatic Renewal (which happens once in a while).

b) Concerning the objections of other church representatives, I had to admit that the objections such as those which are mentioned in the Bossey report are real. But they are signs of immature Christians which one cannot only find in Charismatic Renewal groups but also in other Christian circles. I also tried to show that Charismatic Renewal in other parts of the world and other denominations may be quite different from the special groups which are the reason for those objections.

Concerning the opinion that there are "two types of Christians" I tried to clarify the historical roots of the teaching of "baptism with the Spirit" and to demonstrate that the normal use of this expression in charismatic circles is misleading. Since I am considered as one of the leading representatives of Charismatic Renewal my theological conviction is accepted as an alternative to those teachings. My conviction is: there are no phenomena which are charismatic in themselves. Whatever a Christian does or speaks is charismatic if it is a vehicle of God's love and grace and it is not charismatic if God's love does not break through (I Cor. 13:1-3) There are also no Christians who are "charismatic" and others who are not. We all act sometimes charismatically, and sometimes not. (Compare Matt. 16: 17 & 23.)

c) Concerning heathen elements I try to demonstrate that those elements are not only in Third World countries but also in so-called "Christian" countries. It does not depend on the phenomenon but on the functions of those phenomena. However, it must be admitted that some phenomena seem to be difficult to integrate in some areas, because they are so heavily loaded with heathen significance.

In ecumenical conferences it was not always easy to get adequate statements into the reports of those conferences. Sometimes they were even deleted in drafting committees and I had to fight in order to get them in again. But when the report finally appeared especially those passages were widely quoted (mainly by those who were interested and responsible for the renewal of the church).

4. What should be done in the future?

a) After the Central Committee has approved the Bossey report it should be sent to all member churches together with a slip for ordering the documentary volume. On this slip it should be indicated when the volume will be ready (I can get it ready at the end of December 1980).

b) Churches should be encouraged to "repeat" the Bossey conference on regional basis (for instance for the USA, Latin America, Australia and so on). At this stage it would be good if the churches take the initiative.

c) Churches should initiate theological courses for pastors in order to give them a clear biblical teaching on the whole realm of "charisma". These courses should be organized by the churches. It would be enough to have a period from Monday to Saturday. These courses shoul be ecumenical and held by the best experts who are able to build bridges (I have made preliminary plans with David Gill for such courses in Australia and New Zealand; I have already initiated two courses in Switzerland).

II. Interpreting to Charismatic Renewal Groups the Significance of the Churches and of the WCC

1. To whom did I speak?

a) In the USA and in Europe I have had close contacts with CR groups and leaders for many years. I deepened and widened these contacts through talks at the international charismatic conferences at Lausanne (1977) and Berlin (1979) and through my cooperation at the European Charismatic Leaders conference in Brussels (1978). I also was actively involved in the Ecumenical Charismatic Conferences in Koningstein, FRG (1978 and 1979) and Aich, Austria (1978).

I also visited some Charismatic Renewal Centres (in
Germany: Hartenschwand, Hurlach, Lindau, Gnadental; in
the USA: Community of Jesus in Cape Cod) and had con-
versations with many charismatic leaders such as Demos
Shakarian, Ralph Wilderson, Volkard Spitzer, Denis and
Rita Bennett, David du Plessis, Betty Lowe, Aril Edvardsen,
Stanley Sjöberg and others.

b) In Latin America (September 1979) I visited charisma-
tic groups and centres in Trinidad (Pentecostal, Roman
Catholic and Evangelical Neo-Pentecostal). Colombia
(Renewal Communities "Minutos de Deos" at Bogota).
Equador (Iglesia Unida, Quito). Chile (Iglesia Pente-
costal de la Trinidad and social work of Bishop Labbe,
contacts with Anglican and Catholic charismatics).
Argentina (Ecumenical Charismatic Leaders meeting in
Buenos Aires).

In Brazil, I visited the following places: Sao Paulo
(Church of Manuel de Mello, Presbyterian Charismatic
Centre, Roman Catholic leaders conference). Rio de
Janeiro (Nuova Vida Pentecostal Church, Roman Catholic
leaders conference and Buon Pastor Charismatic group,
Evangelical Maranata Charismatic Rally). Queluz (Ecu-
menical Charismatic community), Guaringueta (social
work of charismatics among the poor). Belo Horizonte
(ecumenical charismatic hospital), Peniel Baptist
charismatic rehabilitation centre for drug addicts,
Bethany Fellowship, (Lutheran Charismatic Fellowship).
Brasilia (Charismatic Coordinator Paul Lewies and Bra-
zilian Centre of the Wycliffe Bible translators).
Salvador (Conversation with Anglican and Roman Catholic
Church leaders). Recife (Favella Work of Roman Catholic
charismatic group, ecumenical charismatic leaders meeting, conversation with Bishop Dom Helder Camara).

c) On my way to and from Australia (May 1978) I used the
stops of the aircraft to interrupt my journey to visit
charismatic groups in some Asian countries and in Australia:

India (ecumenical charismatic leaders meeting and a
Roman Catholic rally in Bombay). Singapore (ecumenical
charismatic banquet and conversations with charismatic
church leaders of the Anglican and the Methodist Church).
Australia (ecumenical charismatic leaders meeting and
Anglican charismatic prayer meetings in Melbourne where

I also was the main speaker at the final Ecumenical Charismatic Service of the "Festival of Faith", St. Patrick's Cathedral. I also spoke at charismatic rallies of the Uniting Church in Sydney, Newcastle and Sutherland).
Sri Landa (Roman Catholic charismatic community, Colombo, Presbyterian City mission in Kandy with charismatic work among the poor).

Besides these visits I got many more invitations to speak at CR conferences which I could not accept for time reasons.

2. What were the main problems?

a) In the USA, Australia and Europe I occasionally discovered within neo-Pentecostal groups disinterest in the organized church (some pointed to negative experiences such as "our pastor does not want charismatic worship in his parish"). I also found quite often the opinion that "charismatic meetings are enough and no further church engagement is necessary". In some cases there was real danger that charismatics who did not find adequate understanding in their churches were inclined to form or attend "charismatic churches" (such as the "house church movement" in England). I encountered also questions as are listed in the Bossey report under B. II. a) to h).

b) Some charismatic groups had a very distorted view of the World Council of Churches because they had read the propaganda of evangelical fundamentalist groups (which are mainly the same groups which write also negatively against Charismatic Renewal!).

c) Charismatic churches in the Third World often are uninformed about the WCC. They also have very little possibility to inform themselves about the WCC because they can neither read nor write the official languages of the WCC.

3. How did I react?

a) Quite often charismatics were puzzled by my position because they did not expect that the WCC is officially and seriously interested in Charismatic Renewal (e.g. when Demos Shakarian saw my card he wondered "how is this opssible: CR and WCC are on the same card!"). But

224

when I explained my work people became very interested
(thus Demos Shakarian asked if his worldwide organization among laymen "FGBMFI" which is "Full Gospel Busi-
nessmen Fellowship International" could become affiliated
with the World Council of Churches). The Iglesia Pentecostal de la Trinidad in Chile also became interested
in memberhsip.

b) Charismatics are interested and confused when I tell
them of other charismatic groups throughout the world
which have a totally different style than the North
American pattern (which they think is the only real
CR pattern!).

c) I tried to teach them theology. Normally I do this
with success because my books are known and estimated
for many years among charismatic leaders. This theological teaching has a chance because it is biblically
rooted and it takes seriously some hidden doubts which
many charismatics have about the classical Pentecostal
teachings (but which they do not dare to attack because
they don't have adequate arguments or fear to be no
longer in the "main stream" of Charismatic Renewal).

4.   What should be done in the future?

a) The next important step should be to get in contact
with the chairmen of the confessional charismatic groups
(such as the Lutheran Charismatic Fellowship, Presbyterian Charismatic Fellowship, Anglican Charismatic
Fellowship, etc.) and some other church related charismatic groups (such as vision ministries, Gemeinde-Gabe
Dienste, etc.) in order to share thoughts about the Bossey
report and about the follow-up consultation. (Since
most of the chairmen of those groups are living in North
America, perhaps Minneapolis would be a good place for
such a meeting).

b) Research and contact journeys (which I undertook in
Latin America and in some Asian countries) should be
continued, especially to get more information and more
contacts in Korea, Japan and Africa. But also to investigate charismatic events in the Orthodox Church and
among minority groups.

c) The proposals in the Bossey report C a) to k) should
be taken seriously and detailed steps should be developed to put them into practice (including developing
ideas for Vancouver 1983).

III. Models of Integration

1. What did I do?

a) In Stony Point (1978) the RCL Working Group decided,
that a consultation should be held in March 1980 on the
significance of the CR for the churches.

In order to prepare this consultation I organized a
meeting of a consultative group at Schloss Schwanberg/
FRG (December 1978) and asked Walter Hollenweger to be
its moderator. At this meeting the paper "Towards a
Church Renewed and United in the Spirit" was written (it
was approved as consultation background paper by the
executive group which met at Bossey July 1979). The
consultative group also made suggestions for participants and speakers of the consultation. For detailed
planning of the consultation members of the consultative group met a second time in Nidelbad/Switzerland
(December 1979).

b) From January to June 1979 I conducted in Schaffhausen
an "Introduction into ecumenical/charismatic worship
experience". I also helped to initiate a Healing Home
in Munich/FRG for wholistic and charismatic health care
and organized a conference on "Healing and Wholeness for
the whole person" (Nidelbad, November 1979, co-sponsored
by Renewal and Congregational Life (RCL) and (CMC) - Christ
Medical Commission). In Schloss Hünigen, Switzerland
I organized in July/August 1978 and 1980 two ecumenical/
charismatic theological seminars for pastors and priests.
The quality of these seminars was such that they were
officially recognized by the in-service training department of the Bernese church.

c) As representative of the WCC I was elected into the
ecumenical core-team of the "Ecumenical Church-day" of
the Schweizericher Diakonieverein. This church-day
takes place every year on the third week-end of June
in Nidelbad/Switzerland and is much older than the WCC.
The core-team meets three times a year in order to prepare the annual church-day. In 1979 the theme of the
church-day was on the Holy Spirit (I was one of the
speakers). I also helped to prepare the church-day of
1980, where also Jews and Muslims were involved.

Amongst others the particular contribution of these contacts mentioned under b) and c) consists of loosening up
the antagonism of evangelicals towards the WCC and furthermore in demonstrating to Swiss and German churches
the WCC's concern for spirituality.

2.   What was the main emphasis?

a) In preparing the WCC consultation at Bossey my concern
was to integrate the different CR streams such as church-
related and free charismatics, charismatic communities,
Pentecostals and African Independent Churches. I also
was concerned that the different cultures found adequate
expression, such as American-European cultures (which
heavily dominate the literary market) and Third World
cultures (Roman Catholic and ecumenical grass-root groups
in Brazil, the different expressions of black spirituality
in Africa, England, the Caribbean and the USA).

b) In the field of charismatic healing my concern was to
help to promote a wholistic approach which may include
among others psychotherapy creativity, group therapy,
Bible meditation, prayer, prophetic insights and laying
on of hands.

c) In organizing theological seminars (and in helping to
prepare the church-days of Nidelbad) I was concerned that
a blend of different theological approaches was guaran-
teed. My main effort was to help to provide an atmosphere with "a piety which is not embarrassing and a
theology which is not arrogant" (eine Frömmigkeit die
nicht peinlich und eine Wissenschaft die nicht arrogant
ist").

3.   How were the reactions?

a) The reactions to the Bossey Consultation were on the
whole mainly positive (see Minutes page 11f and Report
A. II. c), second paragraph). In many countries the
Bossey Report was duplicated and widely discussed in
such different churches as the Uniting Church in Australia
and the Evangelical Church in the GDR. In a number of
letters people expressed their gratitude for the Bossey
report and made helpful suggestions for further meetings.

b) Concerning other models of integration sometimes some
"charismatics" had difficulties in accepting "worldly"

methods such as psychotherapy and medical care as "charismatic" or "spiritual". They also wondered how a person whom they did not consider as being "baptised in the Spirit" could perform "charismatic" gifts. On the other hand "non-charismatics" had sometimes difficulties with some charismatic expressions such as prophecy or laying on of hands. But there are many examples that these difficulties were overcome by talking and living together.

c) Concerning the theological seminars some participants complained that they were too "theological" and not enough "spiritual". Other participants however were happy that such solid theology was being taught which gave them a good theological base in their attempts to work for congregational renewal.

4. What should be done in the future?

a) The next major event will be the follow-up consultation of November 1981. I suggest that it should be prepared again by a consultative group. This group could also develop preliminary suggestions for "charismatic" input in the Vancouver Assembly of the WCC.

b) The suggestions under D of the Bossey report should be put into practice. A group of specialists (the consultative groups strengthened by additional members of the Working Group?) should make suggestions for practical steps.

c) In order to coordinate and channel CR concerns the Roman Catholic Church has created an International Charismatic Communication Centre in Brussels. This centre is "unofficially" linked to the Vatican in the person of Cardinal Suenens who was asked by the Pope Paul VI to act as bridge-builder (all over the world I saw the excellent effect of this centre!). It would be of high value if the non-Catholic charismatics could have a similar centre. Besides communication and information this centre could offer ecumenical, theological and experimental training courses for pastors and leaders in Charismatic Renewal.

Final Remarks

In his speech at the consultation and in a contribution at the meeting of the Working Group Philip Potter expressed his surprise about the unexpected large number of reactions of the member churches to his letter concerning the consultation on CR. In travelling through many countries and in talking with many CR leaders I was also surprised to see how large and how fast the Charismatic Renewal is growing (in the USA a recent "Christianity Today - Gallup Poll" indicates that 19% of all Americans 18 years or older - or 29 million consider themselves to be Pentecostal-charismatic).

CR cannot be reached by the normal ecumenical network (church leaders and ecumenical offices are very often not well informed about what is going on in CR!). Therefore the competence and expertise of specialists are necessary.

CR could be a potential danger or blessing for the churches. It is therefore very important that the WCC develops the necessary sensitivity in dealing with this issue.

I cannot conclude this report without mentioning that my activities as consultant on Charismatic Renewal would not be possible without the generous understanding of the Reformed Church of the Canton of Schaffhausen and the help of my wife who faithfully takes over the responsibility for the parish when I am away.

Presented to the meeting of the executive group of the sub-unit on Renewal and Congregational Life, Geneva, August 1980.

C. STATEMENT TO CENTRAL COMMITTEE FROM WORKING GROUP OF THE SUB-UNIT ON RENEWAL AND CONGREGATIONAL LIFE

According to the decision which was made at Stony Point (1978), the sub-unit on Renewal and Congregational Life has held a consultation at Bossey (March 8-13, 1980), whose purpose it was to clarify understanding of the Charismatic Renewal and its meaning for the churches.

The sub-unit was encouraged to proceed with the consultation by the unusually large number of responses to the letter which the General Secretary wrote to the member churches concerning their experiences of the Charismatic Renewal.

Sixty persons took part in this consultation, among whom were the Working Group and the General Secretary of the World Council of Churches. Everybody agreed that this conference has been highly meaningful and that the very fact that it "happened" will have a real impact on the churches.

A result of this consultation is that it has begun to develop a mutual trust and build a bridge between representatives of the World Council of Churches and of the Charismatic Renewal.

The Working Group is well aware that this consultation offered only the beginning of a conversation and therefore requires a follow-up so that some crucial issues might be thoroughly dealt with.

The Working Group recommends that the Central Committee

- pay attention to the report from the consultation, comment on it, and pass it on through the General Secretary, to the member churches, together with its own comments;

- encourage member churches, where relevant, to engage in dialogue with representatives of the Charismatic Renewal on the basis of this document, in places where it has not already started;

- request member churches to share with the World Council of Churches their reactions to this report and any results from dialogue with Charismatic Renewal based on this report;

- include the whole matter of renewal of congregational life as an integral part of the 6th Assembly in Vancouver.

It is the intention of the sub-unit to continue the study and the consultative process which has been undertaken in order to fulfil more adequately its purpose of clarificatio and understanding.

This statement was unanimously accepted by the Central Committee of the WCC in August 1980.

SELECTED BIBLIOGRAPHY

(Most of the titles listed below were suggested as helpful supplementary reading by participants at the Bossey Consultation.)

Becken, Hans-Jürgen. Theologie der Heilung: Das Heilung in den Afrikanischen Unabhängigen Kirchen in Südafrika. Hermannsburg: Verlag der Missionshandlung, 1972.

Berkhof, Hendrikus. The Doctrine of the Holy Spirit. Richmond: John Knox Press, 1964.

Bittlinger, Arnold. Gifts and Graces. London: Hodder & Stoughton, 1967; Grand Rapids: Eerdmans, 1968. Also available in Danish, French, German, Portuguese, and Swedish.

-----. Gifts and Ministries. Grand Rapids: Eerdmans, 1973; London: Hodder & Stoughton, 1974. Also available in Danish, French, German, and Portuguese.

-----. Papst und Pfingstler: Der Röm.-Kath. Pfingstliche Dialog und seine ökumenische Relevanz. Bern and Las Vegas: Peter Lang, 1978.

Christenson, Larry. The Gift of Tongues. San Pedro, 1963.

-----. A Message to the Charismatic Movement. Minneapolis: Bethany Fellowship, 1972.

-----. The Renewed Mind. Minneapolis: Bethany Fellowship, 1974.

-----. The Charismatic Renewal among Lutherans. Minneapolis: Bethany, 1976.

Clark, Stephen. Man and Woman in Christ. Ann Arbor: Servant Books, 1980.

-----. Building Christian Communities. Notre Dame, Ind.: Ave Maria Press, 1972.

-----. Where Are We Headed? Notre Dame, Ind.: Charismatic Renewal Services, 1973.

Davis, Rex. Locusts and Wild Honey. Geneva: World Council of Churches, 1978.

Dunn, James D. G. Baptism in the Holy Spirit. London: SCM Press, 1970.

-----. Jesus and the Spirit. London: SCM Press, 1975.

-----. Unity and Diversity in the New Testament. London: SCM Press, 1977.

DuPlessis, David. A Man Called Mr. Pentecost. Plainfield, N. J.: Logos, 1977.

-----. The Spirit Bade Me Go. Oakland, 1963.

Engelsviken, Tormod. Den Hellige Ands gjerning i Kirkens liv. Oslo: Luther Forlag, 1981.

-----. The Gift of the Spirit: An Analysis and Evaluation of the Charismatic Movement from a Lutheran Theological Perspective. Dubuque, Ia.: Aquinas Institute of Theology, 1981.

Gelpi, Donald. Charism and Sacrament. New York: Paulist Press, 1976; London: SPCK, 1977.

-----. Pentecostalism: A Theological Viewpoint. New York: Paulist Press, 1970.

Green, Michael. I Believe in the Holy Spirit. London: Hodder & Stoughton, and Grand Rapids: Eerdmans, 1975.

Hamilton, Michael P., editor. The Charismatic Movement. Grand Rapids: Eerdmans, 1975.

Harper, Michael. A New Way of Living. London: Hodder & Stoughton, 1973.

-----. Let My People Grow. London: Hodder & Stoughton, 1977.

-----. Bishops Move. London: Hodder & Stoughton, 1978.

-----. You Are My Sons. London: Hodder & Stoughton, 1980.

Heitmann, Claus and Heribert Mühlen, editors. Erfahrung und Theologie des Heiligen Geistes. Munich: Kösel, 1974.

Hocken, Peter. "The Charismatic Renewal, the Churches, and Unity," in One in Christ, No. 4, 1979.

Hollenweger, Walter. The Pentecostals. London: SCM Press, and Minneapolis: Augsburg, 1972. Also available in German and Spanish.

-----. Pentecost Between Black and White. Belfast: Christian Journals Ltd., 1974. Also available in Dutch and German.

-----. Erfahrungen der Leibhaftigkeit. Munich: Chr. Kaiser Verlag, 1979.

-----. "Roots and Fruits of the Charismatic Renewal in the Third World: Implications for Mission," in Theological Renewal, No. 14, Feb. 1980.

Hummel, Charles E. Fire in the Fireplace: Contemporary Charismatic Renewal. Downers Grove, Ill.: Inter-Varsity Press, 1978.

Jensen, Richard A. Touched by the Spirit. Minneapolis: Augsburg, 1975.

Kelsey, Morton. Healing and Christianity. New York: Harper & Row, 1973.

-----. Encounter with God. Minneapolis: Bethany Fellowship, 1974; London: Hodder & Stoughton, 1974.

MacNutt, Francis. Healing. Notre Dame, Ind.: Ave Maria Press, 1974.

McDonnell, Kilian. Charismatic Renewal and the Churches. New York: Seabury Press, 1976.

-----. Charismatic Renewal and Ecumenism. New York: Paulist Press, 1978.

-----. Presence, Power, Praise: Documents on the Charismatic Renewal. 3 volumes. Collegeville, Minn.: Liturgical Press, 1980.

-----, and Arnold Bittlinger. The Baptism in the Holy Spirit as an Ecumenical Problem. Notre Dame, Ind.: Charismatic Renewal Services, 1972.

Martin, Ralph. Fire on the Earth. Ann Arbor: Word of Life, 1975.

Montague, George T. The Holy Spirit: Growth of a Biblical Tradition. New York: Paulist Press, 1976.

Mühlen, Heribert. A Charismatic Theology. London: Burns & Oates, 1978; New York: Paulist Press, 1979. Also available in Dutch, French, German, Hungarian, Croatian, Polish, Portuguese, and Spanish.

-----. Die Erneuerung des christlichen Glaubens. Munich: Don Bosco, 1974.

-----. Morgen wird Einheit sein. Paderborn: Pattloch, 1974.

Samarin, William J. Tongues of Men and Angels. London and New York: Collier-Macmillan, 1972.

Smail, Thomas. Reflected Glory: The Spirit in Christ and Christians. London: Hodder & Stoughton, and Grand Rapids: Eerdmans, 1975.

-----. The Forgotten Father. London: Hodder and Stoughton, 1980.

Spittler, Russell. Perspectives of New Pentecostalism. Grand Rapids: Baker Book House, 1976.

Strachan, Gordon. The Pentecostal Theology of Edward Irving. London: Darton, Longman and Todd.

Suenes, Léon-Joseph. A New Pentecost? London: Darton, Longman and Todd, 1975.

Synan, H. Vinson. Charismatic Bridges. Ann Arbor: Word of Life, 1974.

Taylor, John V. The Go-Between God: The Holy Spirit and the Christian Mission. London: SCM Press, 1972.

Tugwell, Simon. Did You Receive the Spirit? London: Darton, Longman and Todd, 1972.

Tidings, Judy. Gathering a People: Catholic Saints in Charismatic Perspective. Plainfield, N. J. : Logos, 1977.

Usdorf, Werner. Afrikanische Initiative. Das aktive Leiden des Propheten Simon Kimbangu. Frankfurt: Lang, 1975.

Watson, David. I Believe in the Church. London: Hodder & Stoughton, and Grand Rapids: Eerdmans, 1978.

234

Wilkerson, David. The Cross and the Switchblade. New York: Bernard Geis Associates, 1963.

Williams, Rod. The Era of the Spirit. Plainfield, N.J.: Logos, 1971.

-----. The Pentecostal Reality. Plainfield, N. J.: Logos, 1972.

-----. The Gift of the Holy Spirit. Plainfield, N.J.: Logos, 1977.

Yokum, Bruce. Prophecy. Ann Arbor: Servant Books, 1976.

LIST OF PARTICIPANTS

1. Rev. Adeolu ADEGBOLA
   C.A.R.E.
   P.O. Box 9270
   Ibadan, Nigeria (Methodist)

2. *Mr. John ADEGOKE
   100 Bushley Close
   Woodrow North, Redditch, U.K.
   (Senior Apostle of Cherubim
   & Seraphim, U.K.)

3. Mr. Henry Asige AJEGA (Ind.)
   General Secretary, African
   Israel Church Nineveh,
   P.O. Box 701, Kisumu, Kenya

4. *Mrs. Deborah BAILEY
   6 Kendale Road
   Luton, U.K. (Calvary Church
   of God in Christ)

5. Fr. Assam BITAR
   c/o Mr. Gabirel Habib
   Middle East Council of Churches
   P.O. Box 5376 - Beirut, Lebanon
   (Orthodox Church, Antioch)

6. *Pastor Alvin BLAKE
   90 Beechwood Road, Luton, U.K.
   (Calvary Church of God in Christ)

7. *Ms. Nova BLAKE
   90 Beechwood Road, Luton, U.K.
   (Calvary Church of God in Christ)

8. Most Rev. Bill BURNETT
   Bishopscourt, Claremont,
   Cape, 7700 S. Africa (Anglican)

9. Rev. V.M. DAVID (Anglican)
   Indian Charismatic Centre
   Mary Villa Vattaparampil
   Pooventuruthu P.O. Kottayam
   686-012, India

10. Dr. J.D.G. DUNN
    University of Nottingham
    Dept. of Theology, Nottingham
    U.K. NG7 2RD

11. Mrs. Ylva EGGEHORN (Lutheran)
    Grödy 5
    140 41 Sorunda, Sweden

12. *Mr. Melvin ELLIS
    27 Brunel Road, Lewsey Farm
    Estate, Luton, U.K.
    (Calvary Church of God in Christ)

13. Rev. Tormod ENGELSVIKEN
    Kjaernes
    N-1400 Ski, Norway (Lutheran)

14. Sister EVANGELINE (Reformed)
    Communauté des Diaconesses de Versailles,
    10 rue de Porte de Buc
    F-7800 Versailles, France

15. Rev. Peter FELBER (Reformed)
    Pfarrhaus
    8211 Beggingen, Switzerland

16. *Ms. Minette FRANCIS
    132 Bradley Road, Luton, U.K.
    (Calvary Church of God in Christ)

17. Pastorin Hildegard FUHR (United)
    Bund der Evangelischen Kirchen
    in der D.D.R.,
    Auguststrasse 80, 104-Berlin, DDR

18. *Ms. Doreen GRANT
    62 Tweed Tower
    Birchfield Road, Perry Barr,
    Birmingham, B20 3JR - U.K.
    (First United Church of Jesus Christ Apostolic)

19. Rev. Gordon GRAY (Presbyterian)
    26 N. Circular Road
    Lisburn, Co. Antrim, N. Ireland

20. Rev. Michael HARPER
    Holy Trinity Church
    High Street, Hounslow,
    Middlesex TW3 1HG, U.K.
    (Anglican)

21. Rev. Peter HOCKEN
    281 Dawlish Road, Selly Oak
    B29 7AU - U.K. (Catholic)

22. Dr. Walter HOLLENWEGER
    Department of Theology
    University of Birmingham
    Birmingham B15 2TT - U.K.
    (Reformed)

23. Metropolitan IRENEOS
    Holy Metropolis
    Chania, Crete, Greece
    (Ecumenical Patriarchate, Crete)

24. Dr. Jonas JONSON
    Stiftsgarden
    795 00 Rättvik - Sweden
    (Lutheran)

25. Rev. John KITAGAWA
    209 East 16th Street
    New York - N.Y. 10003
    USA (Episcopalian)

26. Dr. John KUREWA (Methodist) &
    Mr. Pontas NASUTION
    Commission on World Mission and Evangelism
    WCC, Geneva

27. Mr. Nelson Lemus ZAMBRANO
    (from Santiago de Chile)
    Haus Rissen, Rissenerlandstr. 193
    2000 Hamburg-Rissen, FRG
    (Pentecostal)

28. Rev. Ben LENTURUT
    The United Church in Papua New Guinea and the
    Solomon Islands
    Douglas Street, P.O. Box 3401
    Port Moresby, Papua New Guinea

29. Rev. J. Oscar McCLOUD
    United Presbyterian Church in the USA,
    Program Agency
    475 Riverside Drive, Room 1108
    New York - N.Y. 10027, USA

30. Rev. Kilian McDONNELL
    Institute for Ecumenical and Cultural Research,
    Collegeville, Minnesota 56321 - USA
    (Catholic)

31. Dr. Loren B. MEAD
    The Alban Institute, Inc.
    Mount St. Alban
    Washington, D.C. 20016 - USA

32. Mgr. Basil MEEKING (Vatican)
    Secretariat for Promoting Christian Unity,
    Vatican City 00120, Italy

33. Professor Herbert MUHLEN
    Scherfederstrasse 70
    D-4790 Paderborn, FRG

34. Dr. Pong Bae PARK
    Methodist Theological Seminary
    P.O. Box 45 West Gate, Seoul
    South Korea (Methodist)

35. *Ms. Erica PATTERSON
    39 Macaulay Road, Luton, U.K.
    (Calvary Church of God in Christ)

36. Archpriest Antonios RAGHEB
    123 Elteraa Elbolakia Street
    Shobra, Cairo, Egypt
    (Coptic Orthodox)

37. Mrs. Ingrid REIMER
    Engelbergstr. 32
    7000 Stuttgart - FRG
    (Lutheran)

38. Very Rev. Andrew SACUY-AP
    Cathedral Church of St. Mary
    St. John, P.O. Box 655, Manila
    Philippines (Anglican)

39. Sister Lucida SCHMIEDER O.S.B.
    (From Orlinda, Brazil)
    Warburgerstrasse 2
    4790 Paderborn, FRG

40. Rev. Matthias SENS
    Theologische Studienabteilung Bund der Evangelischen
    Kirchen in der Deutschen Demokratischen Republik,
    Auguststrasse 80, Berlin 104, D.D.R. (United)

41. Dr. William P. SHOWALTER
    Parkminster Presbyterian Church (UPCUSA)
    2710 Chili Avenue
    Rochester, N.Y. 14624, USA

42. Mr. Bena SILU
    Eglise de Jésus Christ sur la Terre par le
    Prophète Kimbangu
    87 rue de Monkoto
    B.P. 7069, Kinshasa, Zaïre

43. *Ms. Carolyn SMITH
    14 Mostyn Road
    Leagrave, Luton, U.K.
    (Calvary Church of God in Christ)

44. Rev. Canon David TATCHELL
    3602 8th Street, S.W.
    Calgary T2T-3A7, Canada

45. *Ms. Marjorie THOMAS
    32 Reginald Street
    Luton, U.K. (Calvary Church of God in Christ)

46. Dr. Andrew WALKER
    12 Herbert Morrison House
    Clem Attlee Court
    London - S.W.6 - U.K.
    (Russian Orthodox Church, U.K.)

47. Rev. Rodman WILLIAMS
    Melodyland School of Theology
    10 Freedom Way
    P.O. Box 6000
    Anaheim, California 92806 - USA
    (Presbyterian Neo-Pentecostal)

240

48. Rev. Lois WILSON
    33 Marley Street
    Kingston, Ontario K7M 2M4
    Canada (United Church of Canada)

OBSERVERS/VISITORS

49. Mr. George EGGEHORN
    Grödy 5
    140 41 Sorunda, Sweden

50. Father J. LUCAL (Catholic)
    SODEPAX
    150 Route de Ferney
    Geneva 1211 - Switzerland

51. Rev. Harold MERRITT
    Church of Christ
    23 Bluestone Avenue
    Burslem, Stoke-on-Trent
    ST6 7EE, U.K.

52. Ms. Judith TYDINGS (Catholic)
    Mother of God Community
    10413 Boswell Lane
    Potomac, Maryland 20854, USA

STAFF

53. Ms. Evelyn APPIAH

54. Dr. Arnold BITTLINGER

55. Ms. Tamara GERBER

56. Dr. Philip POTTER

57. Mr. Ralph YOUNG

INTERPRETERS

58. Ms. Renate SBEGHEN

59. Ms. Roswitha GINGLAS

* Charismatic group from U.K.

LOCUSTS AND WILD HONEY

This book is about the charismatic renewal and the ecumenical movement. Rex Davis, Canon of Lincoln Minster, draws on his experience to provide a personal account of the "wild ecumenism" he sees among charismatics, dividing his criticism between the excesses of the renewal movement and the inflexibility of the ecumenical establishment. The book is illustrated and written in a lively style.

"This book is a must for all who care for the unity and renewal of the Church." (Church of England Newspaper)

"The untypical, thought provoking cover is matched by the contents." (Renewal)

Risk Book series, Sfr. 8.90, US$4.75, £2.50

a WCC publication